The Twisted Road to Auschwitz

*And Haman said unto King Ahasuerus,
There is a certain people
scattered abroad and dispersed
among the people in all the provinces
of thy kingdom; and their laws
are diverse from all people;
neither keep they the king's laws:
therefore it is not
for the king's profit to suffer them.*

ESTHER 3:8

The Twisted Road to Auschwitz

NAZI POLICY TOWARD GERMAN JEWS
1933–1939

KARL A. SCHLEUNES

*With a New Bibliographical Essay by the Author
and a Foreword by Hans Mommsen*

UNIVERSITY OF ILLINOIS PRESS

Urbana and Chicago

∞ This book is printed on acid-free paper.

Library of Congress Cataloging-in-Publication Data
Schleunes, Karl A.
The twisted road to Auschwitz : Nazi policy toward German Jews,
1933–1939 / Karl A. Schleunes ; with a new bibliographical essay by
the author and a foreword by Hans Mommsen.—Illini Books ed.
p.   cm.
Reprint. Originally published: 1970.
Includes bibliographical references and index.
ISBN 0-252-06147-0 (pb)
1. Jews—Germany—History—1933–1945. 2. Germany—
Politics and government—1933–1945. I. Title.
DS135.G3315S34   1990
943'.004924—dc20   90-35944
CIP
ISBN 978-0-252-06147-9 (pb)

Contents

Foreword

SINCE the publication of Karl Schleunes' *The Twisted Road to Auschwitz* in 1970 an almost inconceivably broad variety of scholarly books and articles has dealt with why and how the Holocaust came into being and what kind of mechanisms lay at the bottom of the unimaginable cruelties committed by the Nazi regime against the Jews. Schleunes demonstrated that the fanatical anti-Semitism that guided Hitler and his chiefs cannot in itself provide a sufficiently coherent explanation of the genesis of the Holocaust. At least partly because of his analysis, the internal structure of the regime, the role of its bureaucracies, and the rivalries between competing power groups became the focus of research. In conjunction with this, anti-Jewish policy during the prewar years has been the object of further analysis. Additional evidence was also made available that had been partly ignored or was disclosed only in local and regional studies. In the light of our extended knowledge of the history of the Nazi system generally, as well as anti-Jewish policies in particular, Schleunes' study stands reaffirmed in its effort to trace the early stages of discrimination against the Jews and their exclusion from public life that led ultimately to their deaths. Moreover, the specific methodological approach displayed in Schleunes' book has proved indispensable for an adequate interpretation of Jewish persecution in the Third Reich.

At the time Schleunes' book appeared its pioneering quality was appreciated by only a minority of scholars, and it took a couple of years before the perspective from which it was written gained a wider currency with historians in the field of Holocaust history. It has remained a controversial contribution ever since. For the great majority of historians there was not the slightest doubt that the course of the Nazi persecution of the Jews had been preconceived in the minds of the Nazi leaders, and they had steered the anti-Jewish measures deliberately from step to step until the conditions of World War II permitted the systematic implementation of a long-cherished ambition: the annihilation of all Jews under German rule. Most observers took their lead from the theory of totalitarian dictatorship and assumed that from the start to the very end anti-Jewish policy was deliberately planned and put into practice because of Hitler's personal involvement.

Schleunes, however, broke the narrowness of the previous interpretive patterns by analyzing Nazi Jewish policy as a political process driven not only by the ideological prejudices and Jew hatred of the Nazi leadership but at least as much by the social dynamics inherent in the Nazi movement and the self-induced pressures to preserve the unity of the Nazi party. Starting from the assumption that racial anti-Semitism served as a means to integrate otherwise incompatible targets, Schleunes argues that in the long run, Hitler felt he could not afford to accept any retreat from anti-Semitism. Simultaneously, the German dictator was not, as many historians maintained, continuously at the center of the anti-Semitic escalation. On the contrary, Hitler usually avoided official involvement in anti-Jewish policies. Though Hitler's anti-Semitism was obviously insatiable, he frequently delayed anti-Jewish measures requested by party radicals, and he was often only indirectly involved when the escalation of anti-Jewish policy started anew in November 1938.

From this proposition Schleunes arrives at the crucial conclusion that the acceleration of anti-Jewish persecution was due less to the ideological pressure from the rather restricted group of fanatical anti-Semites in and outside the Nazi party than to the empire building and the never-ending struggle between competing public and party agencies for control over anti-Jewish policy. Schleunes was the first historian to show that from the Nazi point of view the different strategies against the Jewish population appeared as failures because neither the boycott in

April 1933 and the early anti-Semitic legislation that replaced "wild" actions nor the so-called voluntary Aryanization effectually reduced the increasing number of Jewish inhabitants in the expanding German empire through voluntary or forced emigration. Hitler's inability to accept setbacks together with his extreme anti-Semitic prejudices explain why the failure of the various efforts to achieve or postulate "final" solutions of the Jewish problem did not lead to indifference and passivity, as was the case in other areas of policy.

By analyzing the political decision-making process, Schleunes concludes that even in Jewish policy Hitler was uncertain about the strategic choices and that this uncertainty allowed a decision-making vacuum to emerge. The actual process, Schleunes points out, frequently turns out to be the exact opposite of what the *Fuehrerprinzip* would lead one to expect. Not until November 1938 did Hitler decide in favor of a centralized and coordinated procedure in the Jewish question by vesting Goering and, indirectly, Heydrich with the requisite powers. Hitler himself lacked a clear-cut concept of how to achieve his visionary goal of getting rid of the Jewish population. Schleunes argues that a long, drawn-out process of trial and error was needed until enforced emigration could be replaced by systematic deportation and annihilation of the Jewish victims.

Originally, Schleunes' interpretation met with strong apprehensions from many historians who stood under the prevailing influence of the Hitler-centrist approach. Even today *The Twisted Road* is still occasionally accused of revisionism and a hardly intentional exculpation of the dictator. Despite this, many of Schleunes' conclusions were taken up by ensuing researchers and developed further. For instance, Martin Broszat, in "Soziale Motivation und Führer-Bindung des Nationalsozialismus," took up Schleunes' observation that in certain conditions Hitler would act mainly under pressure from Nazi hardliners. Broszat argued compellingly that Hitler's rhetoric was taken literally by his fanatical supporters who then put him under the pressure of a self-fulfilling prophesy.

In some respects Schleunes cleared the road for later research by describing the anti-Jewish policy of the Nazi regime as a multifaceted process with its ups and downs and as a series of shortcomings rather than a chain of successful operations, though the victims certainly viewed these measures differently. Schleunes argues correctly that the actual course of events leading to the Holocaust can only be explained by a combination of events. Ideological fanaticism was a precondition, while the cumulative radicalization of rivaling agencies worked as the motivating force behind anti-Jewish policies. He stresses the interaction between divergent interests and influences, including foreign policy that in his view deserve even closer attention than the ideological factors. Schleunes traces the developmental stages up to the pogrom of November 9 and 10, 1938, which he regards as a crucial turning point. His specific approach, however, induced functionalist historians to demonstrate that Hitler's rather responsive attitude toward anti-Jewish activities did not change qualitatively even during the ensuing implementation of the genocide. The extent to which Hitler interfered directly in the extermination procedures and whether he in fact delivered a formal order to start the systematic annihilation program will remain controversial, but it is by now universally accepted that the process as such was strongly dependent on the empire building of the competing Nazi subleaders.

In recent years several authors have tried to describe the process of Jewish persecution in Germany. None of them has succeeded in presenting such a well-balanced account of its early stages as Karl Schleunes. Schleunes' contention that "the Final Solution as it emerged in 1941 and 1942 was not the product of a grand design" still is controversially received, but has not been convincingly refuted in spite of the opposing view of several Israeli scholars, especially David Bankier, who regards Hitler as the central promoter of the individual anti-Jewish actions throughout the course of the Third Reich. The general picture as presented by Karl Schleunes still seems convincing to me. His book remains an indispensable contribution to our understanding of the origins of and the preconditions for the Nazi persecution of the Jews. Moreover, Schleunes' contribution paved the way for a tremendously productive debate that contributed decisively to a better understanding of the destructive and inhuman nature of the Nazi regime.

Hans Mommsen

Introduction

THERE IS no single phenomenon in our time so important for us to understand as the one which identified itself in Germany during the 1920's, 30's and 40's as National Socialism. By the time this movement was swept from the stage it had destroyed the lives of at least thirty million and perhaps as many as forty million people. Violent death accompanying war in an age of industry and technology, by the 1940's, had its precedents. The institutions which most appropriately symbolize the Nazi era—Auschwitz, Dachau, Treblinka, and some fifty other concentration and extermination camps—had none.

These factories of death are now permanently cataloged in the darkest annals of the human story. Their existence casts a long shadow over the hopes for our own future. The realization that some men will construct a factory in which to kill other men raises the gravest questions about man himself. We have entered an age which we cannot avoid labeling "After Auschwitz." If we are to begin to understand ourselves we must somehow come to grips with the reality of Auschwitz.

The study which follows is an attempt to come to grips with a part of that reality. It is not an attempt to analyze the functioning of Auschwitz or what the Nazis chose to call "The Final Solution to the Jewish Problem." Since Raul Hilberg's impressive study of this period such an effort has become unnecessary.[1] It is instead an examination of the period which immediately precedes Auschwitz, the period from 1933, when Hitler came to power, until late 1938 and early 1939, when the machinery which eventually administered a Final Solution was established.

[1] Raul Hilberg, *The Destruction of the European Jews* (Chicago, 1961).

It was during these first five years of Hitler's rule that the Nazis stumbled toward something resembling a Final Solution to the Jewish Problem. The Final Solution as it emerged in 1941 and 1942 was not the product of a grand design. In fact, when the Nazis came to power, they had no specific plans for a solution of any sort. They were certain only that a solution was necessary. This commitment carried the Nazi system along the twisted road to Auschwitz.

* * *

I am indebted to the goodwill and friendship of my colleagues in the history department at the University of Illinois at Chicago Circle. Their advice at critical stages of this study has been extremely valuable. Special gratitude is also due Professor Harold C. Deutsch of the University of Minnesota whose guidance in the early stages of this study was invaluable. At both the research and writing stages I have received the generous financial support of several foundations and institutes. These include the Fulbright Commission, the National Foundation for Jewish Culture, the Leo Baeck Institute, and the Summer Fellowship Program of the University of Illinois. To Dr. Max Kreutzberger and his successor as Secretary of the Leo Baeck Institute, Dr. Fred Grubel, and to Mrs. Ilse R. Wolff of the Wiener Library I am grateful for having put the research facilities of their libraries at my disposal. Their interest, advice, and encouragement have been important to me.

I have also imposed unduly upon the friendship of Earl and Lydia Ann Talbot and Stephen and Elaine Klemen whom I asked to read this manuscript before its final draft. Many of their suggestions have been incorporated into the final text.

Chicago, Illinois
July 22, 1969

The Twisted Road to Auschwitz

1. The Jewish Problem in the Second Reich

On April 29, 1945, twenty-four hours before his suicide, Adolf Hitler dictated his final testament. It was an extraordinary document created in extraordinary circumstances. Outside his underground bunker the Soviet Army was grinding Berlin into total submission. The Third Reich was choking in its own ashes. In these last moments of his life Hitler was displaying a remarkable calm. The towering rage to which Hitler had become so susceptible in times of crisis was absent. With the destruction of his last bastion raging above him, Adolf Hitler, once the dictator of an empire ranging across Europe from Le Havre to Leningrad, contemplated the future.

After expelling the traitors Himmler and Goering from the party and after naming a successor government, the Fuehrer ended his testament with his most important message: "Above all, I charge the leadership of the nation, as well as its followers, to a rigorous adherence to our racial laws and to a merciless resistance against the poisoner of all peoples—international Jewry."[1] That Hitler should deliver a warning about international Jewry as his final and most significant message to the future is a chilling reminder of the role played by the Jew in the Nazi world view. Such reminders are hardly necessary, however. From the very outset of the Nazi movement, Hitler and his henchmen had expended untold energies making clear their antipathy for the Jew. The Allied armies had, upon invading Hitler's fortress Europe, uncovered during the last months of the war death camps in which the Nazis had attempted to manufac-

[1] See the facsimile of "Hitler's Last Will and Testament" in Joseph Tenenbaum, *Race and Reich: The Story of an Epoch* (New York, 1956), following p. 238.

ture what they chose to call the "Final Solution to the Jewish Problem."

No single aspect of Nazi policy proved to be more permanently successful than this Final Solution. By the time of its collapse the Nazi death machine had managed to destroy an estimated five to six million Jews, roughly sixty to seventy percent of European Jewry. It is doubtful that Hitler was aware of precisely how successful his Final Solution had been. His final warning shows, however, that in his view the policy had failed. How else could he have explained the Nazi defeat, now that even he had finally to accept it? All his efforts had been brought to ruin by international Jewry. This was the only explanation his intellectual and psychological makeup allowed. The Soviet, American, and British armies were no more than another manifestation of international Jewry's power, whose ultimate aim had always been to bring Germany to its knees. Now that it had finally succeeded, the only thing left to Hitler was the strength to give one last warning and, then, suicide.

The Jew had given form and structure to Hitler's world since his years in Vienna, just prior to the outbreak of the World War in 1914. It was here, Hitler later claimed, that he met the Jew for the first time and learned of the real nature of the Jewish problem. From that time forward the world made sense to Hitler because of the Jew and his inherently evil nature. All that was evil, be it the German defeat in 1918 or the collapse of his own Reich in 1945, could be laid at the feet of the Jews. When after 1918 he became involved in the jumbled world of Weimar politics Hitler assigned to the Jew the ultimate responsibility for all the difficulties Germany faced. The hated republic itself was the product of a Jewish seizure of power; the building of divisive parliamentary factions only the means through which Jews could weaken the German fiber. During the years of the Weimar Republic Jewish malevolence, according to Nazi pronouncement, reached unprecedented proportions. Jews had captured control of the government, the press, the professions, the arts, economic life, and worst of all, through intermarriage, had made great inroads in corrupting the biological purity of Aryan racial stock. This was the Jewish problem to which the Nazis incessantly referred and to which they gave unqualified promise of finding a solution.

That unqualified promises should ultimately yield attempts at an unqualified solution does not appear illogical, at least not in retrospect. Perhaps one should not be surprised that a movement which writes a segment of humanity out of the human race should eventually give birth to a policy of physical extermination. The fact remains, however, that the world was surprised when the full extent of the Nazi atrocity was made known. It was surprised first at the extremes of inhumanity which the Nazis had reached and, upon reflection, it was surprised that this had happened in Germany.

It is often noted that anyone who listened seriously to Hitler or read *Mein Kampf* carefully might have expected something approaching a Final Solution if Hitler ever came to power. But then is not a politician's bark usually worse than his bite? Especially when that politician is as erratic as was Hitler? Hitler, whether in *Mein Kampf* or in his last testament, was not, after all the only observer of the German-Jewish relationship. To dwell solely upon his reflections would lead to a serious misreading of the traditional relationship between Germans and Jews. Jews themselves had for decades been optimistic about their future in Germany. It is illuminating on the one hand to consider the importance of Hitler's reflections upon the Jews, and on the other the observations of a German Jew, Professor Hermann Cohen, the renowned Kantian philosopher, who during World War I noted that:

Despite the universal contrary prejudice I venture to assert that in Germany equal rights for Jews have deeper roots than anywhere else. Everywhere in the world Jews may win a higher share of political rights and government. We German Jews seek this share on the grounds of participation, inwardly recognized, in German morality and religiosity. Hence our road to liberation is harder and more erratic, for it is bound up with the fluctuations of social feelings; but it has deeper historical and cultural roots. And our limited Jewish rights in Germany are of higher value for religious survival than the apparently absolutely equal rights of Jews abroad. . . .[2]

In the light of Auschwitz, Buchenwald, and Dachau, Cohen's observations seem tragically naive. At the time, however, his confidence in Germany seemed well placed; at least it was widely shared. The Germany with which Cohen and his contemporaries were familiar hardly seemed to forecast disaster. Jews had rallied to the defense of the Kaiser's empire in 1914 as enthusiastically as any other Germans. There was legitimate reason for hoping their contributions to the war effort might quell the lingering anti-Jewish resentment which occasionally stirred. But even these stirrings had subsided during the last prewar decades. The enthusiasm of most Jews for being or becoming German was rarely dampened by the anti-Semitic attacks from the fringes of German society. When a Zionist movement was born in eastern Europe following pogroms in Russia and Poland, it found very few adherents in Germany. Zionism failed to make deep inroads here because it seemed an answer to a problem German Jews did not see as their own. The Jews of Poland or Russia might need a homeland; German Jews had one.[3]

If there was a Jewish problem in Germany, said some of Judaism's leaders, it was the quite different prospect of complete assimilation. Since 1880 the percentage of Jews to the total German population had been in decline. By 1900 the 497,000 Jews comprised less than one percent of the total population in Germany. In the larger cities, where most Jews lived, marriage to German Gentiles was becoming increasingly common. Germany, more than any other country at the time, seemed to have gone furthest in destroying the reality and the memory of the

[2] Quoted by Emil L. Fackenheim, "Hermann Cohen: After Fifty Years," Leo Baeck Memorial Lecture 12 (New York, 1969), p. 9.

[3] See Richard Lichtheim, *Die Geschichte des deutschen Zionismus* (Jerusalem, 1954).

medieval ghetto. So noticeable were the trends that leaders in the German Jewish community feared the complete assimilation or fusion of their community into German society by the end of the twentieth century.[4]

The promulgation of the Bismarckian constitution in 1871 brought to legal fruition the process of Jewish emancipation begun during the Prussian reform period early in the century. Emancipation heralded the new day of full and equal participation for Jews in a united and dynamic new Germany. A Jewish member of the Prussian lower house rejoiced that "finally after years of waiting in vain we have landed in a safe harbor."[5] Jewish energies turned to taking advantage of the new opportunities. An expanding economy based upon capitalist and liberal principles occasioned opportunities unheard of to previous generations of Jews. For the first time the business and learned professions were fully open to them. The economy demanded new business and professional services as well as an increase in the quantity of older services and Jews were quick to answer the challenges.[6] By World War I Jewish contributions to the various dimensions of German life had become rich and varied. The names of Eduard Bernstein and Rudolf Hilferding were central to the development of German socialism. Emil Rathenau's *Allgemeine Elekricitäts Gesellschaft* (General Electric Company) had, by around 1900, literally illuminated Wilhelmian Germany, and Emil's son, Walther, through allocating resources, probably contributed more than any other single person to Germany's war effort after 1914. A new marketing technique, the chain department store, was introduced during the 1880's and 90's by Oskar Tietz and, because its volume sales enabled it to undersell competitors, allowed the German consumer to

[4] Arthur Ruppin, *Soziologie der Juden*, vol. 2 (Berlin, 1930), pp. 319-320.

[5] Quoted by Jacob Toury, *Die politischen Orientierungen der Juden in Deutschland, von Jena bis Weimar*, Schriftenreihe Wissenschaftlicher Abhandlungen des Leo Baeck Instituts 15 (Tübingen, 1966), pp. 138-139.

[6] The extent to which Jews came to participate in German economic, professional, and cultural life is examined in Chapter II.

buy an increasingly wide variety of goods more cheaply.[7] In all fields—medicine, the physical sciences, philosophy, literature, the arts as well as business—Germany benefitted from an impressive Jewish contribution. More important than the quantity of the Jewish contribution, however, was the recognition that it was German, not Jewish life which was being enriched. Albert Einstein was not dealing with Jewish physics (later Nazi allegations notwithstanding) any more than Franz Werfel was producing Jewish literature or Kurt Weill, a few years later, was composing Jewish music.

To most observers the Jewish problem did not seem to have a serious German dimension. Nowhere did the promise of the modern world seem more secure. Elsewhere in Europe the situation of Jews appeared to be much more precarious. For the decade spanning the turn of the century France was torn apart by the Dreyfus Affair. In eastern Europe the final decades of the nineteenth century witnessed the most massive Jewish persecutions of the pre-Hitlerian age. The situation there made it appear as if anti-Semitism were primarily an east European phenomenon. In Russia, where Jews had traditionally been restricted to the western Pale of Settlement, a policy of "Russifying" ethnic minorities was accompanied by one aimed at driving Jews into pauperism. When a Jew was implicated in the 1881 assassination of Czar Alexander II a series of "spontaneous" police-initiated pogroms erupted. The following year a succession of regulations—the so-called May Laws—established limits to the number of Jews allowed into Russian schools and restricted Jews from entering the learned professions. Such measures served as the prelude to the spectacular Kishenev pogrom of 1903 during which Jews were hunted down and murdered in the streets by the czarist police.[8] The anti-Jewish legislation and actions of czarist Russia resemble the Nazi persecution of a later

---

[7] Kurt Zielenziger, *Juden in der deutschen Wirtschaft* (Berlin, 1930), pp. 206-220.

[8] Howard Morley Sacher, *The Course of Modern Jewish History* (New York, 1963), pp. 240-260.

day—with one striking exception. Unlike the Nazis, the czarist regime halted its anti-Jewish activity when in 1904 it became involved in war. For the Nazis war was the signal to accelerated persecution.

Poland was second only to Russia in the size of its Jewish population with about three and one-quarter million Jews, or ten percent of her population. Jewish life in Poland was rooted in the general backwardness of the country, a backwardness which nurtured a richly religious, but largely exclusive life, greatly influenced by the Hasidic movement of the eighteenth century. Those Jews who had not entered into secular Polish society were closely tied to the pietism and emotionalism of Hasidism, and consequently less prepared to enter into the secular ways of modern Europe when persecution drove them westward. This Jew was known to western Europeans as the *Ostjude*, or eastern Jew, whose mannerisms and bearing came to be so bitterly despised by the anti-Semites. In Poland clerical alarm at a growing atheistic socialism and the customary fear of "Jewish capitalism" gave birth to an anti-Semitism as vigorous as any pre-Nazi variety. Anti-Semitism proved to be the only force able to fuse the conservative political factions in Poland during the turbulent latter years of the nineteenth century.[9]

The closest parallel to the eventual German experience with the Jewish problem is to be found in Romania. Like Germany, Romania did not become unified and independent until the latter part of the nineteenth century. The principalities of Moldavia and Wallachia which made up Romania had long been the battlefield for Russian, Turkish, and Habsburg armies, a function German territory had performed for centuries in central Europe. Romanian nationalists of the nineteenth century, like their German contemporaries, often pointed to their ethnic exclusiveness. Culturally and racially they claimed themselves to be of Latin origin, the descendants of Roman settlers, and therefore distinctly different from their Slavic neighbors. To

[9] Raphael Mahler, "Antisemitism in Poland," in Koppel S. Pinson, ed., *Essays on Antisemitism* (New York, 1946), pp. 145-172.

protect this exclusiveness alien influences had to be extirpated. Since the most immediately available alien influence in Romania was a Jewish one, the government quickly instituted repressive measures which soon threatened the continued existence of Romanian Jewry. Jewish children were excluded from the schools; Jewish religious observances were curtailed; Jews were barred from business and professional pursuits; at election time the regime instituted anti-Jewish riots—all in the name of promoting Romanian purity.[10]

Similar patterns of anti-Jewish activity emerged throughout eastern Europe. A process of "Magyarization" in Hungary worked to exclude Jews from the national identity developing there. In Russia Nicholai Danilevsky added scientific substance to the Pan-Slavic movement by stressing the blood ties between the various Slavic peoples,[11]—an observation which served to emphasize the differences between the emerging Slavic nationalities and the Jewish minorities living in their midst. The new sense of national identity emerging in eastern Europe, whether it was Russian, Polish, Romanian, or Hungarian, appeared inevitably to exclude the Jew. If the basis of nationality was race, as an increasing number of people seemed to believe, the only prospect for Jewish assimilation was through intermarriage, the mixing of the races. Given the obvious manifestations of growing anti-Jewish resentments, however, the likelihood that "race-mixing" would offer a solution to the Jewish problem appeared increasingly remote.

In contrast to eastern Europe the situation in Germany seemed much more promising. Rather than closing off secular life to its Jewish inhabitants, the Bismarckian empire was opening the way for fuller Jewish participation. German Jews were not alone in regarding Germany as a safe harbor. Talented young Jews from eastern Europe regarded Germany as the one hope for their future. German universities, for example, offered them educational opportunities which their own governments

---

10 Sacher, *Modern Jewish History,* pp. 255-259.
11 Hans Kohn, *Pan-Slavism* (New York, 1966), pp. 190ff.

had just closed off. One of the many east European Jews to receive his university education in Germany was Chaim Weizmann, later to become one of Judaism's foremost Zionists and the first president of Israel. Born in the Russian Pale of Settlement in 1874, the young Weizmann, finding Russia's restrictions on Jewish students impossible to circumvent, joined what he called the "educational stampede" of Jewish students to Germany.[12]

The oppressed Jews of eastern Europe came to view Germany as a haven from pogrom and persecution. Thousands fled their homes at the turn of the century, many of them coming to Germany hoping to acquire citizenship or at least to use Germany as a way station in their emigration to the United States.[13] If there was a worldwide Jewish problem it did not appear to have an important German dimension.

That there was to some extent a Jewish problem even in Germany was, of course, undeniable. Even Professor Cohen in all of his optimism noted limitations to Jewish rights in Germany, but only to conclude that these limited rights were of more value "than the apparently absolutely equal rights of Jews abroad . . ." Presumably German Jews would eventually gain these absolutely equal rights as well and then enjoy the additional advantage of having them rooted deeply in the German tradition.

German Jews had not been shielded from the currents of anti-Semitism spreading across Europe in the latter half of the nineteenth century. While they did not suffer the pogroms or persecutions of eastern Europe, or even the degrading spectacle of a Dreyfus Affair, the Jewish question was very much alive in many German circles. Even outside the most vigorous anti-Semitic circles the Jewish question was a much discussed issue. It had become part of the larger question of giving meaning and identity to the Germany created by developments of the 1860's.

[12] Chaim Weizmann, *Trial and Error: The Autobiography of Chaim Weizmann* (New York, 1949), pp. 29-30.
[13] S. Adler-Rudel, *Ostjuden in Deutschland, 1880-1940*, Schriftenreihe Wissenschaftlicher Abhandlungen des Leo Baeck Instituts (Tübingen, 1959), p. 112.

It was under Bismarck during the 1860's that Prussian power finally achieved a German political unity. In a succession of quick victories against Denmark, Austria, and France, Prussia's army and Bismarck's wile forged a German Empire—a Second Reich—declared at Versailles in 1871. The new Reich excluded many Germans living on its fringes in Austria and Bohemia and was therefore based on the "small German" or *kleindeutsch* conception of German unity. There were those who were disappointed, but Bismarck nonetheless looked upon his work of a decade and declared it to be good. Germany, he announced, was a satisfied power. Her task now was to solidify the gains of the past decade and convince her jittery neighbors that she had no further designs on their territory. Bismarck's commitment to turn away from further expansion brought with it a rather arbitrary geographical definition of the new Germany. To the east the Germans living in Bohemia and Austria served as a reminder that the geographical definition could still be enlarged.

The problem of precisely defining Germany assumed immediate importance when early in the nineteenth century German sentiment developed the aim of unifying the German peoples into a single sovereign political unit. When the revolutionaries of 1848 saw the opportunity for unification the question of defining Germany was one of the most crucial questions they faced. Two basic attitudes emerged at the Frankfurt Parliament where German nationalists struggled with this question. The *Kleindeutschers* were willing to accept a small Germany, one which excluded Germans living within the legitimate boundaries of neighboring states. They based their thinking upon the political and power realities of the day. The *Grossdeutschers*, less mindful of these realities, envisioned a large Germany which would incorporate all Germans into the new state regardless of who presently ruled over them. Failure of the two groups to resolve their differences largely precluded adoption of a strategy sufficiently realistic to achieve unification of any kind. For the next decade and a half both the constitutional and national aspirations of German nationalism foundered. Until the Bismarckian solution resolved the issue in favor of the *Kleindeutschers* the question remained largely academic.

Those who had championed the *grossdeutsch* approach to unity were for a time neutralized by their own exhilaration at Bismarck's achievement. If German power could achieve this, could it not achieve even more? The exhilaration wore off, however, as it became clear that Bismarck, true to his word, would not use German power to effect a *Grossdeutschland*. Unwittingly the Iron Chancellor had also kept *grossdeutsch* hope alive through the annexation of Alsace-Lorraine from France in 1871. Here was a territory populated in part at least by German-speaking peoples, one which had been part of the German Holy Roman Empire until gobbled up by the wars of Louis XIV and his *Chambres de réunion*. Its incorporation into the new Reich served as a constant reminder that *grossdeutsch* aims were only partially realized.[14] Germany, Bismarck's pronouncement notwithstanding, was not complete.

The connection of the *grossdeutsch-kleindeutsch* issue to the development of anti-Semitism and racism later in the century is by no means a simple one. The important element here is, however, that the issue raised the question of who belonged to Germany, and more critically, who did not belong. The essence of the Jewish problem as it developed in Germany (and elsewhere) ultimately reduces itself to that question.

The question of belonging was particularly important to the *Grossdeutschers* who were anxious to include all Germans in Germany. *Grossdeutsch* attitudes had their intellectual roots in an organic concept of nationhood which had developed during the late eighteenth and early nineteenth centuries. The organic concept was a response to the peculiar political situation of central and eastern Europe and therefore in sharp contrast to the predominantly mechanistic concept of nationhood developed in western Europe. In France and England, for example, there already existed by the eighteenth century a relatively high de-

[14] Walter Lipgens, "Bismarck, die öffentliche Meinung und die Annexion von Elsass-Lothringen, 1870," *Historiche Zeitschrift* 199 (1964): 31-112.

gree of uniformity in ethnic composition (some ethnic groupings having merged, others having been assimilated) as well as general conformity of language and religion. This relative homogeneity, fostered and often demanded by central state authority, allowed these countries to develop the idea of nationhood within the political matrix of the state.[15] Consequently nationality developed as a political concept. The connection of the individual to the nation was a legal one; he was the citizen of a distinct and sovereign political entity—France or England. Theoretically an individual could change his nationality by moving to another state and declaring allegiance to its government. For him, the nineteenth century French philosopher, Renan, that the existence of a nation rests upon a daily plebiscite of its citizens was perfectly applicable. There was nothing inherent in his makeup which would prevent him leaving one nationality and deciding to become part of another one. The procedure was a mechanical one, in theory open to selection and choice if he was willing to subject himself to being assimilated into the ways of his new society, its language and its value structures.

In central and eastern Europe, in which Germany had been, according to Metternich, nothing more than a geographical expression, nationality perforce could not be tied to the state. There were no states in the western European sense, only the remnants of once great empires whose boundaries were ill-defined and which purportedly governed over peoples deeply fragmented by ethnic, religious, language, and social divisions. No authority—political, religious, or otherwise—could foster the bridging of these divisions. Indeed, the imperial structures oftentimes continued to exercise limited authority in the nineteenth century only because of these divisions.

The concept of nation which emerged in central and eastern Europe came to be tied to a recognition of the separateness of the various groups living in these regions. This separateness was

15 See Hans Rothfels, "Grundsätzliches zum Problem der Nationalität," *Historische Zeitschrift* 174 (1952): 339-358; and Otto Pflanze, "Nationalism in Europe, 1848-1871," *Review of Politics* 28 (April, 1966): 129-143.

most evident in the various languages, but was usually reinforced by differences in religion and social status, both of which served to promote and reinforce mutual antagonisms. Out of this cultural separateness emerged an eastern European concept of nationality distinct from that of Britain or France. Rather than the mechanistic matrix of politics, it was culture which gave birth to the idea of nationhood. Each nation came to be considered the unique creation of a unique culture, an organic expression of that culture's intrinsic generative powers. Its literature, art, religion, and music were the various attributes of a distinct culture and the characteristics of a unique nationality. The result for eastern Europe was what the distinguished German historian, Friederich Meinecke, called the *Kulturnation,* to be distinguished from western Europe's *Staatsnation.*[16]

It was the German philosopher Johann Gottfried Herder (1774-1803) who gave shape to the ideas of culture and nationality in the latter half of the eighteenth century. Herder saw in each culture a *Volksgeist* or spirit which inspired the unique expressions of language, literature, and art of each nation. Nationality was for Herder a cultural organism, as much the product of nature as was a tree or a flower. The members of a nationality were joined to one another by inner spiritual bonds; together they comprised the *Volk.* Because of the spiritual bonds, the *Volk* was more than merely the sum of its parts; it was an organic entity, a creation of nature held together by shared culture. The implications of this organic conception of nationality are easy to see. Assimilation and acculturation, possible within the legal mechanistic concepts of western Europe, were more difficult when the differences of nationalities were seen to be resting on qualities inherent in the *Volk* itself. The law could be changed by an act of man's will; the spirit of the *Volksgeist* could not.

Herder scrupulously avoided assigning greater value to any one culture or nationality. There was only one race—the human

16 Friedrich Meinecke, *Weltbürgertum und Nationalstaat, Werke,* vol. 5 (Munich, 1962), p. 10.

race—which for him was divided into a variety of different or unique cultures, all of equal value. He used the concept of *Volk* to designate those who belonged to the German nationality or to any other. The chief tangible attribute of nationality was language; understandably so, for it was about the only point of contact for the German or any peoples in the world in which Herder moved. For the nationalists of Herder's generation the *völkisch* concept was immensely useful in allowing them to see a unity where none had previously existed. Herder yearned for a politically unified Germany which would embrace all Germans. "The most natural state is one nationality with one national character," he wrote. Arguing against the multinational political structures of his day, he warned that "Nothing therefore appears so indirectly opposite to the end of government as the unnatural enlargement of states, the wild mixing of all kinds of people and nationalities under one scepter."[17]

The logic of Herder's humanitarian nationalism was to fulfill itself when each *Volk* developed its own sovereign government. This political self-fulfillment would yield an age of peace between nations which by their nature would be satisfied within the state structures. Herder's influence on the development of nationalist ideology in Germany and in eastern Europe was profound. Fichte, the prophet of a German nationalism during the Napoleonic occupation, drew upon Herder's conception of national cultures as unique organisms to rally the Germans to a war of liberation. The idea of the *Volksgeist* was widely adopted in areas outside of politics as well. The Grimm brothers searched for it in the German folk tales they collected. In legal theory Carl von Savigny discovered a uniquely German historical school of law. Friedrich Schlegel and Georg Friedrich Hegel elaborated upon Herder's conceptualizations and constructed rigorous philosophical systems in which the individual national cultures played a central role. Goethe, who read Herder's books

[17] Quoted by Robert R. Ergang in *Herder and the Foundations of German Nationalism* (New York, 1966), pp. 243-244.

avidly, stated that Herder's work had been borrowed so extensively by others that it became a commonplace.[18]

To the awakening peoples of eastern Europe Herder's ideas inspired a generation of nationalist intellectuals. His concept of cultural nationalities legitimized the longings of those who, in the face of control by a foreign emperor, be he Habsburg, Romanov, or Turk, hoped for a greater measure of self-determination. For these people Herder was a prophet. One of Herder's disciples, the historian Heinrich Luden at the University of Jena, decisively influenced young east European intellectuals. His lectures during the decade following the Congress of Vienna attracted students from all over eastern Europe, from Poland, Hungary, Bohemia, Serbia, and elsewhere who shortly became instrumental in spreading nationalist ideas among their own people.[19] His most immediate influence was upon the development of Czech nationalism through his student František Palacký and upon the early stages of the Pan-Slavic movement through Jan Kollar.[20]

For all of these people Herder's conceptualization of *Volk* was useful for defining who belonged to a national culture. It made legitimate and desirable the separation of people into different national groups, and was therefore a powerful weapon against the cosmopolitanism of the conservative imperial structures of eastern Europe. Throughout these areas of Europe variations on Herder's ideas served as the backbone of nationalist movements.

Theoretically, the idea of *Volk* liberated the Germans and east European peoples from the sleep induced by centuries of imperial control. In practice it was not quite that simple. The Habsburgs, Hohenzollerns, and the Romanovs did not simply

18 Ibid., p. 103.

19 Hermann Oncken, "Deutsche geistige Einflüsse in der europäischen Nationalitätenbewegung des 19. Jahrhunderts," *Deutsche Vierteljahrsschrift für Literatur —Wissenschaft—und Geistesgeschichte* 7 (1929): 607-627.

20 Josef Pfitzner, "Heinrich Luden und František Palacký: Ein Kapitel deutschslawischer Kulturbeziehungen," *Historische Zeitschrift* 141 (1930): 54-96.

roll over and play dead in the face of a new idea. They formed a Holy Alliance in 1815 at least in part to protect themselves from such views. Then, too, the *völkisch* idea itself had implications which its liberal champions had failed to see. The idea of *Volk* could indeed be used to define those who belonged, but it could also be used to define those who did not belong. What about minority groups who lived in the same geographical area as a *Volk?* Or lived scattered throughout the areas inhabited by several *Volk?* Specifically, what about the Jews who lived scattered across central and eastern Europe? Were they a separate *Volk* which might have made their concentration in one area with their own political structures desirable? Or could they continue to exist as a minority among a variety of different nationalities? If so, would they have to maintain their separateness from the majority people around them, or was their assimilation into the majority possible or even desirable?

It is within the framework structured by these questions that one can see a specific central and east European dimension to the Jewish problem as it developed in the nineteenth century. The central and east European nations were confronted with a Jewish problem which was itself an intrinsic part of their own struggle for identity and independence, a struggle which was given its shape in large part by the influence of the German idealistic philosophers and particularly their popularizing disciples. We have seen the direction which this struggle took in Russia, Poland, Hungary, and Romania later in the century, where Russification, Magyarization, and the maintenance of Romanian purity came at the expense of Jewish minorities. It would be foolish to suggest that the persecutions and pogroms were motivated merely by the need for securing a national identity; certainly many of its participants had never heard of such a thing or would not have understood it if they had. Yet the rationale of the instigators of discrimination and persecution was rooted in precisely that argument. At the very least, there was serious question as to whether Jews could belong to a national community, a *Volk,* or a *Kulturnation.*

The question of the Jewish relationship to the German *Volk* was raised very early in the nineteenth century. The raucous nationalist *Turnvater* Jahn who organized gymnastic societies during the Napoleonic occupation so that German youth might be fit to expel the hated foreigner, excluded Jews (and Poles and priests) from his group because they were not part of the *Volkstum*.[21] The Jewish question was raised also by the patriotic *Burschenschaft* student movement which grew out of the disappointment of the failure of the Congress of Vienna to create a united Germany. At a *Burschenschaft* congress in 1818 the question of Jewish eligibility for membership in the student societies was debated. The decision, which came to be anchored in the *Burschenschaft* constitution, was that Jews "as such, because they have no Fatherland and can have no interest in ours, are not eligible for membership unless they prove that they are anxious to develop within themselves a Christian-German spirit."[22] The same attitude was adopted toward foreigners. It is significant to note, however, that on this level a solution to the Jewish question was relatively simple. Jews could still become part of the German *Volk* simply by adopting its basic values— Christianity and German patriotism. It would be incorrect to see in this formulation of the Jewish question merely the first step in the development of a situation which eventually closed off entirely the Jewish entry into German culture. In the context of its own time it was a significant step forward. It offered Jews for the first time in modern history the concrete opportunity to move out of the spiritual ghetto of separateness and to join a mainstream of European life. The young Heinrich Heine went so far as to say that the adoption of these values was "the entry ticket for Jews into European culture." What is significant is not so much that the Jewish question was raised, but that a solution to the question was considered possible. There was a deeper im-

[21] Simon Dubnow, *Die neueste Geschichte des jüdischen Volkes, 1789-1914* (Berlin, 1920), p. 204.

[22] Georg Heer, *Die Geschichte der deutschen Burschenschaft*, vol. 2 (Heidelberg, 1920), pp. 19, 24.

plication to the solution proposed by the liberal nationalist movement, however—one so obvious that its recognition would have been comparable to a fish discovering water: the view of what Germany was, rooted in an organic conception of nationhood, did not admit the possibility of an ethnically plural society. Consequently, the Jewish question was rooted not in the Jews themselves, but in the nature of the German self-identity. This situation, more than anything else, was to plague the Jewish-German relationship into the next century.

The *grossdeutsch-kleindeutsch* issue was part of a larger identity question. On the geographical level the question had been settled, temporarily at least, by the events of 1871. But unification had also raised the identity question to other levels. In part this is what Bismarck must have been talking about when he spoke of consolidating the gains of the past decade. It is certainly what the *Grossdeutschers* had in mind when they expressed dissatisfaction with the incompleteness of Bismarck's creation. The socialists, who eventually managed to establish something approaching a working class subculture, quite obviously did not share in the identity envisioned by either Bismarck or the *Grossdeutschers*.

Bismarck's situation in the first two decades after unification is particularly instructive. He brought to Germany a tailor-made constitution to provide the formal context in which an identity could be developed. While it is doubtful that he had any highly developed notions about organic community (having little respect for professors and their academic musings), it is clear that he too was concerned about the consequences of pluralism. His attacks upon Catholics and socialists in the 70's and 80's were undertaken out of the fear that these groups could not maintain their own identity and also fit into the Germany he envisioned. The Catholic, he feared, would be loyal to Rome; the socialist to international revolution. Bismarck's struggles with the Catholics and socialists were essentially no different, however, from the struggles political authority had had in western Europe with potentially dissident groups. Louis XIV and Elizabeth I had both sought to enforce religious conformity and were largely successful. At least so far as the Catholics were concerned, Bismarck discovered that he could get along with less than conformity so long as they accepted political allegiance to Germany and its way of doing things.

The most articulate definition of Germany's identity problem came from the historian Heinrich von Treitschke. When Treitschke came to the University of Berlin in 1873 he found the historical school there engrossed in the study and criticism of sources. Treitschke wanted none of that. To him the purpose of history was to imbue the German people with pride and idealism, qualities he found peculiarly lacking in the new Reich. Bismarck's accomplishment he considered a diplomatic-military accomplishment, only the shell of a nation. History alone could fill this vacuum and give Germany its identity.[23]

As Treitschke set out to fill the vacuum with his multivolume *German History in the Nineteenth Century* a wave of anti-Jewish feeling erupted. Essentially it was triggered by resentments stemming from the economic depression which came in the wake of the astonishing prosperity following the Franco-Prussian War. The stock anti-Jewish accusations were retreaded and applied to the present situation. Jews were widely rumored

[23] Andreas Dorpalen, *Heinrich von Treitschke* (New Haven, 1957), p. 226. The concept of identity as used in this chapter is borrowed from Erik H. Erikson's concept of ego-identity. The identity concept has been applied to an analysis of Burmese society by Lucian Pye, *Politics, Personality, and Nation Building: Burma's Search for Identity* (New Haven, 1962). Pye suggests that the identity concept "can serve as a powerful intellectual tool for understanding the process of nation building in transitional societies" (p. 52). Certainly Germany found herself in a transitional situation during the 1860's, 70's, and 80's—her years of nation building. In the early history of the United States the struggle between the federalists and antifederalists would be another case critical in the development of identity. M. S. Lipset deals with this problem, observing: "It was from this struggle (the federalist and anti-federalist controversy) that values and goals became defined, issues carved out, positions taken, in short an identity established." See Martin Seymour Lipset, *The First New Nation* (New York, 1963), p. 16. With slightly different contours, the identity concept has been applied to a study of public opinion in Canada. See Mildred Schwartz, *Public Opinion and Canadian Identity* (Berkeley, 1967).

to have engaged in fraudulent practices on the bourse and to have profited unfairly from the collapse. Treitschke suddenly found himself confronted with the Jewish question. While he did not fall prey to the simple prejudices expressed around him, neither could he ignore the question. What he did was to raise the Jewish question to the level of Germany's identity problem. The Jews were dangerous to Germany, he said, because they were an alien, cosmopolitan element in a national society which did not yet have firm traditions. This German weakness had enabled Jews to gain control of vital aspects of German life and culture—and now the economy too.[24] Their cosmopolitanism made the Jews, in Treitschke's much quoted phrase, "Germany's misfortune."

The coarseness of Treitschke's anti-Jewish rhetoric has left him open to the charge of being one of Hitler's intellectual fore-runners. Indeed Treitschke's contribution to German anti-Semitism should not be underestimated. The widespread influence of his lectures and writings certainly helped to drive an awareness of a Jewish problem into the consciousness of Germany's educated classes. Still, Hitler's intellectual forebears are hardly as respectable as this renowned professor from Berlin. For Hitler the Jewish problem was the only problem; for Treitschke it was part of a larger problem of German unity. Treitschke was still in the tradition of the *Burschenschaft* movement in that he asked Jews to abandon their own traditions in order to be accepted as Germans. His anger with the Jews, he said, arose from their failure to take full advantage of the opportunity for assimilation offered by emancipation.[25] Alien though they were, Treitschke still believed that Jews could eventually share in and become part of the German community. In this tradition it was the unassimilated Jew who was dangerous. In the tradition of which Hitler represented the culmination, it

24 Dorpalen, *Treitschke,* pp. 241-247.
25 Hans-Günther Zmarzlik, "Der Antisemitismus im Zweiten Reich," *Geschichte im Wissenschaft und Unterricht* 14 (1963): 273-286.

was the assimilated or disguised Jew who was most dangerous to German culture.

Germany's real misfortune was the fact that her quest for identity coincided with a period of severe economic dislocation. Economic crisis brought to the surface the older anti-Jewish prejudices and helped create the climate in which these prejudices found a new footing in racism. The racist dimension to anti-Semitism developed after 1870 during an era which Fritz Stern has characterized as one of "cultural despair."[26] The crisis to which Stern points arose out of the response to the crises any society undergoing rapid transition must face. It was during the first decades following unification that Germany suddenly found herself to be modern. Industrialization proceeded at a pace unparalleled anywhere during the nineteenth century. Coal and iron, noted John Maynard Keynes, had by the 1870's replaced the already outdated "blood and iron" of the 1860's. Here was an economic crisis more far-reaching in its implications for Germany than the financial depression of 1873. In the wake of industrialization came the dislocations associated with urbanization and the breaking up of traditional economic and social relationships.

Modernity in its industrial, capitalist, and liberal forms stirred a wide variety of resentments. The urban working classes, spurred by socialist ideology, began increasingly to look for a revolution which would maintain an industrial society, but reorganize it within a noncapitalist framework. Other socioeconomic groups were less optimistic about an industrial society. The modernity it represented threatened to pass them by completely. Hardest hit were elements of the lower middle classes— the shopkeeper, the skilled craftsman, the small businessman— who had great difficulty competing with the large industrial, business, and financial institutions of an industrial capitalist economy. The inability to adjust to this new situation threat-

[26] Fritz Stern, *The Politics of Cultural Despair: A Study in the Rise of the Germanic Ideology* (New York, 1965).

ened the economic and social status of these groups. In a society as conscious of its class divisions and class privileges as Germany, the prospect of being stripped of this status had highly unsettling implications. For the individual it meant slipping into the proletariat; for the society at large it meant a highly dissatisfied and potentially revolutionary social class. Just as the upheavals of 1848 had been inspired largely by the resistance of craftsman, artisan, and peasant to modernization,[27] so the new dislocations of the 1870's became crucial in shaping the attitudes of a new lower middle-class generation.

The individual shopkeeper and artisan might not have been able to adjust to this modernity or even to understand it, but he knew very well that the department store and the new methods of manufacture threatened his livelihood and the status associated with it. More articulate critics such as Treitschke felt that materialism was replacing the time-honored values of community or *Gemeinschaft* as the sociologist Tönnies called it. The cold rationality of capitalism precluded the growth of the spiritual, organic community. Political liberalism, with its stress on the individual, led to a divisive system of political parties whose function seemed to be to rupture the bonds of *Volk*. Those whom the new Germany for one reason or another left behind understandably became its severest critics. The despair they felt found its outlet in a variety of isms: racism, anti-Semitism, anti-industrialism, anticapitalism, antiliberalism, and antimodernity in all its manifestations. Many of these critics soon began to call for a conservative revolution, one which would return Germany to its premodern and "pre-Jewish" stage of development.

The transformation of anti-Jewish feelings into racial categories occurred in this atmosphere of the 1870's and 80's. The transformation had its beginnings with the coining of the term "anti-Semitism," used for the first time in 1873 by an obscure German pamphleteer, Wilhelm Marr. Marr assigned to Jews the attri-

[27] Theodor S. Hamerow, *Restoration, Revolution, Reaction: Economics and Politics in Germany, 1815-1871* (Princeton, 1958), pp. 102-106; 150-155.

butes of a race. His pamphlet, *Der Sieg des Judentums über das Germanentum* (The Victory of Judaism over Germanism) mentioned for the first time a perpetual racial conflict between Jews and Germans, a conflict which, as his title indicated, he thought the Jews were winning. Very little is known about Marr. When his pamphlet was published in 1873 he was an unemployed journalist removed from his position, he claimed, by Jews.[28] Not only were the Jews ruining Germany; they had already ruined him.

Because Marr was the first in Germany to equate the racial question with the Jewish problem his views serve as a useful model in explaining the direction anti-Jewish feelings were eventually to take. In attacking the Jews, Marr was also criticizing the Germany in which he lived. The basic weapons in the Jewish arsenal—political and economic liberalism—had been handed them in the process of political emancipation. A Germany based upon false liberal doctrines had allowed for the Jewish emancipation and led to its seizing of the leading positions in German finance, industry, and professional life. Germany's fault, he told the Jews, lay in the fact we "did not possess the ethical strength to confine you to yourselves and to intercourse among yourselves."[29] Assimilation, far from being the answer to the Jewish problem, as it was for Treitschke, was for Marr its cause. Because their qualities were racially determined there was no possibility of Jews accepting the values of Germanism. The struggle between Jews and Germans would have to be to the death.

Perhaps because of his belief that he himself had been done in by the Jews, Marr concluded that the victory of Judaism over Germanism was almost complete. Only a desperate counterattack by an aroused Germany might possibly bring a reversal of the seemingly inevitable. Otherwise, he wrote, "Let us sub-

[28] Brief treatments of Marr and his influence appear in Paul W. Massing, *Rehearsal for Destruction: A Study of Political Anti-Semitism in Imperial Germany* (New York, 1949), pp. 6-10; and P. G. J. Pulzer, *The Rise of Political Anti-Semitism in Germany and Austria* (New York, 1964), pp. 47-52.

[29] Massing, *Rehearsal for Destruction*, p. 8.

mit to the inevitable if we are unable to change it. Its name is: FINIS GERMANIAE."[30] In what must have been a desperate attempt to stem the Jewish tide of victory, Marr founded in 1879 an Anti-Semite League.[31] It was the first German organization committed to combatting the danger presented by a Jewish race.

Except for his advice about submitting to the inevitable, Marr anticipated by half a century most of what the Nazis were going to say about the Jewish problem. Hitler agreed that emancipation lay at the root of the Jewish problem; that there was no point in distinguishing between good and bad Jews; that the question of German identity had reached the point where Germany's very survival lay in the balance.

Marr, by placing the Jewish problem into racial categories, appropriates for himself an important role in the development of a racist dialectic in Germany. To call him the father of German racism, however, would be to overestimate his importance, if only because so many others have willingly claimed its paternity. Whether Marr was influenced by the man who is most often considered the father of racism, the French aristocrat and diplomat Count Arthur de Gobineau, is difficult to say. When applied to Germany, however, Gobineau's reputation is questionable. Here his influence was limited until the late 1890's when a Gobineau Society was founded at the University of Göttingen by a man who was also preparing a translation of Gobineau's four-volume *Essay on the Inequality of the Human Races*,[32] published forty years earlier. By the time the German translation appeared in 1898, an independent German school of racism was on the verge of publishing its own racist synthesis, one with a definite German stamp. Racism was apparently unconcerned about the nationality of her suitors.

Marr's significance had been to tie the Jewish question to race, though he had left undefined the essence of what distin-

---

30 Ibid., p. 9.
31 George L. Mosse, *The Crisis of German Ideology* (New York, 1965), p. 130.
32 Pulzer, *Political Anti-Semitism*, p. 236.

guished the Jewish race from any other. That gap was filled by Eugen Duehring, whose *Die Judenfrage als Frage der Rassenschädlichkeit* (The Jewish Question as a Problem of Race Deterioration) in 1881 suggested blood as the distinguishing mark of race. Duehring's views were in many ways those of the later Nazis writ small. Aside from the link between blood and race, Duehring advocated a type of "national socialism" (quickly assigned to the scrap heap of socialist doctrine by Friedrich Engels) which defined itself against what he called Jewish liberalism and capitalism. Germans could defend their racial honor by removing the nefarious Jew from his position in government, business, and finance. German blood could be guarded from contamination by annulling racially mixed marriages between Jews and Germans and by preventing any future ones.[33] Duehring's discovery of the link between blood and race brought anti-Semitism to a new stage in its development. While his idea did not catch on immediately, it was to be of great future importance for the Nazis in giving their anti-Semitic propaganda a pseudoscientific base.

The writings of Duehring and Marr were only part of a sizable anti-Semitic literature reflecting the new racial twists to the resentment of Jews. There would be little value in outlining or summarizing in detail the views presented during these years. A rich variety of opinion on nonessentials could not hide general agreement that Jews were a race, that they threatened German cultural, biological, and national purity, and that, therefore, they were incapable of becoming Germans.

The power of this resentment was demonstrated by the formation of an anti-Semitic political party in the late 1870's. In 1878, Dr. Adolf Stoecker, the court chaplain to Kaiser Wilhelm I, organized a Christian Social Workers' Party. Stoecker had come a long way up the social ladder in Imperial Germany. He was the son of a modest lower middle-class family whose parents had sacrificed their own comforts so that he might study at the univer-

[33] Tenenbaum, *Race and Reich*, p. 12.

sity. It was their suffering during the depression of the 70's which moved him to political action. He directed his party's appeals to those lower middle classes, the shopkeeper and crafts-man, who had reason to fear the new capitalist-industrial order. Their suffering, Stoecker told them, was the product of Jewish materialism. Stoecker was no racist, but like the racists and many other critics of society he hoped to establish for Germany a tighter sense of community. According to Stoecker such a community could be created through a Christian International of Love, an anticapitalist program of economic reform and a restriction on "Jewish liberties."[34]

Stoecker and his politics fell into disgrace with the new Kaiser after 1890, not so much for his anti-Semitism as for his peculiar brand of socialism. By electing a handful of representatives to various state parliaments and to the imperial Reichstag during the 1880's, however, anti-Semitism had made its first concerted effort to influence the political course of the Second Reich. The relevance of Stoecker's contribution to anti-Semitism was not lost upon the Nazis. Walter Frank, their chief historian and an organizer of anti-Jewish scholarship for the Third Reich, earned his doctorate with a dissertation on Stoecker.

It remained for a half-German, the son of an English admiral and a German mother, Houston Stewart Chamberlain, to pro-vide for Germany the first detailed synthesis of racial thought. His *Foundations of the 19th Century* which appeared in 1899, one year after the Gobineau translation, was an immediate suc-cess. Chamberlain offered his readers a complete theory of his-tory based on race. Real history, he informed them, began just prior to the Middle Ages with the migrations of the Germanic peoples. The ancient civilizations of China, India, Persia, Greece, and Rome he dismissed as prolegomena to real history. The appearance of Germans upon the historical stage had rescued a dying humanity whose civilizations had already de-clined. It had been their inherent racial superiority which

---

[34] Massing, *Rehearsal for Destruction*, p. 22.

allowed Germans to accomplish this historical task. The undoers of civilization on the other hand were the parasitic Semites, a race of inferior peoples.[35]

Chamberlain's work was heady stuff for a people whose national ego was already puffed out of proportion. The impetuous Kaiser Wilhelm II read the book and complimented Chamberlain for bringing "order to confusion; light to darkness [and] proof for what we suspected. . . ."[36]

Chamberlain, although his synthesis climaxed some three decades of racial thinking, did not draw his ideas directly from predecessors such as Marr or Duehring. His system was constructed out of his own materials. In that sense at least he was original. The blood component of Duehring or of the later Nazis was still absent. It is difficult to say whether he chose to ignore Duehring's contentions or was unfamiliar with them; in any event he espoused the then more fashionable theories of phrenology as an explanation for race. Chamberlain hit upon skull length as being the mark which differentiated one race from another. Nothing had been achieved in the way of history or science, but Chamberlain, who by virtue of his marriage to Richard Wagner's widow had entry into Germany's highest circles, had lent authority to a set of ideas systematizing a theory of Jewish racial inferiority.

Chamberlain, Stoecker, Duehring, Marr, and Treitschke were critics of Imperial Germany. Each one of them abhorred in somewhat different fashion the spiritual emptiness of their society. Each one agreed in one way or another that Jews were responsible for this emptiness. Except for Treitschke and Stoecker, they also agreed that Jews could not share in a German *Volksgeist*. If that was true, under no circumstances could Jews be integrated or absorbed into the Germany they envisioned. For them Germany had to go a step beyond being a *Kulturnation* to become a race-nation.

35 Gerd-Klaus Kaltenbrunner, "Houston Stewart Chamberlains germanischer Mythos," *Politische Studien* 175 (1967): 568-583.
36 Ibid., p. 581.

Chamberlain's racial explanation for human history was only one of the many intellectual syntheses produced in the latter half of the nineteenth century. Most of the isms which have profoundly influenced the twentieth century have their genesis in these decades. Considering its influence upon our own century, racism must rank with Marxism in its importance. Certain parallels between the two are obvious. Each has subsequently served as the ideological underpinning for a twentieth-century totalitarian dictatorship. In its most extreme form each has stressed the inevitability of conflict and the totally dichotomous nature of good and evil. Each has offered an explanation for historical phenomena, a motivating force for the process of history. Where Marxism suggested economic interest as the basis for historical causation, racism explained it on the basis of varying genetic or blood qualities. The basic unit of society for the Marxists was the social class; for the racists it was the race. In place of Marx's economic determination the racists established a racial determinism.

The recital of such surface parallels obscures, of course, the fact that these two isms were bitterly opposed to one another. Duehring's efforts to combine socialism and racism were rejected immediately by the Marxists because they were not based upon the scientific principles discovered by Marx. The racists rejected Marxism on the other hand because Marx failed to recognize what they had considered the obvious differences between peoples. Marx's claim to having discovered a science of society, if not accepted as dogma, at least warranted and received serious attention. The nearest racism came to scientific repute was through its self-claimed link with a third great synthesis of the nineteenth century, the Darwinian theory of natural selection and survival of the fittest.

The publication of Darwin's theory of biological evolution in 1859 had an immediate impact in Germany. At the national congress of German scientists in 1863 the debate on Darwin's theory was led by a young biologist, Professor Ernst Haeckel of the University of Jena. Already in 1863 Haeckel went beyond

Darwin's views on biological evolution to see in them a general theory of human and social development.[37] For the next four decades he acted as the chief apostle for Social Darwinism in Germany. His writings popularized the basic notions of Darwinism and employed them to explain the historical and social development of civilization. The interpretation of Social Darwinism to a mass audience became his life work. While his academic reputation suffered, his books were extremely popular. In 1899 his mission was capped by providing a Social Darwinist answer to *The Riddle of the Universe,* a book which by 1914 had sold more than 300,000 copies.[38]

The popularity of Social Darwinism among Germany's educated classes occasions little surprise. It offered German nationalists a new and meaningful interpretation of the recent past. German military success in the Bismarckian wars fitted neatly into Darwinist categories. Almost before the rest of Europe could draw its breath German armies had swept aside the forces of the Austrian and French Empires, two of Europe's great powers. In the struggle for survival, the fitness of Germany had been clearly demonstrated. Was not this expressive of a superior spirit or *Volksgeist?*

Haeckel had not been a racist, but the susceptibility of views such as his had immediate implications for the race question. One of the problems of the humanitarian concepts of *Volk* and *Volksgeist* had been their inherent ambiguity. Pinning down a nationality by its traditions in literature, folk-music, and philosophy left the fringes of national definition very unclear. If, however, the nationalist could demonstrate a distinctive racial composition to his nation, if the *Volk* was also a race, these ambiguities could be swept aside.

Darwin's notion of struggle for survival was quickly appropriated by the racists once the Social Darwinists raised the struggle

[37] Wilhelm Bölsche, *Haeckel: His Life and Work,* trans. Joseph McCabe (London, 1906), pp. 150-151.

[38] Hans-Günther Zmarzlik, "Der Sozialdarwinismus in Deutschland als geschichtliches Problem," *Vierteljahrshefte für Zeitgeschichte* 11 (July 1963): 246-273.

from the biological to the social plane. Such a struggle, legitimized by the latest scientific views, justified the racists' conceptions of superior and inferior peoples and nations and validated the conflict between them. The racists' appropriation of these scientific categories won for racist thought a much wider circulation than its ideas warranted. What satisfaction there must have been to find that one's prejudices were actually expressions of scientific truth. What greater authority than science could the racists have invoked? A populace astounded by the changes in its physical and social environment already attributed most of these changes to science and technology. The addition of a racial science seemed no more than logical. Not all Social Darwinists were anti-Semites or even racists in any specific sense, any more than all anti-Semites were Social Darwinists, but the development of Social Darwinism gave to racism and anti-Semitism and the *völkisch* movement a foundation it would not have found for itself.

The anti-Semitic movement in late nineteenth-century Germany was an integral part of the *völkisch* and *grossdeutsch* opposition within the Second Reich. *Grossdeutsch* sentiment, rooted as it was in the idea of a German *Volk,* was exceedingly vulnerable to the idea of maintaining a German racial purity. The link between anti-Semitic and *grossdeutsch* sympathies is demonstrated clearly by the history of the Pan-German League. Founded in 1891, the Pan-German League had the unmistakably *grossdeutsch* purpose of creating a community of all German-speaking peoples and resisting all nonnational tendencies which might hinder the development of complete nationhood. At first the League was not particularly anti-Semitic. Jews were allowed membership if they were fully assimilated into German culture. By 1903 the influence of racist ideas was reflected in the League's new program which stressed for the first time the racial affinity of the German peoples. Among its influential members by then were Ludwig Scheman, the Gobineau translator, and H. S. Chamberlain whose *Foundations of the 19th Century* was currently enjoying popularity. A few years later, in 1912, the League took the next step by declaring itself to be based upon racial principles. The final steps of proclaiming the Jews to be the non-German element which threatened the creation of an effective community of Germans came very shortly thereafter.[39]

The attacks of Marr, Duehring, Chamberlain, or even the Pan-Germans did little to dampen the enthusiasm of most Jews in Germany for becoming German. The anti-Semitic racism which emerged during the Second Reich had, with the exception of the Pan-Germans, very limited organizational strength. A view of how deeply German Jewry identified itself with Germany and wanted to be German is afforded by the debate in Jewish circles over how this identification should be expressed. Usage finally came to settle upon "German Jew," to which a leading anti-Semite, Konstantin Frantz, answered, "One speaks of German or French Jews, but never of Jewish Germans or Jewish Frenchmen."[40] To Frantz the distinction was important. The Jew remained Jewish; his claim to nationality was only an affectation.

Whatever the distinctions between Jew and German made by the anti-Semites, they seemed to represent by and large the views of those on the fringes of German society. The racists and anti-Semites were almost without exception protesting developments over which they had very little control. The indices of assimilation served to convince most Jews that Germany was indeed a safe harbor.

The problem for German Jewry seemed to be much more one of overcoming the traditional anti-Jewish attitude based upon religious and economic stereotypes. By no means had the racists succeeded in channeling all anti-Jewish resentments into the racial mold. The fact remained, however, that Jews were far from having free access into the most prestigious professions. The German military was exceedingly reluctant to allow the

[39] Alfred Kruck, *Geschichte des Alldeutschen Verbandes* (Wiesbaden, 1954), pp. 10, 130-131.
[40] Toury, *Orientierungen der Juden*, p. 139.

commissioning of Jewish officers for reasons ranging from the belief that Jewish dietary laws might restrict their military effectiveness to the far more revealing contention that Jews might not be able to command the respect due a superior officer.[41] Similarly the federal and state civil services and judiciary prevented—particularly at their upper levels—a significant Jewish representation.[42] The same situation prevailed in education at the secondary and university levels, where Jews were granted professorships only with great reluctance. The resistance of the traditionally prestigious professions to Jewish participation forced them into the newer professions and occupations where ability and performance counted more heavily than birth and status. This fact in itself served to associate Jews more closely with modernity and change in the minds of those groups and classes whom change had passed by. These people became the built-in audience for those who charged that liberalism, capitalism, and materialism were all Jewish inventions to dupe the honest well-meaning German.

Not all such charges stemmed from the crackpot elements of German society. They were given considerable repute by the eminent economist Werner Sombart whose treatise on *The Jews and Modern Capitalism* in 1911 linked the Jews with the growth of the entrepreneurial system.[43] Sombart saw in what he called the restless spirit of the Jews, the motive force in the development of a market economy. This same spirit, he now concluded, was the basis of the Jewish aptitude for operating within a modern capitalist system. Sombart was not a racist, not even anti-Jewish, at least by his own definition. Yet the course of his own career which he began as a nineteenth-century liberal and ended as a blood-nationalist follower of Adolf Hitler illustrated the adaptability of his ideas to a variety of purposes.

[41] Karl Demeter, *The German Officer-Corps in Society and State, 1650-1945*, trans. Angus Malcolm (New York, 1965), pp. 224-225.

[42] Toury, *Orientierungen der Juden*, p. 126.

[43] Werner Sombart, *The Jews and Modern Capitalism* (London, 1913).

The Jewish identification with liberalism was not one merely imputed to them by their enemies. A recent study indicates that nearly 90 percent of Germany's politically conscious Jews identified themselves with liberal or progressive parties after 1870.[44] For good reason Jews saw a liberal Germany as the foundation of their security. It guaranteed them equality of treatment and opportunity together with the protection of their religious right to be "German citizens of the Jewish faith." The attacks by Marr and others reinforced these liberal political attitudes and encouraged the efforts of German Jewry to strengthen what obviously was not yet a fully liberal society. At the same time their efforts in this direction underlined their alienation from right-wing, *völkisch* and racist critics of Imperial Germany.

When weighed against the situation of Jews elsewhere in Europe, and against the progress German Jews had made during the past century, the anti-Semites did not seem to represent a serious threat. Hermann Cohen had taken them into account when he talked in 1915 of the deep historical and cultural roots Jews had been able to set down in Germany. Taken more seriously by Jews themselves was the Jewish question as it had been posed by Treitschke. He had demanded of Jews that they become German. By 1914 that demand seemed well on the way to being met.

---

[44] Toury, *Orientierungen der Juden*, p. 131, n. 45.

11. The Promise and the Threat of Weimar

JEWISH PREDICTIONS on assimilation might well have been realized, had the twentieth century run its course without a Hitler or a Nazi party. It was finally this extreme product of the right wing in German politics which completely reversed what reason had once dictated to be the course of Jewish development in Germany. The story of German Jews from 1919 to 1933 is largely one of how the Jewish situation in the Second Reich was transformed into the Jewish problem of the Third Reich.

The establishment of the Weimar Republic in 1918 seemed to guarantee the continued assimilation of German Jewry. The rights of man, based on an assumption of human equality, were anchored in a constitution which a Jew, Hugo Preuss, had been instrumental in writing. The measure of Jewish participation in the life of the old Reich and its promise in the new republic gave unquestioned substance to the future of German Jews. Not even the victorious powers of 1918, so anxious to guarantee minority rights in the new states of eastern Europe, had required any special assurances of Germany in the Versailles Treaty. Jews simply were not regarded as a minority. By losing some of its territory to surrounding states, Germany lost whatever minorities she had once had.[1]

Many of the problems Jews had faced, even in the wake of emancipation, the republic promised to solve. Careers in the military and higher civil service which traditionally had been reserved for the aristocracy were at least legally opened to talent. The disarmament clauses of Versailles precluded in effect a military career for Jews, but the civil service was now opened to any

[1] Oscar I. Janowsky and Melvin M. Fagen, *International Aspects of German Racial Policies* (New York, 1937), p. 28.

citizen. The abandoning of traditional legal restrictions on mobility only served to improve the prospects for an accelerated process of assimilation.

The vast majority of Germany's Jews was in a position to take advantage of the new opportunities, particularly because the past warranted no special doubts about the future. The Jewish contribution to the war effort between 1914 and 1918 had placed them firmly in the tradition of German patriotism. Some 80,000 had served in the Imperial Army during the war.[2] Whether or not this was a sufficient contribution came to be disputed by the anti-Semites during the 1920's. What could not be disputed was that 12,000 Jews had died for the fatherland and that 35,000 had been decorated for valor. The home front, too, had been well served by Jews. Walther Rathenau, who organized German economic mobilization, and Fritz Haber, head of the German chemical industry, led the list of those prominent in the waging of war. Many of these later banded together in the *Reichsbund der Jüdischen Frontsoldaten,* a Jewish veterans organization, to recall how they had fought for their Kaiser and his empire.

One of the things which had bothered Jewish leaders at the turn of the century and seemed to support their fears of total assimilation was the relatively small size of the Jewish community. Of Europe's ten million or so Jews, less than five percent lived in Germany. Compared to the large Jewish communities in Russia or Poland, German Jews had no large population reserves to fall back upon. The census of 1925 revealed 568,000 Jews who comprised less than one percent of the total German population. Since 1880 the percentage of Jews to the total population had declined steadily. Had it not been for the influx of thousands of foreign Jews after 1900, a decline in absolute numbers would have been noted as well.

It was this small community which was being weakened steadily by the assimilation process, a process which the new republican institutions promised to accelerate quantitatively

[2] Hugo Valentin, *Antisemitism: Historically and Critically Examined* (New York, 1936), p. 109.

and qualitatively. The most immediately striking index of
assimilation was the rapid increase in the number of marriages
between Jewish and non-Jewish Germans. In the larger cities,
Berlin and Frankfurt, where the Jewish population was concentrated, one of every three Jews was marrying outside of his

TABLE 1. JEWISH POPULATION IN GERMANY, 1861-1933

Year	Population of Germany	Jews	
		Number	Percentage
1861	33,652,000	353,000	1.05
1871	36,323,000	383,000	1.05
1880	40,218,000	437,000	1.09
1890	44,230,000	465,000	1.05
1900	50,626,000	497,000	0.98
1910	58,451,000	539,000	0.92
1925	63,181,000	568,000	0.90
1933	66,029,000	503,000	0.76

Source: "Die Glaubensjuden im Deutschen Reich, Volks-, Berufs- und Betriebs-
zaehlung vom 16 Juli 1933," Statistik des Deutschen Reiches 451, no. 5 (Berlin,
1936), p. 7.

faith by the late 20's. For Germany as a whole between 1910 and
1929, the number of Jews marrying non-Jews rose from 8 to 23
percent.[3] For the assimilation-minded, these marriages represented the last stage of a process begun when the Jew emerged
from the medieval ghetto. Others, of course, saw them as weak-
ening the fibers of the Jewish communal consciousness. The
Nazis were shortly to classify such marriages as a deliberate effort
by Jews to defile the purity of German blood, the basest of all
Jewish crimes.

The mixed marriages were understandably most common in
the large cities where the ease of social intercourse undermined
the traditional authority of religious and social caste lines. Berlin, where the percentage of these marriages was highest, was
also the city with the largest Jewish population, 160,564 or

[3] Arthur Ruppin, The Jews in the Modern World (London, 1934), p. 319.

nearly one-third of Germany's Jews.[4] With 71 percent of her Jews living in cities of 100,000 or more inhabitants, the pressures reinforcing the trend to urbanization were considerable. The extent of Jewish urbanization is made especially clear when looking at the other end of the scale. Only 15 percent lived in towns with less than 10,000 residents.

TABLE 2. JEWISH POPULATION IN GERMAN CITIES

City	Population	Jews[*]	Percentage of Jews in Germany
Berlin	4,242,501	160,564	32.1
Frankfurt/a.M.	555,857	26,158	5.2
Breslau	625,198	20,202	4.1
Hamburg	1,129,307	16,885	3.4
Cologne	756,605	14,816	3.0
Leipzig	713,470	11,564	2.3
Munich	735,388	9,005	1.8
Essen	654,461	4,506	0.9
Dresden	642,143	4,397	0.9
Dortmund	540,875	4,108	0.8
Total	10,595,905	272,205	54.5

Source: *Glaubensjuden*, p. 9.
[*] Includes only *Glaubensjuden* or confessing Jews and excludes Jews from the Saar.

The socioeconomic position of Jews in the Weimar Republic was overwhelmingly middle class, a position which reflected the historical circumstances of the Jewish situation in a Christian society and the opportunities offered by a rapidly expanding industrialized Germany of the late nineteenth century.[5] In 1933 over 147,000, or nearly 30 percent of Germany's Jews, were engaged in commercial activity of one sort or another. This was

[4] *Die Glaubensjuden im Deutschen Reich, Volks-, Berufs- und Betriebszählung vom 16. Juli 1933, Statistik des Deutschen Reiches* 451, no. 5 (Berlin, 1936), p. 9.
[5] Esra Bennathan, "Die demographische und wirtschaftliche Struktur der Juden," in Werner E. Mosse, ed., 2nd ed., *Entscheidungsjahr 1932, Zur Judenfrage in der Endphase der Weimarer Republik* (Tübingen, 1966), pp. 87-131.

well over half of all Jews gainfully employed. The 1933 census, taken shortly after Hitler came to power, revealed the breakdown into commercial activities shown in Table 3. Next to the 137,048 Jews dealing in light merchandise, real estate brokers comprised the largest category. In view of Nazi charges, it should

TABLE 3. COMMERCIAL ACTIVITIES OF GERMAN JEWS

Commercial Activity	Number of Jews
Commercial Enterprises	137,048
Light Merchandise	114,659
Small Business	2,196
Publishing	1,831
Real Estate	17,100
Business Services	1,262
Banking, Insurance, Stockbrokers	6,170
Bankers and Stockbrokers	4,085
Private Insurance	1,908
Transportation	988
Restauranteurs, etc.	3,006

Source: Glaubensjuden, p. 23.

be noted that the number of Jewish bankers and stockbrokers represented only two percent of that category in Germany.

The second largest grouping of economic activity for Jews was in industry. Except in some selected areas such as food or the chemical industries, however, Jews were underrepresented in proportion to the rest of the population.

TABLE 4. REPRESENTATION OF JEWS IN GERMAN INDUSTRY

Industry	Jews	Total for Germany
Food	10,568	1,629,645
Chemical	2,223	362,751
Metal	7,220	3,068,509
Textile	3,517	1,118,715
Construction	2,291	1,948,366

Source: Glaubensjuden, p. 24.

TABLE 5. REPRESENTATION OF JEWS IN GERMAN CLOTHING TRADES

Occupation	Number of Jews	Total for Germany
Tailor	14,823	865,029
Furrier	1,735	32,829
Milliner	1,962	73,944
Shoemaker	2,262	366,428

Source: *Glaubensjuden*, p. 24.

Certain trades, especially tailoring, had a proportional over-representation of Jews. Jewish tailors constituted nearly 27 percent of all Jews employed in a nonlaboring capacity in trades or industry. For non-Jews the figure was only seven percent. A similar overrepresentation, although to a lesser degree, existed for the Jewish furriers, milliners, and shoemakers.

A final significant category of Jewish activity was in sales and the various learned professions: law, medicine, university teaching, and journalism. The professions were particularly attractive to the bright young sons of the Jewish shopkeepers and tradesmen because they provided the most immediate openings for upward social mobility. They were also within the financial reach of the classes whose capital was limited. Furthermore, these were the professions which enjoyed considerable prestige and in which success depended more upon ability and initiative than upon background or status.

TABLE 6. REPRESENTATION OF JEWS IN GERMAN PROFESSIONS

Profession	Number in Germany	Jews	
		Number	Percentage
Lawyers	18,000	3,000	16
Medical Doctors	51,000	5,500	10
University Teachers	5,000	200	3
Journalists and Writers	17,000	900	5
Accountants	13,000	515	4
Dancers, Actors, Artists	23,000	703	3
Sales Representatives and Agents	216,000	24,000	9

Source: *Glaubensjuden*, p. 24.

In view of Nazi propaganda it should be pointed out that Jews dominated in none of the professions, trades, industries, or commercial occupations. The only exception would be the department store chains where names such as Tietz, Wertheim, and Karstadt were dominant. To highlight their resentment against the department store the Nazis promised their dissolution in the party platform. Jewish success in department store enterprises pointed to a situation which worked to the Nazi advantage. The solid middle-class position of German Jews tied them to modernity in all its forms: capitalism, urbanism, socialism, republicanism. The antimodern predilections of most Nazi assumptions left the Jews exposed as the agents of modern ideas and, by Nazi definition, the subverters of traditional German values. The department store, which introduced new marketing techniques to the disadvantage of the small shopkeeper, had been an invention of the late nineteenth century. The same period had given birth to the great expansion in the demand for the services provided by the learned professions. The business expansion following German unification had greatly increased the need for lawyers. Advances in science and education had similar effects in medicine, journalism, and teaching. That large numbers of Jews should respond to these opportunities in the wake of emancipation is hardly surprising. The rapid assimilation of Jews into German society and culture following 1870 must be explained in this context.

An instance of Jewish success and visibility became especially apparent in the newspaper business. The German press, like many other aspects of German cultural and intellectual life, flowered during the 1920's. Papers such as the *Vossische Zeitung* in Berlin and the *Frankfurter Zeitung* enjoyed international renown. The *Vossische Zeitung* was published by one of the two large Jewish publishing houses in Germany, the Ullstein concern, which also published the *Morgenpost* and several dailies of the boulevard press variety. The other large Jewish publisher, the Rudolf Mosse concern, put out, in addition to its highly regarded *Berliner Tageblatt*, the *Boersenkurier* and the *8—Uhr*

Abendblatt. During the 20's and pre-Nazi 30's editorship of these papers had generally been in Jewish hands. Many of the journalists who staffed these papers were also Jewish.[6]

Although the leading papers of both the Ullstein and Mosse houses were regarded highly at home and abroad they in no sense dominated the German newspaper industry. In fact, neither the *Vossische* nor the *Franfurter Zeitung* ever exceeded a circulation of 100,000. Control of the German press, after 1919, had fallen largely into the hands of Alfred Hugenberg, a director in the Krupp works, chairman of the conservative-nationalist German National People's Party (DNVP) from 1929 to 1933 and later a partner in Hitler's first coalition cabinet.[7] Hugenberg's empire encompassed over half the German press, dominated the advertising business and eventually extended into the new motion picture industry with the purchase in 1927 of the *Universum Film A.G.* or UFA. Contrary to anti-Semitic claims, the German press during the 1920's took on an increasingly conservative and nationalist bent as Hugenberg's tentacles spread wider and wider.

To at least one person, however, Jewish dominance of the press seemed real enough by the early 20's. During 1921 and 1922 an aspiring young journalist from Rheydt, fresh with Ph.D., was receiving manuscript refusals from Mosse and Ullstein editors on the average of once a week.[8] He was particularly eager to have his pieces appear in the prestigious and liberal *Berliner Tageblatt,* edited by the distinguished Theodor Wolff, a Jew. His accounts with these Jewish publishers and editors went unsettled until 1933 when Hitler established a special Ministry of Propaganda from which Dr. Joseph Goebbels could mete out revenge.

The impression that Jews dominated important areas of German life reached far beyond the right-wing circles in which

[6] Ernst Kahn, "Die Judenpresse," *Leo Baeck Institute Bulletin* 1 (1958): 13-18.

[7] Oron J. Hale, *The Captive Press in the Third Reich* (Princeton, N.J., 1964), pp. 308-309.

[8] Helmut Heiber, *Joseph Goebbels* (Berlin, 1962), p. 39.

Goebbels was eventually to move. In March of 1933 the British ambassador to Berlin cabled an assessment of Germany's Jewish problem back to Whitehall which reflected how widespread the impression had become: ". . . they [Jews] have practically monopolized some professions and have obtained the plums of a great many others. The teaching professions, medicine, law, the press, imaginative literature, architecture, and the like, might, in time become completely monopolized by the Jewish element if we are to judge by the strides made in the last fifteen years."[9]

The notion that a people who comprised less than one percent of the total population could actually dominate large areas of German life was in itself evidence that assimilation was far from complete. The visibility of Jews in the various professions and branches of industry and commerce was kept very much alive by the charges emanating from anti-Semitic circles. Obviously the indices of assimilation which offered Jews hope for the future did not tell the whole story of the Jewish situation in Germany.

The Jewish position in the Germany of the early 1920's seemed anchored nonetheless in the promise of the Weimar constitution. By the latter part of the decade, however, that promise had been transformed into the Jewish problem. It was not the position of the Jews, but the situation of Germany which had changed. A kaleidoscopic shift in focus transformed the healthy signs of assimilation into the unwholesome marks of Jewish predominance. Those forces which were undermining the republic were also eating away at the foundations of the Jewish assimilation. Ultimately the position of German Jewry depended upon the vitality of liberal institutions created by the republic.

In his study on the dissolution of the Weimar Republic, K. D. Bracher stresses two fundamental weaknesses which eventually led to the republic's demise. On the one hand democratic values were not firmly anchored in the German consciousness;

[9] E. L. Woodward and Rohan Butler, eds., *Documents on British Foreign Policy, 1919-1939*, series 2, vol. 5, 1933 (London, 1956), p. 5.

on the other, antirepublican forces had been subdued only temporarily by defeat and revolution.[10] These weaknesses did not necessarily preordain the dissolution of the Weimar system. Democracies, like Rome, are not built in a day. Their histories are invariably marked by growth and development. In no instance has one begun with a full-fledged and mature system of liberal institutions. The potential for development as well as collapse must be kept in mind when analyzing the Weimar Republic.

Whatever the difficulty of gauging the allegiance the German masses might someday have paid the republic, it is safe to say that in 1918 they would not have chosen the government by themselves. The November revolution which gave birth to the republic was itself a product of defeat, not of a popular uprising against the imperial system. A nation which four years earlier had answered the call to arms so enthusiastically had not been prepared by its leaders for the collapse of 1918. The defeat delivered a stunning blow to the German self-image. Victories at Königgrätz, Metz, and Sedan in the previous century had buttressed notions of German invincibility. How could this defeat be explained after the great victories on the eastern front in 1917, after the *grossdeutsch* ideal of the expansionist forces in Germany seemed on the verge of being realized?

Even in defeat the armies of the Fatherland were still occupying foreign soil. Aside from her dead and wounded the war had brought little apparent physical damage to Germany. Cities had not been bombed, homes were not destroyed. In his novel, *The Road Back*, Erich Maria Remarque tells of the soldier who returns from the front to find his home town very much as he left it. Even the books and clothes in his room are the same. "Everything has been left exactly as it was," his sister tells him. There was little physical evidence that a way of life had been destroyed.

The seeming disparity between appearance and reality led to speculation about the defeat being unreal, or at least unneces-

---

[10] Karl Dietrich Bracher, *Die Auflösung der Weimarer Republik*, 3rd ed. (Villingen/Schwarzwald, 1960), p. 17.

sary. Perhaps Germany had not been defeated after all. Perhaps she had been betrayed from within, as General Ludendorff suggested, by a stab-in-the-back or a surrender at five minutes to twelve. If so, a measure of pride could be salvaged. Righteous indignation is an emotion more easily borne than humiliation. An admission of military defeat was tantamount to a recognition of Allied superiority, a pill too bitter for the stomach of national pride. But if the defeat had been engineered from within, matters stood differently. For the thousands of ultranationalists who regarded the events of November 1918 as an incomparable and incomprehensible disaster, things suddenly began to make sense. Germany had been the victim of treason. The traitors were in their own midst: the liberal, the socialist, the communist, the democrat, the republican. These enemies had conspired to bring Germany to ruin and to foist upon her a hated republic.

The success of the stab-in-the-back legend constantly whittled away at the republic's underpinnings. Democracy itself became associated with defeat and revolution and ultimately with economic failure as well. It was to Weimar's great misfortune that it was not attended by economic stability. The balm of prosperity might well have healed the wounds and covered the scars of 1918. Even a promise of economic security would have robbed the political extremists, including the Nazis, of their basic appeal. During the brief prosperity between 1925 and 1929, extremist groups on the right and left found life exceedingly difficult. Twice during the 1920's, however, Germany was struck by economic disaster. First came the inflation of 1922 and 1923. Savings were wiped out; pensions and earnings became meaningless. They would not buy so much as a loaf of bread. The middle-class values of frugality and thrift so important under the empire were now useless. Five years later economic crisis struck again, this time in the form of depression. By 1932 nearly 20 percent of the German laboring classes were unemployed. Once again the middle classes lost what they had managed to build up since the inflation. The class and status position of thousands of small businessmen and shopkeepers, to say nothing of the workers, was again threatened. And this time there was to be no recovering as there had been in 1924. Defeat, democracy, and depression came to be linked in large sectors of the popular consciousness, partly through the accident of history, partly as a consequence of antirepublican propaganda.

The effectiveness of this propaganda lay in its focusing the resentments generated by these crises upon the shoulders of a single diabolical enemy, the Jew. The traditional political liberalism of German Jewry laid it open to the charge that the Weimar Republic was really a Jewish republic. To the right wing which had equated the republic with defeat from the outset, anti-Semitism was given a new underpinning. Under the empire the Jew was a stranger; now, under the republic, he had also become an enemy.[11] Had this republic been able to steer clear of, or at least through, an economic depression it is unlikely that the cry of "Jewish republic" would have echoed in such ever-widening circles. Once it became clear, however, that economic crisis had paralyzed the republic, it was set upon by a steadily increasing number of enemies.

A National Socialist ideology was devised during the 1920's to explain the difficulties which beset Germany after 1918. Its central theme focused on the Jew. "In whatever direction one follows Hitler's train of thought," Hitler's biographer Alan Bullock has observed, "sooner or later one encounters the Satanic figure of the Jew."[12] In the Landsberg prison Hitler himself had written, "The efficiency of a truly national leader consists primarily in preventing the division of the attention of the people, and always concentrating it on a single enemy."[13] The single enemy was the Jew. No stone was left unturned in ferreting him out. At every level the rhetoric of Nazi ideology and propaganda (the two were inseparable) was replete with references to the pernicious Jew. To the socialist wing of his

11 Rudolf Hagelstange, "Metamorphosen des Antisemitismus," *Deutsche Rundschau* 80 (1954): 1255-1260.

12 Alan Bullock, *Hitler: A Study in Tyranny*, rev. ed. (New York, 1964), p. 407.

13 Adolf Hitler, *Mein Kampf* (New York, 1939), p. 152.

party Hitler offered the Jew as the creator of the exploiting bourgeois and capitalist institutions. To the nationalists he offered the same Jew as the destroyer of the conservative, *völkisch* German community. Everywhere he turned, Hitler found a corrupt Jew promoting such diverse evils as bolshevism, capitalism, democracy, jazz, modern abstract art, and above all racial assimilation. Their spiritual and moral standards made them, he said, "germ carriers of the worst sort."[14] Their aim was to subvert Nordic racial superiority and true Aryan or Germanic values. That which was evil in this world could be laid at the feet of the Jews, be it the German defeat in war, the revolution, the republic, the inflation, the depression, the party system, or whatever.

The devil theory of history which emerges from this view was the basic premise of this ideology—if these ideas warrant such a respectable title. History had gone wrong with the French Revolution which had given rise to notions of individualism and human equality and which had begun the emancipation of Jews. From this starting point Jews had introduced into European society the tensions and conflicts which disrupted the peace and well-being of the innocent but superior peoples of the world—especially the Germans or Aryans. The immediate purpose of Nazism, Hitler claimed, was to end the Jewish conspiracy aimed at undermining true civilization and culture.

The struggle between Jews and Aryans was in this view basically a racial one, despite its many manifestations in areas of politics, economics, and social life. The aim of the Jew was to infuse his own parasitic blood into the veins of superior Aryans. Since the French Revolution and emancipation he had made great strides in that direction. The indices of assimilation during the Weimar Republic were sufficient evidence to prove Hitler's point. It was no accident that in one of his first radio addresses to the German people after the Nazi seizure of power, Joseph Goebbels declared: "With the Nazi revolution the year 1789 is stricken from history." Liberalism in all its forms was

14 Ibid., p. 76.

to be overthrown. The community of the *Volk*, without the conflicts inspired by Jews, was to be revived.

Racial conflict was as essential to Nazi ideology as the class struggle was to the Marxists. In either case conflict, be it racial or class, was the moving force in history. Jew or capitalist, the enemy was a total one who had to be destroyed. The destruction of the enemy led, for the Marxists, to the classless society. For the Nazis it led to a *judenrein* Germany, one free of Jews. For both it meant a society which had transcended the tensions and conflicts of history and could exist in peace and harmony.

The society of peace and harmony was for the Nazis essentially in the tradition of the *völkisch* community envisioned by the romantic racists of the nineteenth century. In this sense the Nazis were very much part of a German tradition, one which had its roots in the failure of a large segment of German society to adjust to the Germany which developed after 1870. Hitler appropriated elements of this tradition and gave them a peculiar Nazi stamp. Even before Hitler had emerged as a prominent political figure this tradition had created a loose fusion between *grossdeutsch, völkisch,* and racist ideas. Hitler was to reshuffle these elements and cement them together with a rigid dogma of anti-Semitism.

That a German nationalist born in Austria should be in the *grossdeutsch* tradition is no surprise. For someone such as Hitler no other route to political leadership was open. That he should also be a strident racist and Jew-hater seems less necessary. The route by which these racist ideas were transmitted to a young Adolf Hitler has been traced in an elaborate reconstruction of Hitler's years in Vienna by Wilfried Daim.[15] The personal frustrations Hitler suffered in Vienna were in themselves sufficient to fashion a rather jaundiced view of life. He had come to Vienna from Linz in the autumn of 1907 at the age of eighteen to prepare himself for a career as an artist at the Academy of Fine Arts. His two applications for admission were turned down. Rather than return to Linz he remained in Vienna where he

[15] Wilfried Daim, *Der Mann der Hitler die Ideen gab* (Munich, 1958).

49

was shortly reduced to pawning his meager belongings to live in cheap rooms and eventually flop houses.[16]

At a kiosk near the boarding house where Hitler had rented a room in 1908, there was for sale an unusual monthly journal propagating a racist world view. The journal, *Ostara*, was published by a certain Lanz von Liebenfels, one of many racial prophets in prewar Vienna. Hitler apparently began to buy *Ostara* regularly, for Liebenfels, who survived both world wars, later recalled a young man identifying himself as Adolf Hitler coming to his office about 1909 and asking for back issues of *Ostara*.[17] Liebenfels was, of course, happy to oblige his young reader.

Nearly everything found in Nazi ideology or propaganda has its prototype in *Ostara*. In his interview with Daim during the early 1950's, Liebenfels accused Hitler of plagiarism, especially in *Mein Kampf*. The accusation cannot be discounted, for during the 1920's many of Germany's leading racial theorists, including Hans F. K. Guenther, were given complimentary subscriptions to *Ostara*.

There were other lessons which the Habsburg capital had to teach a budding young racist.[18] Shortly before Hitler came to Vienna, a highly astute politician, Karl Lueger, had captured the ear of Viennese voters with a call to eliminate Jewish influence in the imperial capital. Lueger's strategy, which led him to the mayorality, had been to fuse social resentments with the Jewish question.[19] An admiring Hitler was to reflect in the seclusion of Landsberg prison: "He [Lueger] based his party on the middle classes which were threatened with extinction, and so assured himself a group of followers almost impossible to unnerve, filled with a readiness for sacrifice as well as a tough fighting strength."[20]

[16] Bullock, *Hitler*, pp. 30ff.

[17] Daim, *Der Mann*, pp. 20-21.

[18] See Carl E. Schorske, "Politics in a New Key: An Austrian Triptych," *Journal of Modern History* 39 (1967): 343-386.

[19] Pulzer, *Political Anti-Semitism*, pp. 163-187.

[20] Hitler, *Mein Kampf*, p. 128.

Hitler was quite willing to acknowledge the debts he owed to his Vienna experience, with the exception of the one to Lieben-fels. What led him to pay tribute to Lueger and ignore Lieben-fels is difficult to say.[21] Perhaps Hitler was anxious to believe that he had discovered the Jew for himself. At least he gives that impression in *Mein Kampf*. When he arrived in Vienna, he writes, "I had no idea that organized hostility against the Jews existed."[22] But then, for the first time in his life, he says, he bought some anti-Semitic pamphlets. At first he claims to have been repelled by the accusations he read. Gradually, however, he came to recognize that the things he hated—certain forms of art, social democracy, liberalism, economic exploitation—were all Jewish creations. And then, "from a feeble cosmopolite I had turned into a fanatical anti-Semite."[23] He might have added that he was also transformed into an anti-Semitic crusader. "By ward-ing off the Jews I am fighting for the Lord's work."[24]

The religious dimension to fanatical Nazism is perhaps too commonplace to warrant special note. Any type of fanaticism has in it something which might be called religious. Daim, how-ever, suggests a paradigmatic relationship between the Nazi and Christian views of reality. Every Nazi who believed the Jew to be his total enemy implicitly subscribed to what Daim chooses to call a theology of race, or "theozoology."[25] Racial purity was for the Nazis a state of paradise; the mixing of races—a Nazi equivalent of original sin—defiled this paradise and led to the confusion of good with evil, superior with inferior, and thus to the inevitable decline of civilization. In its concrete form original sin was for the Nazis the mixing of the Aryans with inferior races. The only hope for redemption from this state was a deliberately conceived policy of what came to be called racial hygiene. Upon successful execution of such a policy a state of

[21] Liebenfels claimed to have been kept in silent obscurity by the Nazis after they came to power. See Daim, *Der Mann*, p. 16.

[22] Hitler, *Mein Kampf*, p. 67.

[23] Ibid., p. 83.

[24] Ibid., p. 84.

[25] Daim, *Der Mann*, pp. 191-210.

perfect racial purity would be restored. There is no need to distort Hitler's views to fit them into this framework. His self-image as redeemer of the German *Volk* was secure. He was fighting the Lord's work. His mission, in its purest form, was to save the Germanic soul from Jewish poisons.

Other Nazis often couched their anti-Semitic utterings in similar terminology. Hitler's chief Jew baiter, Julius Streicher, spoke of there being no deliverance for the German *Volk* without a solution to the Jewish question.[26] Arthur Rosenberg, the party ideologue, went even farther in appropriating familiar categories. In *The Myth of the 20th Century* he wrote: "A new faith is awakening today: The faith that blood will defend the divine essence of man; the faith, supported by pure science, that Nordic blood embodies the new mystery which will supplant the outworn sacrament."[27]

When the Nazi program was formulated in 1920 the nineteenth-century appeal for a *völkisch* Germanic religion was not left unheard. Point 24 called for a "positive Christianity" to combat the Jewish materialist spirit which was enslaving Germany. Presumably positive Christianity embodied the "new mystery" which Rosenberg had revealed.[28] Rosenberg's sacramental analogy was an exaggeration even for the Nazis; still, blood did remain their holiest of precepts. In it resided the elemental life-determining forces and soul-like qualities of which they spoke. Who could prove otherwise?

While parallels to a Christian world view do not demonstrate a causal relationship, they do demonstrate that the Nazis were unable to break traditional categories of thought. From a system which juxtaposed positive Aryan values against the negativism so inherent in the Jew there also emerged a simple system of ethics. Whatever served the Aryan cause was good; anything

---

[26] A slogan to this effect appeared on Streicher's business letterhead.

[27] Arthur Rosenberg, *Der Mythos des 20. Jahrhunderts* (Munich, 1931), p. 114.

[28] A German Christian Church was established after 1933, but Hitler never pushed very hard for its expansion. In his wartime conversations he intimated that the delay was mostly tactical. See H. R. Trevor-Roper, ed., *Hitler's Secret Conversations, 1941-1944* (New York, 1961), p. 65.

which did not was evil. Only with the advent of the Final Solution to the Jewish problem were the potentials of this system realized. Until then, racial mixing was seen as a shame or a disease and in Hitler's own formulation as "a sin against the will of the Eternal Creator."[29]

Anti-Semitism was not, to be sure, the only plank in the Nazi platform. In fact it is very unlikely that anti-Semitism was the issue which attracted large portions of the German electorate. There were other issues and problems which aroused the German people and to which Hitler addressed himself. The Nazi genius, however, was to tie all of these questions to the Jewish problem by riveting attention on the single enemy. The single-mindedness with which Hitler pursued this enemy after his release from Landsberg prison in late 1924 showed how well he had learned the lessons of Vienna.

Throughout the period of the *Kampfzeit*—the term applied by the Nazis to the years before Hitler came to power—the Jew was kept in the forefront. It was the Jew who finally allowed Hitler to reconcile the contradictory provisions of the party's program. Not that Hitler was unduly bothered by contradictions. He could hound a party stalwart such as Gregor Strasser out of the country for his socialism, purge the radical SA, order his Reichstag deputies to vote for relief credit to East Prussian estate owners and even come to a secret agreement with big industry without formally abandoning his promise to build a national *socialist* state. When Joseph Goebbels recommended that parts of the program be abandoned so the Nazis could ride in more saddles, Hitler proclaimed the party program to be inviolable—so anyone could join the Nazis in their saddle. Hitler understood very well the utility of a rigid, doctrinaire program. To have abandoned the socialist provisions would have been to write off a large segment of potential support. Later, when he was firmly established in power, this part of the program along with numerous others was silently discarded. The program as such, however, remained inviolable.

[29] Hitler, *Mein Kampf*, p. 392.

The chief problem confronting the Nazi leadership, once Hitler had decided to enter the race for parliamentary majorities, was the carving out of a loyal constituency. As the resentments over defeat, revolution and inflation subsided after 1924 the prospect for extremist movements ebbed as well. Not until 1929 with the beginning of the Depression was there any marked improvement in those prospects. Even then there was no assurance that the Nazis would come to power. Despite an "inviolable" program which seemed to cover the waterfront of resentments, the Nazis had no monopoly on any specific point. They were, to be sure, more extreme in their pronouncements, but the issues had to be shared with numerous other parties. Most parties on the right were in some ways anti-Semitic; most of them were also eager to revive the German *völkisch* tradition; and all of them were nationalistic. Moreover the largest of these parties, the German National People's Party (DNVP), had the financial support of a large portion of Germany's wealthy classes. The anti-capitalist appeal had to be shared with the parties Hitler considered to be Germany's greatest political enemies— the communists (KPD) and the much larger socialist party (SPD). Then, too, the Weimar system of proportional representation had given birth to a multitude of splinter or one-issue parties which seemed to be covering every available base of discontent.

The most immediate rival on most counts, however, was the DNVP, Germany's largest right-wing party until the elections of September 1930. Anti-Semitic, the DNVP at various times directed its campaign to this issue. But after 1929 its leader, Alfred Hugenberg, was more concerned with a Marxist than a Jewish danger. His conscious decision to play down anti-Semitism in his speeches during the Depression hinged upon his fear of Moscow and the Comintern.[30] It is important to note that he based his decision upon tactical considerations. Hitler's tactical consideration led him to an exactly opposite decision.

30 Mosse, *Crisis of German Ideology*, p. 241.

Other groups such as the veteran's organization *Stahlhelm* were also anti-Jewish. Yet *Stahlhelm* leader Franz Seldte, whose conservative credentials were never in doubt, regarded Nazi racism and especially its anti-Semitism as too negative. His preference was for a straightforward, pro-Germanic propaganda. Most *völkisch* groups conformed to this somewhat more moderate pattern. Although generally anti-Semitic, usually on vague racial grounds, they elected to emphasize the positive qualities of being German more than the negative ones of being Jewish.

If other parties called for the redress of the same problems, sometimes even in similar fashion, what explains the rapid growth of the Nazis after the Depression? A partial answer is provided by the political ineffectiveness of the other parties, a point which Nazi propagandists expended great energy in emphasizing. The small, single-issue parties contributed nothing to the solution of Weimar's problems. In fact, by siphoning away support from the larger, more moderate parties, they were actually one of the problems Weimar faced. Their existence made the formation of governments based on a parliamentary majority much more difficult. Furthermore, the impossibility of any single party achieving a majority in the Weimar electoral system made necessary the formation of coalition governments. Whichever coalition took responsibility for governing had, then, to address itself to immediate problems ranging from Ruhr occupation to reparation payments to the Polish Corridor. Any attempt at realistic accommodation to these problems, as witnessed by Gustav Stresemann during his term as Foreign Minister, could become exceedingly unpopular.[31]

Throughout the 1920's most of the older parties, with the exception of the communists, were losing support. They faced a problem common in a multiparty system. The German voter in a Reichstag election received a ballot listing many parties. He voted for the party which appealed most directly to his

[31] Henry Ashby Turner, *Stresemann and the Politics of the Weimar Republic* (Princeton, N.J., 1963), chap. 8.

special interests. As the larger coalition parties failed to meet his interests many a German voter retreated into apathy or began supporting one of the special interest parties.[32] Increasingly after 1929 the parties of the center found themselves unable to cope with the problems of reparations, business collapse, unemployment, and subsequent unpopularity. With the failure of moderate parties to form a coalition after the 1930 elections, the field of political battle was increasingly given over to the KPD and the *Nationalsozialistische Deutsche Arbeiter Partei* (hereafter NSDAP or Nazi party), both of which were dedicated to the overthrow of the republic.

The governing parties, even those deeply committed to civil liberties and the republican system, had shared in many of the resentments stemming from 1918 and had never turned a deaf ear to nationalist sentiment. But a frustrated electorate had tended to lose confidence in them. When the Bruening government-by-decree failed to surmount the problems of depression and reparations, even the forces of conservatism were stigmatized with failure. A vacuum was created on the right in German politics, a vacuum which offered the Nazis their greatest opportunity. In this situation they alone appeared capable of bringing order to chaos, to say nothing of their promise to institute the long-standing *völkisch* dream.

The other extremist party, the KPD on the left, also benefited from the paralysis of the Weimar system. But in its fray with the Nazis it was operating at a distinct disadvantage. Its prospects were limited by an intrinsic inability to adopt pseudolegal means and by the encumbrances of tactical directives from the Stalinized Comintern.[33] Hitler, on the other hand, was able and willing to make tactical shifts as the situation demanded. The worth of Hitler's tactics was reflected in the four Reichstag elections from 1928 to November 1932. Together the KPD and

---

[32] See Enid Lakeman and James D. Lambert, *Voting in Democracies: A Study of Majority and Proportional Election Systems* (London, 1955), pp. 182-187.

[33] See Ruth Fischer, *Stalin and German Communism: A Study in the Origins of the State Party* (Cambridge, Mass., 1948).

NSDAP delegations grew from about 13 percent to just over half of the delegates seated, enough to paralyze the Reichstag completely. While the Nazi delegation had grown from 12 to 196, however, the KPD delegation had grown from 54 to only 100 seats.[34]

The question remains, however: What role did the Jewish issue play in this sudden growth of Nazi support? It has been suggested that "it was not anti-Semitism itself which gained Hitler his votes, but anti-Semitism which made possible the other features of the Nazi program which attracted votes."[35] Anti-Semitism was used to achieve a superficial consistency between economic promises, to reconcile appeals to capital and labor, farmers and consumers. By creating the image of the Jewish bolshevik, the Jewish capitalist, Jewish land speculator, and Jewish department store owner, a wide variety of totally contradictory positions was made possible, positions which were necessary to attract diverse groupings of the electorate.

That a significant portion of the populace was receptive to anti-Semitic appeals is beyond question. What portion of it voted for the Nazis because of their anti-Semitism is another matter. Did the conservative vote switch from the more responsible parties to the Nazis out of fear of the Jews? Such a contention is highly doubtful. As the case of Hugenberg indicates, anti-Semitism was not always a first requirement in *völkisch*-oriented circles. There is reason to believe that many Germans who were anti-Jewish felt somewhat like Kaiser Wilhelm I did in the 1880's when he disapproved of Chaplain Stoecker's anti-Jewish activities. His disapproval was tempered by the belief that things would run their course harmlessly, and might even serve to make the Jews a little more modest.[36]

This was a type of armchair anti-Semitism which resisted self-

[34] Election statistics for these years are available in many sources. Perhaps the most convenient would be the tables appended to Koppel S. Pinson, *Modern Germany*, 2nd ed. (New York, 1966), pp. 603-604.

[35] Martin Needler, "Hitler's Anti-Semitism: A Political Appraisal," *Political Opinion Quarterly* 24 (Winter, 1960): 665-669.

[36] Massing, *Rehearsal for Destruction*, p. 37.

inspired action, but failed to resist the action of others.[37] The diffidence which most of the German people displayed in the face of the first Nazi-organized boycott of Jews reflected this attitude. The later concern of Nazi activists about a decreasing public interest in the Jewish problem lends support to this view.

The virulence of Nazi anti-Jewish propaganda could be credited to over-enthusiasm by an electorate unwilling to swallow all of Hitler's ravings. There was at least ample reason for believing the Nazi bite would not be as bad as its bark, an assumption which allowed many conservatives and business leaders to ally with Hitler in the belief that power would mellow his extremism. Even before taking power the Nazi leadership was worried that people were not taking the party's position on the Jewish question seriously enough. In 1932 a position paper was issued, stating that the assumption in some circles that National Socialist anti-Semitic appeals were used merely for purposes of agitation was incorrect: "If the Nazis should ever assume power, this view holds, their anti-Jewish demagoguery would subside. This assumption is false."[38] An accelerated anti-Jewish campaign did not prevent the loss of 34 Nazi seats in the November elections.

Where, then, in the ranking of Nazi appeals, does the Jewish issue fit? Perhaps part of the answer can be found in an analysis of the social group which was first to follow Hitler's banner—the lower-middle class or *Mittelstand*. Studies of voting patterns in the Reichstag elections of 1930 and 1932 confirm the fact that Nazism began as a movement of the lower-middle classes, the shopkeepers, craftsmen, peasants, and less well-off professionals.[39]

[37] See William Sheridan Allen, *The Nazi Seizure of Power: The Experience of a Single German Town, 1930-1935* (Chicago, 1965), p. 77.

[38] Hauptarchiv der NSDAP, Folder 504, Nazis und Judenfrage, Berlin Document Center (hereafter cited as BDC).

[39] See Theodor Geiger, *Die soziale Schichtung des deutschen Volkes* (Stuttgart, 1932); Ernst-August Roloff, "Wer wählte Hitler?" *Politische Studien* 15 (1964): 293-300; Rudolf Heberle, *From Democracy to Nazism: A Regional Case Study of Political Parties in Germany* (Baton Rouge, La., 1945).

The crises of inflation and depression capped by the collapse of the European financial structure in 1931 raised the frustration level of this grouping and with it the size of the Nazi vote. It is doubtful whether the shopkeeper, teacher, craftsman, or marginal lawyer and doctor was in the end any worse off than anyone else, but to his list of problems was added the fear of slipping back into the ranks of the lower, or working classes.[40] Economic depression threatened him with the loss of class identity and status. A shopkeeper, whose self-sufficiency was his pride, cannot be distinguished from the laborer when he is standing in a breadline.

What options did an election offer this shopkeeper? He certainly could not vote communist or socialist. This would have been a deliberate surrender of status. A vote for the parties in the center or toward the right, all the way to the conservative DNVP, would have been wasted. These had been the parties in power when his problems really began. Furthermore, these parties had declined steadily since the Reichstag elections of May 1928. If he was non-Catholic, the Catholic Center party was too sectarian. Only Hitler's NSDAP seemed to promise a way out of the crisis, at least if he could believe Hitler. And since no one else seemed worthy of his trust, there seemed to be no harm in giving Hitler a try.

In the first Depression election of 1930, the Nazi representation in the Reichstag rose from 12 to 107. From our vantage point today one can only speculate on the priority scale with which Nazi promises were received. The speculation need not be idle, however. Walter Simon, who has studied voting habits in pretotalitarian Germany and Austria, concludes the vote for the Nazis constituted "primarily a nonideological expression of protest."[41] Perhaps there was no special priority scale at all

[40] See Harold D. Lasswell, "The Psychology of Hilterism," *Political Quarterly* 4 (1933), pp. 373-384.

[41] Walter B. Simon, "Motivation of a Totalitarian Mass Vote," *British Journal of Sociology* 10 (1959): 338-345.

which determined the shopkeeper's vote. He felt only that the Nazis would take Germany in a direction quite different from the one in which it seemed to be heading. In that his vote of protest was not entirely devoid of ideological content. The communists too promised a different direction. Hitler's direction was at least more consonant with where the shopkeeper wanted to go. And that was better than no direction at all.

If the above analysis is valid, then Hitler's virulent stance on the Jewish question may have been unnecessary, except for his own need to understand the world in a particular way. William S. Allen, in his study of the Nazi movement in a small town, concludes people "were drawn to anti-Semitism because they were drawn to Nazism, not the other way around."[42] Anti-Semitism may not have been quite as appealing as Hitler imagined. There is insufficient evidence to indicate that it played a significant role in bringing him to power. At the same time it must be remembered that it did not prevent his coming to power either. Perhaps it is not especially surprising that the Nazi view of the Jewish danger should have escaped so many Germans. While much of Nazi propaganda dwelt upon the vicious image of the Jew as the dark-haired, stooped, hook-nosed swindler and seducer of fair-haired Aryan maidens, the problem at its roots was conceptualized somewhat differently. This Jew, if he ever appeared, was all too easily spotted. It was the assimilated Jew, in the final analysis, who was the most dangerous. Walter Frank, the Stoecker biographer and historian for the Nazis, stated the problem this way: "It will always remain a task of paramount importance to unveil the so-called "noble," "German" Jew and expose him as the most dangerous type of alien parasite. . . . This is harder when the "Asiatic" [sic] meets us in the civilized form of a Baruch Spinoza or Moses Mendelsohn, of a Friedrich Gundolf or an Albert Einstein. . . ."[43]

[42] Allen, *The Nazi Seizure of Power*, p. 77.
[43] Max Weinreich, *Hitler's Professors: The Part of Scholarship in Germany's Crimes against the Jewish People* (New York, 1946), pp. 57-58.

The task of "unveiling" this assimilated Jew proved to be more difficult than most Nazis had bargained for. Many of them at first refused to recognize the difficulty. Those who finally solved the problem were also those who were eventually assigned to finding a solution to the whole Jewish question.

III. Boycott: The First Impasse

BEFORE HITLER CAME TO POWER, the energies the Nazis devoted to the Jewish problem had been spent entirely on anti-Jewish propaganda. Self-styled racial experts had drawn their data out of thin air, their legerdemain supported by Hitler's often repeated assertions that propaganda need not correspond to reality. The Jew who emerged from this biological alchemy was far removed from reality. Hitler's assertion had precluded an even slightly empirical analysis of factors which made up the real Jewish situation—a situation with which the Nazis would someday have to deal. Promises of utopia are seldom rooted in practical considerations of reality, but rarely has that truism been more applicable than to the Nazi promise of a *judenrein* Germany.

Throughout the years of the *Kampfzeit* the Nazis could afford the luxury of living in the "higher reality" of Hitler's anti-Semitic dream world. As individuals, the Nazi Jew-haters could search the dark corners of their own prejudices to add their own fantastic constructions to that world. When they came to power, however, that dream world left them ill-prepared to deal with a real Jewish problem. The reality of power forced them to deal with the problem at a level closer to its own terms. The alternative would have been to remain in the world of anti-Jewish fantasy, not dealing with the problem at all.

For a variety of reasons the latter was hardly a real alternative, although the Nazis did their best at first to deal with the Jew of their fantasy. The effect of these efforts was a series of anti-Jewish policies which at the outset harmed the Nazi regime nearly as much as they did the Jews. There could be no question, of course, about de-emphasizing the Jewish issue. To pro-

62

claim on the one hand a conservative revolution and to ignore the Jew who made the revolution necessary on the other was a contradiction not even the Nazis could afford. Since the late nineteenth century, when the call for a conservative revolution had first been raised, it had echoed against the Jewish infiltration of German society. Retreat now would have been tantamount to surrender in the face of Jewish strength. Hitler had no intention of accepting Marr's pessimistic forecast of an inevitable Jewish victory.

The Nazis saw themselves, moreover, as a revolutionary party and the days and months following January 30, 1933 as a revolutionary period. Whether or not theirs was a real revolution is largely a problem of semantics. No established institutions were dashed to the ground to be replaced by new revolutionary ones. Instead, Hitler curried the favor of institutions usually serving as targets of revolutionary wrath. The bureaucratic structure was preserved. Military circles were courted rather than overthrown. German industry, which–given the Nazi ideology–should have been fearful, demonstrated its support for the so-called revolution when it agreed in January 1932 at a secret meeting in Düsseldorf to lend financial aid to Hitler's presidential campaign against Hindenburg. The noise and commotion in Berlin that second last day of January 1933 came not from a society being crumbled into dust, but from the SA bands and columns parading before their Fuehrer, the new Chancellor of Germany.

Hitler viewed these columns far into the night, interrupted once, late in the afternoon, by his first cabinet meeting. His new government was a coalition of conservative and right-wing parties. Only two of his fellow Nazis had received posts in the cabinet: Hermann Goering without portfolio and Wilhelm Frick as Minister of Interior. Frick was hardly a major figure in the party. His appointment was as much payment for years of faithful party service as for his administrative ability. A ministry without portfolio and one headed by the indolent Frick seemed scant reward for a party which since the 1930 elections had been

one of Germany's largest. Hitler's coalition partners reserved
the most important posts for themselves. The first-ranking
Foreign Ministry and Ministry of Defense had gone respectively
to the old-line conservatives Konstantin von Neurath and General Werner von Blomberg, both choices of President von Hindenburg. Alfred Hugenberg of the DNVP headed the two key
economic positions in the Economics Ministry and the Ministry
of Food and Agriculture. The *Stahlhelm* leader, Franz Seldte,
was made head of the Ministry of Labor. With the wily Franz
von Papen as vice-chancellor, Hitler's coalition partners believed they had outwitted the young Austrian upstart. They
were confident their cold professionalism would enable them to
control and even harness Hitler to their own purposes. Their
confidence seemed well-founded. The aging President von
Hindenburg disliked and distrusted his new chancellor. The
army viewed him, at best, with suspicion. Hitler had been
handed the reins of a government paralyzed by depression. The
political machinations which led to the coalition had been carried out with the calculated support of Germany's chief industrialists and large landholders. If Hitler succeeded in reviving
Germany, the plan went, his partners would check the excesses;
if he failed, he would be discredited and cast aside.

Not even Hitler was able to conceive of his office as a mandate
for implementing Nazi reforms. Although most of his political
life had been spent condemning the principle of democratic
mandates, his decision in 1925 to proceed by semiparliamentary
means indicated he had also sought such a mandate. In the most
recent elections of November 1932, the prospect of ever achieving an electoral mandate appeared diminished. For the first time
since 1930 the NSDAP lost electoral support. Though still the
largest party in Germany, the Nazis polled some two million
fewer votes than they had in the previous July elections and lost
34 of their Reichstag seats. The spell of an ever-growing National Socialism spearheading a national resurgence was broken.
Hitler arrived at the chancellorship ten weeks later, not on the

wave of popular support, but by the exigencies of luck and the self-defeating intrigues of the non-Nazi right.

If this was a revolution, it was like no one before it. Unlike other revolutionaries, to be sure, the Nazis had come to restore rather than destroy a traditional society. Still, if Hitler was at all in a pensive mood that Monday in late January of 1933, the marching columns of his paramilitary SA would have made him reflect on the enormous problems he faced. In the cabinet rooms behind the reviewing stand was gathered the clique devoted to blocking the fulfillment of most of his promises. Below, parading in review, was the party army hailing the revolution. Hitler, in top hat and frock coat, was the man in the middle. If he attempted to fulfill the revolution there were those who threatened to depose him; if he did not, the revolution might pass him by.

It was obvious to Hitler that revolution for the time being would have to wait. The more immediate task was to consolidate the Nazi position of power, to maneuver through the obstacles others had deliberately placed in his way. His wits in this case were more useful than the thousands of followers eager for the spoils of victory. A lesser man might have been ensnared by the traps laid by Papen or Hugenberg. The ensuing weeks demonstrated to them both that they were no match for the new chancellor.

By March 24, Hitler had managed promulgation of an Enabling Act which allowed the government to rule by decree during the next four years. This had come on top of the Reichstag fire in February which provided the Nazis with a convenient excuse for outlawing the Communist party.[1] Early in March he had organized another Reichstag election in which the NSDAP took 44 percent of the vote. By the end of the month he had forced all but the socialist deputies to vote for his Enabling Act. The speed and audacity which characterized his moves during these early months of power left most of his enemies dazed and

[1] Fritz Tobias, *The Reichstag Fire* (New York, 1963).

compliant. He was careful, however, not to threaten directly those institutions upon whose tacit support he still depended. Big business, as a result of the agreement concluded at Düsseldorf, was the indispensable ally in aggrandizing his power, and Hitler was careful to guard its interests. The military, deeply suspicious of the Bohemian corporal, as Hindenburg called him, was for the moment neutralized by the presence of General von Blomberg in the War Ministry.

In many respects Hitler was more successful in bridling his enemies than in satisfying his supposed friends. The exhilaration of January 30 led many of his friends to believe that all their hopes could be achieved for the asking. How long their enthusiasm could be contained in closed formation marches was one of the most critical questions Hitler faced. The SA, whose membership by now ranged somewhere between three and four million men, took the party's program seriously. It had been built up in the last years by Ernst Roehm on the promise that a Nazi seizure of power would be a blank check to revolution. Roehm was one of the typical malcontents attracted to the Nazi movement. A freebooting adventurer, his checkered career included a stint as a career officer in the German army during World War I—a position of which the disarmament terms of Versailles robbed him—time in the rowdy Free Corps movement which formed the basis for his first connection with the SA, and a period as military adviser to the Bolivian army. In late 1930 Hitler recalled him from Bolivia to carry out a reorganization of the SA following its revolt against the Nazi leadership in Berlin. Roehm's prodigious efforts in the next years were rewarded by a fantastic growth of the SA. Within a year its membership had tripled; by early 1933 it had grown to roughly four million men. The Depression, of course, had come to his aid by creating the discontented groups which found his paramilitary organization appealing. The offer of pay and some meaningful structure to a disoriented life attracted the unemployed worker, the criminal, the bankrupted shopkeeper, the student unable to find a job. With the eclipse of Gregor Strasser, Roehm's reorganized SA also became the guardian of the socialist objectives proclaimed in the party's Twenty-Five Point Program. Roehm and the SA leadership took seriously the Nazi promise to establish a German community free from the social divisions generated by the disruptive forces of capitalism and finance.

For Hitler the importance of the SA lay not in its self-conceived role as guardian of ideological purity. Whatever ideological pretensions it had could serve only to undermine Hitler's own role as absolute Fuehrer of the entire Nazi movement. It was as an instrument of terror that the SA was useful to Hitler's cause. He had counseled often and long of the respect the masses paid to a ruthless show of force. Terror, he said, attracted as many people as it repelled. As an instrument of terror the SA had been schooled throughout the 1920's in the propaganda of the deed. Street brawls, inciting riots at communist rallies, roughing up Jews—these had become part of the SA man's daily routine. Much, perhaps most, of the SA rank and file was comprised of the hoodlum or thug element of German society and cared little for the ideological niceties which to some extent concerned the leadership. To them power would mean little more than the license to spread terror on an even grander scale. To Roehm and the SA leaders, however, power would also mean the establishment of a national-socialistic Germany and, above all, positions of influence in the new regime. It was unlikely that either element would be satisfied very long by parades and victory celebrations.

Roehm was immediately dissatisfied with the composition of the Hitler-led coalition. He had expected, at the very least, to receive a post in the new cabinet, probably as head of the Labor Ministry.[2] His ambition seemed justified on several grounds. The SA, in addition to being the party's largest auxiliary organization, had the only significant working-class representation. Who better than Roehm could be expected to implement the Nazi brand of socialism? Instead, the Labor Ministry had gone to the archconservative Franz Seldte, hardly a champion of the

2 Hermann Rauschning, *The Voice of Destruction* (New York, 1940), p. 152.

workingman's interests. Particularly galling to Roehm was that no party leftist had received an important government position. The left was represented in the government only by Gottfried Feder, one of the drafters of the anticapitalist platform, and he had been relegated to a subministerial post in the Ministry of Economics to be overshadowed by the conservative minister Hugenberg. "He [Hitler] associates only with reactionaries now," Roehm complained to Rauschning shortly after Hitler became chancellor. "His old friends aren't good enough for him."[3]

Roehm had read the signs correctly. Hitler was not interested in revolution, at least not of the type envisioned by the SA leader. Indeed, the Fuehrer had to allay fears of revolution if he expected the German army and his coalition partners to stay reconciled to Nazi rule. Big business, of course, feared the instituting of any form of socialism, including the crackpot variety proclaimed by Roehm. The army, on the other hand, was deeply disturbed by Roehm's poorly disguised intentions of transforming the SA into a conscription-based mass militia and amalgamating it eventually with the *Reichswehr*.[4] The effect of Roehm's plan for the army would have been the loss of its traditional independence from outside authority.

In these circumstances Hitler had as much cause to fear counterrevolution or intervention by the *Reichswehr* as he did the revolution so eagerly sought by the SA. The coalition with conservatives seemingly tied his hands on economic policy. For the time being he needed the German industrialists at least as much as they needed him. The *Reichswehr* on the other hand had adopted no more than a wait-and-see attitude. Potentially it had the power to unseat Hitler if its interests appeared unduly threatened. Its continued toleration depended upon the course the newly proclaimed Third Reich would choose to take. If the party's radicals—especially the SA—got the upper hand, Hitler

[3] Ibid., pp. 152-153.
[4] J. W. Wheeler-Bennett, *The Nemesis of Power: The German Army in Politics 1918-1945*, 2nd ed. (London, 1964), pp. 307ff.

could well expect the army to step in and dispose of both the SA and himself.

The SA was quick to demonstrate that its aims were not fulfilled merely by Hitler having assumed the chancellorship. It embarked immediately upon a campaign of violence and terrorization directed at Nazism's enemies. A great deal of this activity was completely acceptable to Hitler. Attacks upon communists, socialists, or liberals were perfectly congruent with party ideology and Hitler's sympathies. Terror, moreover, reduced the enemy's capacity to organize resistance against Hitler's tentative grasp on the reins of government. As long as that grasp was tentative, however, SA terror could also generate circumstances harmful to Hitler's aim of gaining more absolute control.

During the *Kampfzeit*, random terror had helped create the chaos which assisted Hitler's climb to power. Once he was in power its uses changed. Terror directed against communist or socialist enemies of the regime served many useful purposes. The danger was that this terror, if not properly directed, could also undermine the basis of the new regime. Hitler's non-Nazi allies had calculated, not unreasonably, that the responsibility of power would ameliorate Hitler's radicalism. Nearly each one of his promises to the German people—an end to economic depression and political instability, national rejuvenation, and even his promise to solve the Jewish question—pointed to an orderly approach to problems and their solutions. If he wanted to establish his position more firmly, he could not afford to dispel these hopes entirely.

It was soon apparent, however, that the SA did not share Hitler's desire for order, not even on Hitler's terms. By early March the enemies which had been the first object of SA wrath had been largely subdued. Many of these—communists, socialists, and democrats—were already incarcerated in the first wildcat concentration camps established by the SA.[5] The next obvi-

---

[5] E. K. Bramstedt, *Dictatorship and Political Police: The Technique of Control by Fear* (New York, 1945), p. 120; also Eugen Kogon, *Der SS-Staat, Das System der deutschen Konzentrationslager* (Frankfurt a.M., 1946).

ous target of SA terror was the Jew and the institutions he ostensibly controlled. Although the Jew had not been forgotten in the first wave of terror, he had not been its primary object. In February and March of 1933, the Jew, even by Nazi standards, was not the most immediate threat. To have halted the terror before striking against the Jew, however, would have been to deal with the symptoms and to ignore the disease. Communism, socialism, democracy, and the other ills of Germany were all Jewish-inspired, according to Nazi belief. On this level Hitler and the SA were in total agreement, an agreement which ended when it came to a consideration of the means to be employed for dealing with the Jews.

Contrary to its pledge, the leadership of the NSDAP did not envisage a massive anti-Jewish campaign immediately following a seizure of power. The only plans it had made by late 1932 called for something less extreme. "Should the NSDAP receive an absolute majority, Jews will be deprived of their rights by legal process. If, however, the NSDAP receives power only through a coalition, the rights of German Jews will be undermined through administrative means."[6] The caution of this directive turned out to be entirely appropriate to Hitler's situation in the first months of 1933. It reflected the realities of the political situation in which he found himself. This document is also the only evidence that the Nazis leadership had ever given thought to concrete methods of dealing with the Jewish problem. What role Hitler played, if any, in drafting the plan is impossible to ascertain, although the first official Jewish policy undertaken by the regime in April 1933 speaks for the fact that Hitler, at the very least, agreed with its terms.

The weakness of the plan, apart from its lack of detail, was that it allowed no expression to the explosive anti-Jewish enthusiasm of the SA. Administrative measures could scarcely satisfy an organization schooled in terror, whose leaders were already discontented with what they considered Hitler's mildness. This mildness became especially apparent after the im-

[6] Hauptarchiv der NSDAP, Folder 504, BDC.

mediate threat of organized resistance from the parties of the left and center had been eliminated. Jews had suffered only incidentally in the terrorization of Nazism's other ideological enemies. But by early March they were clearly next on the SA's list. Yet no directives, not even mild ones, were forthcoming from the offices of Hitler's chancellory or party headquarters to indicate the imminence of an anti-Jewish campaign.

The lack of directives, by itself, was of no particular consequence. The SA was certainly prepared to act on its own accord. It failed to appreciate Hitler's need for masking all of his actions behind a facade of legality. During the first two weeks of March, the SA began its own anti-Jewish campaign. For the moment the chief targets were the persons of Jews themselves. Then, confident that the events of January 30 had handed it a blank check, the SA initiated a series of boycotts along with a general mistreatment of Jews throughout Germany. In effect the SA's actions reflected its shotgun approach to the Jewish problem. There was almost no central direction to any of its activities. Local SA units, eager for blood and spoil, initiated their own campaigns of boycott and violence, unaware that such uncoordinated actions served to undermine rather than strengthen Hitler's position. Many of their actions brought them into conflict with the police authorities which were not yet under Nazi control. Violence against the person of a foreign Jew residing or traveling in Germany immediately raised uncomfortable issues with governments abroad. Frequently an SA unit would simply kidnap a Jew and ask his family for a sizable ransom in order to increase the treasury of the unit, or, more often, the treasury of its individual members.[7] By any definition, even Hitler's, these were criminal acts which sabotaged the creation of order and hence the legitimacy of the regime. At the same time such actions could easily spur the *Reichswehr* to action, destroying in turn everything Hitler had built since the end of January.

An incident in the Silesian capital of Breslau in early March

[7] See Berlin Collection: G—73 of the YIVO Institute for Jewish Research, New York.

brought to a head for the first time the issue between the SA and Hitler. Early on the morning of Saturday, March 11, a unit of the local SA invaded a department store in the city's central district. Department stores had long been an object of Nazi wrath. Point Sixteen of the party program had pledged their communalization and lease to the small *Mittelstand* business-man. Subsequent propaganda by the Nazis had succeeded in instilling the notion that department stores were all Jewish-owned or Jewish-inspired. The Breslau SA unit which invaded the department store that morning apparently hoped to assist the communalization process, but the local police arrived in time to avert violence. From there the unit split into smaller groups, going to the Breslau local and district courts where they began dragging Jewish lawyers and judges from their chambers. A favorite sport of the SA during this period was to drag Jewish professional people into the street and force them into the humiliating act of disrobing in public. This time matters did not get that far. Again, the police arrived in time to prevent it. When the SA then went to a branch of the Jewish-owned Wer-theim department store, the harried Breslau chief of police finally phoned Berlin for advice. He was told by police authori-ties there that battles between his police forces and the SA should be avoided if at all possible.[8] A direct conflict between SA and police was averted once more, but the police chief's luck did not hold out much longer. He was replaced very shortly by the commander of the Breslau SA himself.

What happened in Breslau was merely an example of what was going on elsewhere in Germany, especially in areas where Nazi strength was most pronounced. In parts of Oberhessen and in nearby Prussian territory, where the Nazis had received nearly 75 percent of the vote in recent elections, the SA organized a series of small scale boycotts against Jewish businesses and professional people. Along with general intimidation, these boycotts created a climate of fear which affected Jew and non-

[8] A report of this incident by the Breslau Police Chief can be found in the Schumacher Archiv, Folder 240, I, BDC.

Jew alike. Even non-Jews were afraid to speak to long-time Jewish friends or acquaintances, to say nothing of buying in their shops or seeking their professional assistance.[9]

Acts of SA hooliganism and terror were legion during these first months of Nazi power. Insofar as they intimidated a portion of the population which had not supported Hitler, they served a useful purpose. On other levels, however, SA actions were detrimental to Hitler's aims. For one, it was a terror over which Hitler was not exercising control and, therefore, was not being used to solve the immediate problems he faced. Terror, for his purposes, had to be directed and controlled. The urgency with which a rival terror organization, the Secret State Police (Gestapo) was organized under the aegis of Hermann Goering during March and April pointed to Hilter's concern with SA activities. He was by no means shocked at those activities, but neither could he afford to have his authority breached. Also, such random terror threatened to make a shambles of Hitler's promises regarding legality and order. In the wake of the Breslau incidents, for example, the League of District Court Attorneys complained to the court president that further incidents would "bring justice to a complete standstill."[10] The court president in turn complained to the Prussian Ministry of Justice which turned to Vice-Chancellor von Papen for help. Papen phoned Hitler, who happened to be in Munich, to inform him of the problem in Breslau. The Fuehrer immediately got in touch with Breslau's SA leadership demanding a halt to such independently conceived actions.[11] There can be no doubt that Hitler was serious. The next morning SS guards appeared to protect against further actions by the SA.

[9] See *Central Verein Zeitung*, February 2, 1933. Reports of this nature were frequent in the Jewish newspapers of the time, particularly in the assimilation-oriented papers such as the CVZ.

[10] George Weiss, "Einige Dokumente zur Rechtstellung der Juden und zur Entziehung ihres Vermögens," *Schriftenreihe zum Berliner Rückerstattungsrecht* 7, (n.d.), p. 11.

[11] Dr. h.c. Adolf Heilberg, "Pro Memoria 1933," unpublished memoir in the Leo Baeck Institute archives, p. 4. Dr. Heilberg was President of the Breslau Bar Association.

Several times Hitler attempted to impose greater discipline upon the SA. Following the Breslau incidents he issued a general call to avoid all such uncoordinated incidents, demanding "blind discipline" from all his followers. The campaign of unstructured violence subsided only briefly in deference to Hitler's appeal. Continued appeals were to little avail.[12] The revolutionary fervor of the SA, so long in the making, was not to be extinguished merely by a call to discipline. And the discipline which was imposed served merely to frustrate the SA's penchant for violence. SA leaders accused the first Gestapo head, Rudulf Diels, of subverting the revolution before it could get underway. Had it not been for the Gestapo, they felt, at least thirty thousand "subhumans" (*Untermenschen*—a term the Nazis frequently applied to Jews) could have been laid low.[13]

Faced with these pressures the 1932 blueprint for a Jewish policy was woefully inadequate. It was obvious that legal processes or administrative actions would do little to moderate the radical zeal of the SA. After long training in brawls and boycotts it was not prepared to act as the disciplined bureaucratic executor of so unimaginative a policy. Hitler's admonition for discipline failed to impress the SA, not surprising in the light of his own vitriolic anti-Jewish statements. A way out of this dilemma suggested itself when Gestapo Chief Diels complained about SA excesses to a Berlin SA group. Diels was told that "for very human reasons, certain activity must be found which will satisfy the feelings of our comrades."[14] The SA could not be suppressed, but, perhaps, by finding an activity suitable to its temperament, its actions could be steered into less destructive channels.

[12] Hitler's appeal to the SA is also reported by Sir Horace Rumbold, Britain's Ambassador to Germany. See Woodward and Butler, eds., *Documents on British Foreign Policy*, p. 20.

[13] Rudolf Diels, *Lucifer Ante Portas . . . es spricht der erste Chef der Gestapo* (Stuttgart, 1950), p. 350.

[14] Quote from Karl Dietrich Bracher, Wolfgang Sauer, and Gerhard Schulz, *Die nationalsozialistische Machtergreifung, Studien zur Errichtung des totalitären Herrschaftssystem in Deutschland 1933/34* (Cologne, 1960), p. 862.

Hitler retired to his Bavarian mountain retreat to evaluate the situation. On March 26 he summoned Joseph Goebbels to Berchtesgaden to announce his decision.[15] He had decided upon a nationwide boycott against Jews in the business and professional world, an action with which the SA was already familiar and could not help but applaud. It was to be a bold stroke against the economic position of the German Jew. A fourteen-man committee was commissioned to organize the boycott. Julius Streicher, the Franconian *Gauleiter,* publisher of *Der Stuermer,* Hitler's friend and probably the Nazi's most rabid anti-Semite, was chosen by Hitler to head the committee. The others, all party leaders of the second rank, also came mostly from the radical wing of the NSDAP. Some of them were destined for later prominence in Nazi affairs, particularly Heinrich Himmler whose SS at the time was still within the command structure of the SA, and Robert Ley, Walter Darre, and Hans Frank. Each committee member represented a party agency. Representing the SA was Roehm's powerful henchman, Adolf Huehnlein, commander of the SA Motor Corps. Walter Darre, later Minister of Agriculture, was present in his capacity as party chief for agriculture affairs, and Adrian von Renteln as party leader of the radical Combat League of the German Middle Class, an organization of small trades people who had been among the first to rally to the Nazi cause. The representative of the German Labor Front was Robert Ley. Gerhard Wagner, to be heard from again in connection with the Nuremberg Laws, took part as the party's health chief and Hans Frank, later the governor-general of occupied Poland, as the party's legal chief. Also taking part in the planning were representatives from the Nazi Party Factory Cells, the Hitler Youth, and Nazi League for Public Officials.[16] With the exception of Himmler and Frank, the claim most of these people had to membership on the committee was

15 Joseph Goebbels, *Vom Kaiserhof zur Reichskanzlei, Eine historische Darstellung in Tagebuchblättern* (Munich, 1934), p. 288.

16 A list of the boycott committee's members can be found in Document 2156-PS in *Nazi Conspiracy and Aggression,* vol. 4 (Washington, D.C., 1946), pp. 761-762.

less a capacity for organization than it was a violent hatred of Jews.

As was to become the pattern in Nazi Jewish policy, Hitler served only to give matters their initial push. After having appointed Streicher he removed himself from the scene. There could be no question, in mid-March 1933, of bringing the state's administrative or coercive apparatus into the boycott. It was too early to defy openly the wishes of the coalition partners; furthermore, *Gleichschaltung* or coordination of the state's administrative structures under Nazi control had just begun. The police with few exceptions were still under control of non-Nazi ministers in the various states and provinces. Then too the boycott was specifically designed to siphon the energies of the party's radical elements into a controlled activity. Streicher's committee was constituted accordingly. None of its members held state office. As if to emphasize the states' noninvolvement, the boycott committee had its headquarters in Munich while Hitler was busy in Berlin. Officially, at least, there was to be no connection between the committee and the chancellory.

The work of Streicher's committee exploded for the first time the myth of Nazi thoroughness and efficiency. Within a week, by about March 21, the committee had drawn up its plans. A general, nationwide boycott of Jewish business and professional establishments was to be scheduled for Saturday, April 1. It was to continue indefinitely, presumably until Jews had been eliminated from the German economy. A public justification for the boycott, for consumption abroad, was supposedly to pressure both German Jews and the foreign press into ceasing their attacks upon the Nazi regime.

Reactions in foreign countries, especially in England and the United States, to Hilter and the Nazis had been quite unfavorable. The foreign press had reported in detail the terror campaigns of the SA against political enemies and ordinary citizens. In the first weeks after coming to power the Nazis had taken little note of these foreign reactions. Now, however, it was seen that the Jews could be blamed for inciting the foreign press to lie about the situation in Germany. The official Nazi paper *Voelkischer Beobachter*, began printing articles blaming Jews for defaming Germany's good name. Goering raised the problem of the anti-Nazi campaign for the first time in a Reichstag speech on March 23. Two days later on Saturday, March 25, he summoned foreign correspondents in Germany to his office at the Prussian Interior Ministry and vigorously denied their allegations about maltreatment of political enemies and Jews.[17] He also enlisted the Foreign Minister, von Neurath, and Vice-Chancellor von Papen in the cause. While Goering was lecturing the foreign newsmen, these two telephoned American acquaintances denying that the new regime was mistreating Jews.

After his talks with the newsmen, Goering summoned four of Germany's leading Jews to a special meeting in his office. Invitations for the meeting had originally gone out only to three prominent Jewish leaders—Julius Brodnitz, chairman of the Central Association of German Citizens of the Jewish Faith (*Centralverein*); Heinrich Stahl, president of the Berlin Jewish Community; and Max Naumann of the League of National German Jews—all heads of assimilation-minded Jewish organizations. Zionist leadership had been ignored. Only at the last moment had the head of the German Zionist Federation, Kurt Blumenfeld, managed to get himself invited to this obviously important but secret meeting.

When they arrived at the Ministry, Goering immediately plunged into a violent denunciation of Jewish efforts to instigate anti-Nazi calumnies in the British and American press. "Unless you put a stop to these libelous accusations immediately," he warned, "I shall no longer be able to vouch for the safety of German Jews."[18] Goering ordered them to proceed to London to assure British and American Jewry that reports of Nazi atrocities were untrue.

[17] Reported by Sir Horace Rumbold to Sir John Simon. See Woodward and Butler, eds., *Documents on British Foreign Policy*, p. 3.

[18] Martin Rosenbluth recounts the story of the Goering meeting in his memoirs, *Go Forth and Serve: Early Years and Public Life* (New York, 1961), pp. 250-254.

Brodnitz, Stahl, and Naumann argued they were in no positions to make appeals abroad. Their organizations were oriented toward assimilation and German patriotism; consequently they had no important connections in foreign countries. The only group represented which had such high-level connections in foreign Jewish circles was the Zionist Federation, the group Goering had for some reason overlooked on his first invitation list. Blumenfeld agreed to send a Zionist delegation to London, but only on the condition that it would be allowed to tell the truth about Nazi treatment of German Jews. Goering was furious, but he was forced to admit that some untoward incidents had taken place. These he dismissed with a proverb: "When one uses a plane, there are bound to be shavings."

The circumstances of Goering's meeting with these Jewish leaders reflected the peculiar bent of Nazi anti-Semitism. Apparently believing the propaganda about Jewish cohesiveness and international power, he traced anti-Nazi statements in the foreign press directly to Jewish influence. How else could he have expected the men he confronted to wield such influence abroad? The fact that he initially ignored the Zionists reflected, moreover, the opinion that all Jews were alike. Failure to recognize the differences between assimilation-minded and Zionist Jews pointed to his wholesale lack of understanding regarding the realities of the Jewish situation. Later the much more sophisticated SS was to recognize and exploit these differences to its own advantage. In the early stages of the Third Reich, however, no such realistic appraisals of German Jewry had been made. From Hitler down there was the penchant for dealing with the Jew as Nazi propaganda had created him. The weaknesses of such assumptions soon became clear.

Blumenfeld was dispatched to London early in the week following the meeting in the Interior Ministry. Whatever effectiveness he might have had was cancelled by the public announcement in Germany on the evening of March 28 that a general boycott of Jewish businesses and professions was scheduled for the coming Saturday, April 1.

No announcement of the boycott committee's work or even of its existence had been made previously. The boycott was announced as a defensive measure against the anti-Nazi campaigns in the foreign press.[19] Appropriately, Streicher's committee was now called the Central Committee for Defense Against Jewish Atrocity and Boycott Propaganda. A boycott by all Germans was to be directed against Jewish businesses and trades people, articles produced by Jews, Jewish theaters, Jewish performers, Jewish movie houses and movies produced by German Jews, Jewish doctors, Jewish lawyers and judges, and finally against Jewish newsstands and Jewish news dealers.[20] Care was to be taken that foreign Jews resident in Germany would not be included in the boycott. Their inclusion would have provided additional fuel for foreign propagandists and might have led to diplomatic incidents. Therefore the committee spelled out that American films, even though they were almost all Jewish-produced, had to be exempted from the boycott's provisions. The committee had planned the participation of all dissident Nazi elements in the boycott's execution. Enforcement of the boycott was, of course, to be the task of the SA and its subordinate SS. Care was also taken to enlist the help of party units at the district (*Gau*) and local levels. Here were the most loyal supporters of the Nazi movement, people who had not yet been granted any of the rewards of victory. Local Action Committees were established at these levels to ensure the enthusiastic participation of Nazi followers. Not all of the uncoordinated anti-Jewish action of the previous weeks had come from the SA. The Nazi rank and file, especially in the smaller towns, had frequently initiated boycotts on the local level. Each Local Action Committee was also instructed to popularize the boycott among its townspeople. It was also instructed to agitate for measures which would restrict the number of Jews to be allowed to engage in the various

19 *Voelkischer Beobachter*, March 29, 1933.
20 See *Dokumente zur Geschichte der Frankfurter Juden, 1933-1945*, Herausgegeben von der Kommission zur Erforschung der Frankfurter Juden (Frankfurt a.M., 1963), pp. 18-20 (hereafter cited as *Dokumente Frankfurter Juden*).

professions. This latter directive almost certainly originated from a source higher than Streicher's committee, for it corresponded to the 1932 blueprint which called for administrative and legislative action against Jews. Such measures were already under consideration by the regime and were to be announced in early April. To have their announcement coincide with an apparent wave of public demand would add to their effectiveness as well as to the Nazi image of being responsive to the public will.

A transparent effort to solidify the support of the *Mittelstand* was evident in the creation of a role for the local Combat Leagues of the German Middle Class. Their interests had been championed in the committee by Adrian von Renteln. On boycott day they were assigned the special task of supervising the boycott of the hated department stores. Together with the Local Action Committees, the Combat Leagues organized public meetings after March 28 at which the purposes of the boycott were elaborated.[21] The purpose of these meetings was to insure that no Jew, no matter how insignificant his business or practice, was overlooked. German businessmen were also warned not to advertise in Jewish-owned newspapers or in any way contribute to the success of any Jewish enterprise. It was explained that cases of doubtful Jewishness were likely to arise. In that event no boycott was to be instituted until permission had been received from central committee headquarters in Munich. Strict adherence to all of these instructions was demanded. Presumably Germany was prepared for the boycott which would last, said the *Voelkischer Beobachter*, "until an order from party headquarters declares it ended."

Repercussions, some of them totally unexpected, set in immediately after the boycott was announced. Prices on the Berlin Stock Exchange dropped three to nine points in the next few days.[22] At a cabinet meeting on Thursday, March 30, two days before the boycott was scheduled to begin, President Hinden-

---

21 *Voelkischer Beobachter*, March 30, 1933.
22 *New York Times*, March 31, 1933.

burg spent an hour trying to convince Hitler to have the boycott canceled. Hindenburg was supported by Foreign Minister von Neurath, who persuaded Hitler to agree to a cancellation if American and British Jewry called off its boycott of German goods and admitted to exaggerating reports of Nazi brutality.[23] Hitler emphasized to the cabinet that the boycott was an appropriate countermeasure to Jewish agitation. If the party did not organize it, he said, the countermeasures would come from the people themselves and these might take undesirable forms.

Under no circumstances, once it was announced, could Hitler have afforded to call off the boycott. SA and party pressure would not have allowed it. The boycott's purpose was, after all to steer the SA and party radicals away from the spontaneous actions of the past weeks and into acceptable political as well as ideological channels. Cancellation would have been a certain invitation to a renewal of those actions Hitler was most anxious to avoid. Moreover, it would have been tantamount to a retreat on the most basic ideological issues—anti-Semitism and anti-capitalism. Hitler's anticapitalist position was already weak as a result of his coalition with the forces of big business. A retreat on anti-Semitism would have been unacceptable to almost all ranks within his party.

Despite these formidable pressures from his own party, Hitler could not ignore the sentiments of Hindenburg or of his cabinet. Twenty-four hours before the boycott was to begin, the plans were revised. The boycott was now to be for only one day. If this was not sufficient to convince international Jewry to halt its anti-German activities, the boycott would be resumed the following Wednesday, April 5. The change represented a significant shift in the meaning of the boycott. Unless it was actually renewed, the boycott would become little more than a token which at best would deflect only briefly the attention of the party's radicals. To hope that a one-day boycott might satisfy the

[23] Neurath recounted the details of the meeting to Ambassador Rumbold who in turn cabled the information to the Foreign Office in London. See Woodward and Butler, eds., *Documents on British Foreign Policy*, p. 15.

SA or the local Combat Leagues would have been totally illusory.

The task of glossing over the wide range of inconsistent claims centering on the boycott fell to Joseph Goebbels, head of the newly established Ministry of Public Enlightenment and Propaganda. On Friday evening, boycott eve, Goebbels explained on the national radio network the purpose of the boycott. His speech was a masterful display of his propaganda abilities. It was obvious from what Goebbels said that Hindenburg's intervention in the cabinet meeting had not been taken lightly. A portion of the speech was devoted to assuring the "Honorable Reichs President" of the need for measures such as the boycott. Goebbels accorded Hindenburg the gratitude of the German people for his sacrifices to the fatherland and promised him that in the boycott he was witnessing Germany's rebirth. Goebbels went on to establish an image of the German people determined to take their own revenge upon the Jews; the boycott was simply an attempt to guide German resentments into constructive paths. "The Jews in Germany are guests," Goebbels warned. "If they believe they can misuse our hospitality they are sadly mistaken."[24]

Hindenburg was not the only one who needed reassuring, however. The announcement that the boycott was being limited to one day was likely to draw attention to Hitler's slowness in implementing the party's national socialistic ideology. To allay fears of the *Mittelstand* that the Nazi leadership might be retreating on economic questions, Goebbels promised: "This revolution will not by-pass the fundamental question of economics. If until now the *Volk* has existed to serve the economic system or capital, then this capitalism will be shunted aside. We will reverse the situation. Money will serve the economy and the economy in turn will serve the *Volk*."[25]

While Goebbels was speaking, other last-minute preparations

---

[24] Goebbels' speech is reprinted in a collection of his speeches. See Joseph Goebbels, *Revolution der Deutschen* (Oldenburg, 1933), p. 158.

[25] Ibid.

for the boycott were under way throughout the Reich. Goering's Prussian Ministry of the Interior sent a directive to all police authorities in Prussia as well as the presidents of the various German states. The police were instructed "not to hinder the boycott action in any way; in fact, it should view the boycott with magnanimity."[26] Except in cases of violence against life or property, the police were not to interfere in the boycott. The directive showed clearly that this was to be the day of the SA and the party. At the same time the various chief justices of the district courts and the courts' chief prosecutors were briefed through the police radio by Hans Kerrl, the Reich's Commissioner for Justice in Prussia. Kerrl spoke to them for an hour about the need for and purpose of the boycott. "It is the duty of all constituted authorities," he told the court officials, "to see to it that the Nazi-led boycott removes the cause for previous uncoordinated actions."[27] To achieve that purpose Kerrl requested that court officials encourage Jewish judges and lawyers to take their vacations immediately. In addition, if any local Nazi leaders expressed the desire to stand guard at the court buildings in order to implement the boycott, Kerrl advised that these desires be met.

Despite official invocation of public anger, *Volkswut,* to justify the action, it was apparent that the Nazi leadership was concerned at the last moment about a possible lack of public participation. Streicher's committee had charged the local Action Committees to whip up mass enthusiasm and Goebbels' propaganda machine had supported those efforts. Both Streicher and Goebbels had addressed numerous public gatherings during the past few days in which they tried to generate public enthusiasm for the boycott. There was no question, of course, about the popularity of the boycott in SA or party circles. But without wide-scale public participation the Nazi image abroad was bound to suffer even more than it already had. If the boycott

26 *Dokumente Frankfurter Juden,* pp. 20-21.

27 Quoted by Sievert Lorenzen, *Die Juden und die Justiz,* 2nd ed. (Berlin, 1943), p. 175.

turned out to be little more than a cover for SA hooliganism, the myth of nationwide support for Hitler would be seriously damaged.

The Saturday "boycott editions" of the *Voelkischer, Beobachter* ran a front-page story calculated to dispel public apathy. "Unmistakable evidence has been found," the article charged, "that Berlin Jews, to whom absolutely nothing has happened, have visited the representatives of foreign governments in Berlin in order to spread the most atrocious lies about how they have been mistreated."[28] Could any German be blamed, it went on, if he took steps to halt such a vicious defamation of the German character?

The boycott was scheduled to begin that morning throughout Germany, promptly at 10:00 A.M. Two SA or SS men were to stand at the entrance of every Jewish business or office. A prospective customer or client would be informed that he was about to enter a Jewish establishment. Presumably the decision to enter or leave was left to the customer. Henceforth everyone in Germany, from the capital city to the smallest hamlet would be aware of the Jews in his community or neighborhood.

Despite the detailed preparations and admonitions to rigid discipline, there was no standard pattern to the boycott. In some places discipline broke down very quickly. Actions which went far beyond the limits set by the committee were common in many places. In Kiel a Jewish lawyer reportedly was killed by a "crowd" which forced its way into a police station where he was being held. Supposedly a Nazi picket had been wounded by a shot fired from a furniture store owned by the lawyer's father. Elsewhere there was no discipline left to break down. Earlier in the week in numerous communities in Saxony, Silesia, and the Ruhr area, the SA had proclaimed local boycotts immediately upon learning of the one scheduled nationwide for Saturday.[29]

In Berlin on the other hand, the boycott was slow in getting started. At 11:00 A.M. the SA had manned only the entrances to

28 *Voelkischer Beobachter*, April 1, 1933.
29 *Voelkischer Beobachter*, April 30, 1933.

the big department stores, several cigar shops, and a few restaurants. A holiday mood seemed to prevail among the SA men. They generally ignored the Jewish shops in the city's more remote sections in favor of those in the more exciting streets in the city's center. Even here, however, they did not conform to the patterns envisioned by the boycott committee. Instead of standing by twos in doorways, they preferred to march en masse down the streets, singing "To hell with the Jews" and the choruses of the Horst Wessel party anthem. All day long SA units were stationed in the railway stations, greeting the passengers of incoming trains with anti-Jewish slogans and songs.[30] Late in the evening the SA was still in the streets, trying to lend some permanence to the boycott by photographing people who were patronizing Jewish movie theaters.[31] Throughout the day Jews were subjected to a variety of indignities, of course, but not on the scale or in the fashion the boycott's planners had anticipated.

The boycott was more effective in Frankfurt where the SA was at its posts throughout the city promptly at 10 o'clock.[32] As in many other places, however, the SA overstepped its bounds, especially in an incident perpetrated at the university. At 10:00 A.M. some eighty SA men entered the university buildings looking for Jews and Marxists. Two SA leaders, both students at the university, went to the prorektor's office (the rektor was in Berlin) to tell him of their mission. Outside, the SA was expelling Jews from the buildings and turning others away at the entrances. The various institutes of the university were also checked. In one of these, the Pharmacological Institute, they came upon a Jew, Professor Lipschitz, the Institute's director, whom they ordered to leave the premises.[33]

Actions such as this had not been sanctioned by the boycott

30 See Bela Fromm, *Blood and Banquets: A Berlin Social Diary* (New York, 1942), pp. 100-101.

31 Weiss, "Einige Dokumente," p. 17.

32 *Frankfurter Zeitung*, April 2, 1933.

33 The incident was reported by the prorektor to the state minister for Science, Art, and Education. See *Dokumente Frankfurter Juden*, p. 178.

committee. Although it represented no serious breach of discipline, it indicated that the SA was not to be contained within the boundaries envisioned for it by the party leadership.

Far more serious than the breaches of discipline were the implications of a boycott for the German economy. The boycott had been intended to tie in closely with long-standing National Socialist protests against the department stores. Streicher's committee had envisioned its boycott, however, as being aimed only against a department store if it was Jewish. Superficially, at least, this seemed to present little problem. The Nazi's considered four of Germany's five largest department store chains Jewish. What the committee had failed to take into consideration, however, were the complexities involved in boycotting even a Jewish department store. To the committee's dismay it discovered that many of these department stores were largely in the hands of German banks or foreign creditors. These oversights created situations in which Jewish stores—and other businesses in similar financial trouble—had to be protected rather than boycotted. A boycott would have risked the firm's solvency, exacerbated Germany's unemployment problem and endangered the investments of foreigners expressly excluded from the boycott's provisions.[34] An elementary understanding, or even appreciation, of Germany's precarious economic position would have led to questions regarding the advisability of a boycott of any sort. That these problems became apparent to the party and boycott leadership only after the boycott was in progress points to the peculiar Nazi genius for ignoring reality.

As the day progressed, other problems arose which had never occurred to Streicher or anyone connected with the boycott. For the first time the Nazis were faced with the problem of devising a precise definition of who and what was Jewish. Cases of doubtful Jewishness had been foreseen by the boycott committee. The special section it had established in Munich to rule on such cases soon discovered, however, that a complex business enterprise precluded precise classification. Was a firm Jewish if its stock

34 Heinrich Uhlig, *Die Warenhäuser im Dritten Reich* (Cologne, 1956), p. 52.

was owned primarily by Jews? The Nazis thought so, but what if its directors or a majority of its employees were Aryan? This problem of definition was to plague many later stages of Jewish policy. A solution defied Nazi ingenuity until such considerations of correctness were no longer necessary.

The boycott created problems in other areas as well. One of its prime purposes had been to demonstrate to the party's radicals the sincerity of the regime's commitment to National Socialist ideology. In that the boycott succeeded all too well. Not only were there excesses in Frankfurt and various other parts of Germany, but many people saw the boycott as a signal for making demands the regime could not possibly fulfill. A local party unit in Berlin, for example, wanted the government to compel Jewish shopkeepers to dismiss their Jewish employees immediately and grant their Aryan employees two months' wages in advance.[35]

The weight of these unexpected problems forced cancellation of the boycott the same day it was begun. On Saturday afternoon Streicher announced the boycott would not be resumed the following Wednesday. For fear that Jews might think the Nazi storm had passed, he added that the structure of his committee was being maintained so a boycott could be resumed at any time.

The official reason given for canceling the boycott was that its aims had been realized. In a classic example of Orwellian doublethink, Goebbel's Propaganda Ministry announced: "The Reich government is pleased to announce that the counterboycott against the agitation of Germany's enemies has been a success. With only a few exceptions this outrageous foreign propaganda has been stopped. The government takes the position that it would serve no purpose to continue the counterboycott since now such outside agitation stems only from the communists."[36]

Not all of the repercussions to the boycott were undone

[35] Rumbold to Simon. See Woodward and Butler, eds., *Documents on British Foreign Policy*, p. 22.

[36] *Deutsche Allgemeine Zeitung*, April 4, 1933.

merely by its cancellation. The foreign press had given it extensive and almost universally unfavorable treatment. Reactions abroad forced the government into retreat. Hitler enlisted his newly appointed Reichsbank president, Hjalmar Schacht, into explaining the boycott. In the next days Schacht telephoned British bankers to assure them of the future orthodoxy of German economic policy.[37] Neither had Hitler's rhetoric dissuaded President Hindenburg from his objections to the boycott. On April 4, he sent a letter to the chancellor outlining his objections to various Nazi policies.

Within its own circles the Nazi leadership was prepared to admit failure. On April 17, Curt Menzel, a Nazi jurist, spoke of the boycott's problems to a meeting of the League of National Socialist German jurists in Hamburg. Menzel's analysis stressed what many Nazis considered to be the public apathy evident during the boycott. The spontaneity and enthusiasm of which Goebbels and others had made so much seemed limited to the radical elements within the party. The response of the people had been far from satisfactory. Menzel told of the situation in Berlin where crowds had gathered more out of curiosity than enthusiasm for the boycott. The first task of Nazi propaganda, as he saw it, was to awaken the masses to their role in an anti-Jewish policy, "especially after the many failures of our recent Saturday boycott."[38] Menzel also criticized the failure of Streicher's committee to identify properly the concept "Jewish business." The apathy of the German public could be traced to such oversights, he believed.[39] Lack of public enthusiasm for the boycott was particularly disappointing to the Nazis. This apathy may have been the most characteristic response, but there were enough incidents of resistance and expressions of sympathy from German friends to soften the impact for many Jews. Gifts of flowers and candy from these friends indicated that not all of

---

[37] Lichtheim, *Geschichte des deutschen Zionismus*, p. 253.

[38] Menzel's speech is reprinted in his *Minderheitenrecht und Judenfrage* (Edelgarten, n.d.), p. 18.

[39] Ibid., p. 19.

Germany had gone mad. Many Jewish shop owners, especially those in working-class districts, noted that people were making a point of buying in their store that day.[40]

Failures such as these seriously discredited the party's radicals as formulators and executors of Jewish policy. Attempts to relegate them to a position of secondary influence, however, were not realized without considerable friction. Twice during the following months, once in July and again in August, Streicher's committee had to be restrained by Nazi Party Headquarters. Hitler's deputy, Rudolf Hess, ordered the committee to be more circumspect in its actions and propaganda, emphasizing that its task was limited mainly to investigating cases of Jewish corruption. Eventually Streicher's committee was assigned additional duties such as investigating business firms to determine whether they were Aryan or Jewish, but it never again was commissioned to organize a boycott.[41]

Privately inspired boycotts continued to plague the Nazi leaders, however. The SA in particular was unwilling to forego the pleasure of this "meaningful activity," although other radical units within the party also were eager for another Jewish boycott. Frequently during the next months Rudolf Hess issued orders interdicting such plans. He was not always successful.

By mid-April it had become apparent that in their first attempt at a Jewish policy the Nazis had struck from a position of weakness at what was unwittingly a foundation of Jewish strength. The boycott, as it turned out, was as much an attack on the German economy as it was on the Jews. If Hitler hoped to consolidate his political position, economic problems had to be solved, not aggravated. The economy was in such a delicate state that it could not tolerate negative measures of any sort. Foreign capital investments and loans were dependent upon confidence in German economic policy. Any measures which undermined that confidence served only to increase those prob-

40 Mally Dienemann, "Memoiren," unpublished memoir in the Leo Baeck Institute archives, p. 10.

41 Collection: Streicher, Folder 21, Zentralkomitee für Boykottbewegung, BDC.

lems Hitler was committed to solving. The boycott had taught the Nazi leadership one very essential lesson: concurrent solutions to the Jewish question and the economic problem were impossible. Until some measure of economic progress was visible it was apparent that domestic and external considerations would impose limits on any Jewish policy.

In the boycott action, of course, Hitler's tactical sense failed him, a failure which is at first difficult to understand. The success he had in other areas eluded him on the Jewish issue. For once he was unable to play both ends against the center and emerge on top. Why should that have been? It is not sufficient merely to point to his limited knowledge of economics, although this deficiency played its role. His problem, shared by the entire Nazi movement, was the failure to understand the situation of Jews in Germany. The Jew he talked about and believed in did not exist. When it came to evaluating the Jewish question, neither Hitler nor anyone else had anything other than his own propaganda to draw upon. Goering could invite German Jewish leaders to his office, convinced they had the power to influence governments and the press abroad. His conviction rested upon the categories manufactured by years of Nazi prejudice and propaganda.

The consequences of acting upon these totally illusory premises were demonstrated by the boycott's failure. This perspective also affords an understanding of a series of failures in Jewish policy which followed the boycott. If the Nazis hoped to find a satisfactory solution to the Jewish problem—satisfactory on their own terms—at least a minimum of objective understanding regarding Jews was required.

Whatever disappointment the Nazi leadership registered over the events of boycott Saturday, it was not dissuaded from pursuing the movement's anti-Jewish objectives. The radicals had been discredited for their failures, not for their intentions. Furthermore, when it came to anti-Semitism, it would do Hitler an injustice to classify him with any group other than the radicals. He differed from them only in his sense of tactics and his willingness to compromise today in order to achieve his goals tomorrow.

A sense of tactics or willingness to compromise did nothing to mitigate Hitler's determination to solve the Jewish problem. In the days immediately following the boycott, it would have been politically prudent to play down this resolve. Anti-Jewish activity was offering the Third Reich's enemies abroad untold opportunities to attack the new regime. Internal considerations, arising from the failure of one approach, might have dictated a second look at a proposal for another. Yet one week after the boycott, the regime announced the first in a series of laws discriminating against Jews. Less grandiose than the boycott, these laws demonstrated, nevertheless, the measure of Nazi determination. If the Jew could not be attacked directly on the economic front, perhaps he was more vulnerable at other points.

IV. Legislation: The Second Impasse

REPERCUSSIONS to the boycott demonstrated the consequences of acting upon a fairy-tale conception of the Jewish problem. The broadside attack against "Jewish control" of the German economy had implications which required immediate retreat. Realists such as Hitler were willing—though reluctantly so—to make the retreat. Streicher and other radical Jew-haters saw such retreats as diluting Nazi ideology. The frustrations of the radicals gave rise in the next few years to a series of anti-Jewish initiatives which were ill-conceived and, in the circumstances, doomed to failure.

A striking feature of Nazi Jewish policy after the April boycott was its lack of coordination. Indeed, until late 1938, one cannot speak of a single Jewish policy. There was, to be sure, the official anti-Jewish line of the regime, propagated by Goebbels' Propaganda Ministry and in Hitler's speeches, which masked the inconsistencies and reverses in a multitude of Jewish policies. Behind this facade one notes policies which were pursued without the sanction and oftentimes without the knowledge of the party's central authorities. What appeared to outside observers as steady Nazi pressures against Jews on nearly all fronts, was actually the product of strain and disagreement within the Nazi movement.

The SA's seizure of the initiative in Jewish affairs illustrated clearly that Jews were considered fair game. But the failure of the boycott illustrated just as clearly the dangers inherent in allowing radicals to determine the course of Jewish policy. The dilemma was of Hitler's own making. Years of anti-Jewish propaganda had prepared the SA and others for radical action. To cry in one breath *"Juda verrecke"* (Death to the Jews), and to ask in the next for discipline and restraint was as unrealistic as it was inconsistent. This was, however, the position in which Hitler found himself. There was no way for him to provide leadership from this position. His followers had already taken more than circumstances allowed him to give.

It must be emphasized again that the mildness of the regime's official policy did not stem from top-level doubts regarding anti-Semitism. The boycott had demonstrated, however, the existence of certain realities, the harshest of which was Germany's own precarious economic situation. During the boycott, economic considerations had forced the Nazis to protect several Jewish department stores. In June this embarrassing situation was compounded when Hugenberg's replacement as Economics Minister, Dr. Kurt Schmitt, confronted Hitler with a painful dilemma. Schmitt asked Hitler to approve a governmental loan to save Germany's second largest department store chain, the Jewish-owned Hermann Tietz Concern. In 1932 the Tietz chain had borrowed RM 132.8 million. Now, in mid-1933, it faced the prospect of being liquidated. Schmitt argued the liquidation would add 14,000 people to the list of Germany's unemployed. The confidence of Germany's business community was at stake, he emphasized. Only Hitler's approval for the grant of RM 14.5 million additional credit for Tietz from the Reich-controlled *Akzept und Garantiebank* could rescue the situation. Hitler's choice was between ideological purity and the needs of the moment. After two hours of bitter argument he chose the latter. Reich-controlled credit was used to rescue the most hated of "Jewish institutions"—the department store chain.[1]

Pressures from outside Germany were also making themselves felt. On May 30, the Council of the League of Nations censured Germany for its anti-Jewish measures in Upper Silesia.[2] A few weeks later at the World Economic Conference in London,

---

[1] Reported by Dr. E. Michael, an official in the Reichs Economics Ministry in 1933, to Heinrich Uhlig, *Die Warenhäuser im Dritten Reich* (Cologne, 1956), pp. 115-117.

[2] *New York Times*, May 31, 1933.

Foreign Minister Neurath noted a growing diplomatic isolation of Germany. He delivered himself of his concerns in a letter to President Hindenburg on June 19:

> I have found a mood—at first in the English world and then in wider circles—which cannot be taken seriously enough. It represents a backward step for the political situation of Germany. In my report to the Reichs Chancellor I have explained what I consider to be the cause of this reversal. The Jewish question, which has been used to isolate and harm us at the Geneva meeting of the League Council . . . , is also very much in evidence here at the even more important London meetings.[3]

Another, though less important consideration in the making of Jewish policy had to be public apathy. Public reaction to the boycott had been unsatisfactory. The enthusiasm hoped for by the boycott's planners had failed to materialize. In some cities there had been active resistance with customers deliberately trying to buy in boycotted businesses. The *Voelkischer Beobachter* reported on April 3 that in Hannover some people tried to use force to get into a Jewish-owned store. Such incidents were the exception, but they reflected something less than wholesale sympathy with Nazi aims and policies. In his postmortem examination of the boycott, Kurt Menzel admitted the need for an anti-Semitic awakening among the masses.

Part of the boycott's purpose had been to further such an awakening. Streicher's committee had called upon Local Action Committees to agitate among the masses for measures which would limit the number of Jews engaged in the professions. The 1932 Nazi blueprint had envisioned such measures against Jewish doctors, lawyers, and teachers and the harassment of these individuals by the SA during March left little doubt about Nazi intentions. Within a week after the boycott the first legislation discriminating against Jewish professionals was decreed. Three more laws followed before the end of the month.

There could never be any real doubt that, once they came to

---

[3] Neurath's letter is quoted in Helmut Genschel, *Die Verdrängung der Juden aus der Wirtschaft im Dritten Reich* (Göttingen, 1966), pp. 76-77.

power, the Nazis would tamper with civil rights. Rumors before January 1933 had indicated the civil service would be the first victim. Such rumors disturbed the conservatives to whom the German civil service was a symbol of loyalty and efficiency and one of the few remaining links with the happier pre-Weimar age. In Hitler's first cabinet meeting on January 30, Vice-Chancellor von Papen asked him to deny the rumors.[4] When reports of SA excesses against state employees, including judges and public prosecutors, became common during the weeks prior to the boycott, other high-placed conservatives also protested to the Nazi chancellor. On April 4, just three days after the boycott, President von Hindenburg sent Hitler the following letter:

> In the last few days I have been notified of numerous incidents in which judges, lawyers, and judicial civil servants, who had been wounded in the war, were illegally forced to take their vacations and then dismissed because they were of Jewish origin.
> For myself, one who reveres those who died in the war and is thankful to those soldiers who survived and the wounded who suffered, this treatment of Jewish war veterans now in the civil service is intolerable. I am convinced that you, Herr Chancellor, share these human feelings and so I urge you most heartily to concern yourself with this problem and to see to it that an honorable solution for the entire civil service is found. I feel that civil servants, judges, teachers, and lawyers who were wounded in the war or were soldiers on the front, or are sons of those who died or had sons who died in battle must—insofar as they have not given cause to be treated otherwise—be allowed to continue in their professions. If they were prepared to bleed and die for Germany they deserve to be treated honorably by the Fatherland.[5]

The old soldier had spoken in true soldierly fashion. For Hindenburg, at least, loyalty to Germany was not to be punished for irrelevant reasons.

[4] Herbert Michaelis and Ernst Schraepler, eds., *Das Dritte Reich, Die Zertrümmerung des Parteienstaates und die Grundlegung der Diktatur: Dokumentensammlung*, vol. 9 (Berlin, n.d.), p. 7.

[5] *Dokumente der deutschen Politik und Geschichte*, vol. 4 (Berlin, n.d.), pp. 147-148.

Hitler could not afford to take the president's views lightly. Yet his reply the next day was not altogether conciliatory. He justified Nazi actions by informing Hindenburg that Jews had overrun certain professions, preventing Germans, also wounded in the war, from securing worthy positions. Millions of his brave and loyal followers in the NSDAP were being kept out of good jobs by Jews. Now that the situation was soon to be reversed, Jews were complaining. Nonetheless, Hitler assured him that:

> I share your worthy motives, Herr Field Marshal, and have taken them into consideration in my talks with the Interior Minister Frick. You may be assured that the solution to this problem will be carried out legally, and not by actions of caprice. I have informed the Interior Minister of the cases you would like to see excepted. A law has been in preparation for about a week and will take into consideration those Jews who are veterans, who suffered in the war, who served in some capacity, or who after long service do not warrant dismissal.[6]

The framework for discriminatory legislation had been provided by passage of the Enabling Act of March 24. The Reichstag's action had given the government formal power to govern and legislate by decree, thereby providing the Nazis a cloak of legality with which to cover their official actions. Most important, the act enabled the Nazi regime to set aside those provisions of the Weimar constitution which stood in its way, especially those guaranteeing legal equality to all citizens.

Hitler's suggestion to Hindenburg that a law had been under consideration for only a week indicates that it was hastily prepared, almost as hastily as had been the boycott. There is little reason to doubt Hitler's word on this point. The Nazis could afford a hastily prepared law. Nazi law could be changed or expanded by supplementary decrees (*Durchführungsverordnungen*). The decree powers of the Enabling Act allowed the regime to cover any inadequacies or oversights.

The 1932 blueprint for dealing with the Jewish question had

[6] Ibid., pp. 148-149.

forecast legal action against Jews (*Entrechtungsmassnahmen*) if and when the National Socialists achieved a parliamentary majority. In effect the Enabling Act and the subsequent collapse of the opposition parties established such a majority. Numerous reasons for a legal approach to a solution of the Jewish question suggested themselves. Prudence dictated that the Nazi regime maintain a degree of respectability abroad. The opinions of foreign governments and foreign creditors were crucial during these early months of Nazi rule. If Jews were to be discriminated against, the Nazis could at least point to the "legality" of the discrimination. There were sufficient circles of conservatism abroad whose fear of bolshevism made them willing to overlook the substance of law if the form was maintained.[7] One can even speculate that Hitler's petit bourgeois value system required the correctness of a pseudolegal approach. Whatever else he may have been, the Fuehrer was not a superficial cynic. Legal or pseudolegal tactics had, moreover, served Hitler well in his long struggle for power following the 1923 Putsch.

A most persuasive argument for the legal approach arose out of the situation of March 1933 itself, however. Just as the boycott had aimed at giving form to a chaotic economic persecution engineered by the SA, so legislation could hopefully bring order to the uncoordinated actions against Jewish professionals. Hitler had promised the German people order. For that he needed the law.

Throughout March Jewish judges and lawyers had been subjected to frequent indignities and even injury by SA terrorists. The SA was particularly zealous in its intimidation of a professional class it did not trust. In connection with the Breslau incident mentioned earlier, the SA soon was making a practice of preventing Jewish judges and lawyers from entering their courtrooms and offices. Until mid-March this sort of activity was confined primarily to the lower courts. After that, however, it be-

[7] See, for example, Margaret George, *The Warped Vision: British Foreign Policy*, 1933-1939 (Pittsburgh, 1965).

gan to threaten the president of the District Court of Appeals (*Oberlandesgericht*) as well.[8]

To prevent a complete breakdown of the judicial process, the Breslau police chief, now the former SA leader who had led the earlier action, ordered that henceforth only seventeen Jewish prosecutors would be allowed to argue cases before the court.[9] Some 72 Jewish prosecutors were affected by the order. As a further measure the district and local courts in nearby Oels were occupied by the regular police to assure "orderly court proceedings." At the same time in Breslau all Jewish judges and magistrates were placed on the retired list, their posts opened to racially suitable officials.[10]

Dismissals and forced vacations—the type which had prompted Hindenburg's letter to Hitler—were common elsewhere in the Reich. On March 25, the Bavarian Ministry of Justice ordered the replacement of Jewish judges in cases involving criminal and disciplinary action. Likewise state attorneys and court officials of Jewish origin were no longer allowed to act as prosecutors in the Bavarian courts.

In Berlin matters went even further. In early April Hans Kerrl, the Prussian Justice Minister, ordered: "The number of Jewish lawyers to be admitted to the Berlin courts will henceforth be equal to the percentage of Jews in the German population."[11] This, Kerrl's order continued, would leave about 35 lawyers of Jewish descent who could be admitted to the Berlin courts. Kerrl was not satisfied with regulating the Jewish situation merely in his own domain. Earlier, on March 30, he had dispatched his assistant, Dr. Roland Freisler, to help clear up confusion which developed in the Frankfurt court system. Freisler, whose moment of glory was to come in 1944 as judge in the trials of Hitler's would-be assassins, was already the strident bully eager to prove himself. He explained to the judges of the

8 Weiss, "Einige Dokumente," pp. 11-12.

9 Ibid., p. 12.

10 Rumbold to Simon. Woodward and Butler, eds., *Documents on British Foreign Policy*, p. 23.

11 *Voelkischer Beobachter*, April 4, 1933.

Frankfurt court what measures Berlin had in mind for its Jewish judges and lawyers. Following the meeting the president of the Frankfurt District Court issued an order requiring all Jewish judges associated with the court to take an immediate "vacation." Those who failed to comply, he warned, would be locked out of their courtrooms.[12]

In Munich and Wuppertal city officials, not all of whom were Nazis, decided upon their own authority that municipal contracts should not be granted to Jewish firms. The mayor of Düsseldorf issued instructions that all Jewish doctors and pharmacists were to be dismissed from the National Health Service (*Krankenkasse*). Not only lawyers, judges, and doctors, but Jewish professionals of all types were being forced to relinquish their positions. As long as he was employed in one fashion or another by a branch of the government—local, state, or federal—the Jewish judge, lawyer, doctor, or teacher was subject to dismissal.

Wherever local officials were slow in ordering dismissals or vacations for Jews, the SA was quick to help enforce the party's will. In Cologne, for example, where officials of the courts did not immediately ban Jewish lawyers and judges, SA units marched into the chambers and simply removed them. To dramatize its hatred of Jews, the SA carried them out into the streets and forced them to disrobe. Such actions on the part of the SA tended to elicit greater cooperation from reluctant authorities.

From the Nazi point of view these were purely administrative actions, fully in accord with the proposals in the 1932 blueprint. More important, these administrative actions bore the promise of success. Jews were being expelled from German professional life in great numbers. The prospect of complete elimination, moreover, promised to become brighter as the states' administrative apparatus fell increasingly into Nazi hands.

Despite the promise of administrative measures, the arguments for legislative regulation of Jewish participation in the

---

12 *Voelkischer Beobachter*, April 1, 1933.

professions were unusually persuasive. The need for some degree of consistency was an immediate one. Without it the breakdown of essential judicial services was threatened. The anarchy which would have resulted ran contrary to Hitler's promise to the German people as well as his own conception of the Nazi revolution. It was apparent, as the Cologne case demonstrated, that the existing bureaucracy could not be entrusted to applying administrative measures uniformly. As yet the various levels of the German civil service had not been subjected to an effective *Gleichschaltung.* Furthermore, Hitler's letter to Hindenburg notwithstanding, the shortage of capable party members to fill essential civil service positions was acute. Those few party members who had managed to secure posts in the municipal and *Land* or state bureaucracies were rapidly promoted to the Federal civil service.[13] If they were to operate effectively they needed the authority of law to enforce their decisions. Without the law, they would have to depend upon the SA to persuade recalcitrant officials at the lower levels. Dependence upon the SA raised more problems than it solved, however. Its past performance gave little evidence that it would be satisfied to act within the guidelines set by the Nazi authorities in Berlin. When these considerations were added to the pressures from Hindenburg and the importance of the Nazi image abroad, the need for a legal definition of the Jewish situation became overwhelming.

The first anti-Jewish legislation of 1933 was a direct response to the pressures operating from inside and outside the Nazi movement. As had been the case with the boycott, Hitler was caught in a dilemma. He, too, was absolutely convinced of the need for solving the Jewish problem. Yet, he was vulnerable from two sides. Hindenburg and the forces he represented demanded order; the SA and the party radicals demanded action which threatened that order. Neither side could be ignored. The four anti-Jewish laws of April were designed to bridge the gap.

13 Bernhard Lösener, "Als Rassereferat im Reichsministerium des Innern," *Vierteljahrshefte für Zeitgeschichte* 9 (July, 1961): 267.

The biological premises of Nazi anti-Semitism prescribed a specific approach to anti-Jewish legislation. It would have been reasonable to predict in 1932 that the first anti-Jewish laws of a Nazi regime would be designed to halt the process of biological assimilation and perhaps end the immigration of the *Ostjude*, or even require his expulsion. From Nazi propaganda throughout the *Kampfzeit* one might have expected an immediate ban on marriages between Jews and Germans, a requirement of racial anti-Semitism since the days of Karl Lueger. At the very least, ideology demanded some action which would halt and ultimately reverse the assimilation process.

It is not surprising, therefore, that the first concrete proposals for anti-Jewish legislation were aimed at de-assimilating the Jew from the German. The proposals came not from Hitler or anyone in his coterie, but from Dr. Paul Bang, a conscientious Nazi official in the Economics Ministry. Bang had seen the logic inherent in his anti-Semitism. He wanted to see legislation which would halt the immigration of Eastern Jews, a law which would force the assimilated German-Jew who had changed his name to take back his original and more obviously Jewish name and one which might possibly force the Eastern Jew's emigration from Germany. While he did not touch upon marriage, his proposals for unmasking the disguise of many assimilated Jews seemed the logical first step for the Nazis to take. In early March Bang sent his proposals to the Reichs chancellory office where he expected them to come to his Fuehrer's attention. From there they were sent to Wilhelm Frick in the Interior Ministry and shelved.[14] Not until 1938, when such questions had become largely irrelevant, was something approaching Bang's proposals implemented.

Bang was not alone in seeing the logic of the situation. An official in the Reichs Interior Ministry who was responsible for "legislation in the Jewish question" was besieged almost daily

[14] Bracher, Sauer, and Schulz, *Die nationalsozialistische Machtergreifung*, p. 280, n. 96.

during the first years of the Third Reich with suggestions for measures against the Jewish menace. Advice came from all quarters of the NSDAP, but especially from the radical elements which were anxious for an immediate solution to the Jewish problem.[15]

The set of four laws promulgated in April 1933 had little to do with what Nazi ideology proclaimed to be the heart of the Jewish question. Rather than comprising a frontal attack upon the blood aspects of assimilation, they were directed against the Jewish professionals who had been the object of recent SA terrorism. The same pressures which had led to the boycott now gave rise to legislation. The first two laws, both decreed on April 7, were aimed at the civil service and legal profession. Two more laws, one affecting Jewish doctors practicing within the National Health Service, the other affecting Jewish teachers and students, went into effect on April 22 and April 25 respectively.

Unlike the boycott which initially was directed at driving Jews out of the German economy, the April laws represented a very limited attack upon Jewish professional people. The laws made no specific mention of Jews, nor were they aimed at Jews exclusively. The Civil Service Law, which served as the model for anti-Jewish legislation until late 1935, was officially called the "Law for Restoration of the Professional Civil Service."[16] Its intention was not so much to restore the civil service as to provide a legal basis for eliminating undesirable elements which supposedly had infiltrated the civil service during the Weimar period. This might include anyone with nonnational sympathies, be he communist, socialist, liberal, or Jew. During the first months following Hitler's *Machtergreifung*, or seizure of power, Jews did not lack for company in being the object of Nazi attack. According to Nazi doctrine the political and racial foes had gained their influence during the liberal regime following the revolution of November 1918. The purpose of the conservative revolution, ostensibly at least, was to restore the society

15 Lösener, "Als Rassereferat," p. 267.
16 *Reichsgesetzblatt* I, 1933, p. 175 (hereafter cited as RGB1).

which had preceded one based on liberal principles. In fact, the Nazis' strictly political foes were not even accorded the niceties of legal exclusion. The SA had established wildcat concentration camps at the very outset of Nazi rule and collected communists —or people it called communists—to inhabit them. Ostensibly the experience in these camps would re-educate political enemies. For Jews, whose perversity was biologically determined, such re-education was impossible and the number of Jews incarcerated in these camps was at first very small.

The Civil Service Law was couched in terms which made it applicable to both the political and racial enemy. It defined three groups of undesirable civil servants and provided for their dismissal. Those who had been appointed after November 9, 1918 were subject to removal if they lacked the proper qualification or training. By arbitrary definition nearly anyone could be made to fit into this category. A second group included those civil servants who "judging by their previous political activities do not afford sufficient guarantee that they will always support the national state without reserve." [17] The third group, also subject to dismissal, were civil servants of "non-Aryan" descent.

The term non-Aryan was in obvious reference to the racial enemy. Failure to call him by his Jewish name, however, pointed to a problem of considerable consequence for Nazi legal actions. No adequate definition of the Jew had been established. The problem had first arisen in connection with the boycotting of Jewish department stores. As long as the Nazis felt the need to maintain a legal facade to their anti-Jewish actions, the problem of definition was to plague them. The essence of the problem was simple enough: propaganda slogans about Jewish blood defied translation even into Nazi legal terminology. The inconsistency emerging from the definition of an ostensibly biological phenomenon, the Jew, on the basis of a cultural attribute, religion, was resolved only by fiat. The problem of definition ultimately posed impossible questions. Was the Jew who had married a German, abandoned his faith, and considered himself

[17] Ibid.

German, still a Jew? Hitler, of course, maintained that he was, that he could never leave his Jewishness behind. But what of the children of such a marriage? Or eventually the grandchildren? Or the great-grandchildren?

The problem did not exist for someone like Julius Streicher who maintained he could sniff out Jewish blood no matter how well it was disguised. Hitler's claims were equally extravagant. In one of those endless wartime monologues at Berchtesgaden, he told how Jewish blood always made itself apparent. He used the example of a Baron Liebig he had once met. Liebig's lineage had been purely Aryan, except for one ancestor born of Jewish parents in 1616. Upon seeing Liebig, Hitler claimed to have recognized immediately a pronounced appearance of Jewishness.[18] If his duties as chancellor had not kept him so busy he might have solved the problem of identifying and defining the Jew all by himself. What a formidable team of Jew-searchers the Reich might have had, had Hitler coupled his own abilities with those of Streicher! Those who drafted anti-Jewish legislation for the Third Reich, if they shared Hitler's gifts for identifying the Jews, were not as skillful in pinning them to legal categories. They had to fall back upon the negative concept of non-Aryan, emblematic of what the German was not.

In this connection it is as revealing to look at those who were excepted from the law's provisions as at those who fell under them. Hindenburg's letter to Hitler had not been in vain. With one exception Hitler honored his promise to the Reich's president. His exception was the first category mentioned in the Civil Service Law. He refused to concede the regime's right to dismiss anyone whose position had been attained after November 1918. Otherwise Hindenburg's requests were honored. A civil servant who had fought in the war or whose father or son had served was exempt from dismissal unless he was disqualified for lack of professional or political reliability.

18 Gerhard Ritter, ed., *Hitlers Tischgespräche im Führerhauptquartier, 1941-1942* (Bonn, 1951), pp. 312-313.

Theoretically Hitler's exception overrode Hindenburg's considerations. Judgments on matters relating to proper training and qualifications were to be made by Nazi ministers. A Jew, a liberal, a conservative, a communist, or a socialist could always be accused of lacking the necessary qualifications if he could not be excluded on any other basis. In practice things worked out quite differently. In the first instance very few Jews, communists, or socialists had ever achieved high positions in the German civil service, even during the liberal interlude of Weimar. To that extent the civil service needed little restoring. Given the traditions of efficiency and conservatism in the German bureaucracy, moreover, it was unlikely that either professional or political unreliability was widespread. Unless Hitler was willing and, more importantly, able to demand the dismissal of politically conservative bureaucrats as well, the defenses of the German civil service against the Nazi assault seemed well prepared.[19]

Announced along with the Civil Service Law of April 7 was the "Law Concerning Admission to the Legal Profession,"[20] which affected both judges and public prosecutors. The approximately 3,000 Jewish lawyers in Germany were much more vulnerable to attack than the few Jewish bureaucrats. They were state officials who dealt with public matters under the glaring light of a publicity organized by the Nazis themselves.

The April legislation was completed later in the month with the announcement of a law affecting Jewish medical doctors and another restricting the number of Jewish students in German schools. On April 22, non-Aryans and communists were subjected to the "Decree Regarding Physicians' Services with the National Health Service."[21] Henceforth patients covered by the national insurance were informed their expenses would not be paid if they consulted a non-Aryan doctor. Once again the

---

19 E. N. Peterson, "The Bureaucracy and the Nazi Party," *Review of Politics* 28 (April, 1966): 172-192.

20 RGBl, I, 1933, p. 188.

21 Ibid., p. 222.

Hindenburg exceptions were applied. Jewish doctors who were war veterans or had otherwise suffered from the war were not subject to the decree. Exclusion from the National Health Service greatly weakened the economic position of Jewish doctors. The exclusion technique was shortly to be applied to other professions as well.

The "Law Against the Overcrowding of German Schools"[22] was announced on April 25. Educational policy is usually a first target of revolutionaries. To this the Nazis were no exception. Their regime faced the imperative of perpetuating itself by passing its ideological insights on to a generation of school children. This required an immediate end to the Weimar teachings regarding democracy and equality. Above all it required the inculcation of racial pride into German school children. Administrative efforts preceded the first Nazi legislation pertaining to schools. In Bavaria the Minister of Culture formulated a curriculum around Theodor Fritsch's "standard-setting work on the Jewish question."[23] In Berlin the Nazi school commissioner directed the city's Jewish teachers to take an immediate leave of absence "to prevent incidents and unrest in our schools."[24]

The School Law of April 25 was not, however, a direct response to these pressures. For the most part it was concerned with the overcrowded conditions in German schools. The World War and Depression had led to a lag in school construction which by 1933 had begun to raise serious problems. Rather than embark on a school construction program, the Nazis chose to limit enrollment in general and to reduce the enrollment of Jewish students in particular. In the first instance German higher schools (primary schools were unaffected) were directed to limit the number of students in such overcrowded professional studies as law. Jewish students on the other hand were subjected to a *numerus clausus*. The number of Jews to be admitted to high

22 Ibid., p. 225.
23 *Voelkischer Beobachter*, April 7, 1933.
24 *Voelkischer Beobachter*, April 2 and 3, 1933.

schools (*Gymasien*), technical institutes, and universities was restricted to 1.5 percent of the total enrollment.[25]

With the concentration of German Jewry in the large cities such as Berlin and Frankfurt, the *numerus clausus* worked a particular hardship upon the Jewish community. Exceptions were made in communities where the percentage of Jews exceeded five percent of the total population. Here five percent of a school's students could be Jewish, but in no case was the Jewish percentage allowed to be greater. Consistent with the other April Laws, children of Jewish war veterans were not counted as part of the Jewish quota. The School Law was also the first of the Nazi laws to go slightly beyond the vague Aryan/non-Aryan definition of the Civil Service Law. A non-Aryan child had to have two non-Aryan parents. The child with one Aryan and one Jewish parent was still considered to be Aryan. The generosity of this legal definition did not have long to survive.

The Jewish community was forced by the School Law to set up its own emergency school system. However, those Jewish children who were still allowed to attend German schools can hardly be said to have been advantaged. They suffered the full burden of the anti-Semitism which was being institutionalized into the Nazi education structure. Each school had in its curriculum a course in racial theory which both Aryan and Jewish students were required to attend. Here they learned of Jewish racial inferiority in its many dimensions. The notebook of a young Jewish girl from Offenbach, the daughter of a rabbi, indicates the content of her teacher's lecture on racial theory. The girl was thirteen when she recorded that:

1. The Jewish race is much inferior to the Negro race.
2. All Jews have crooked legs, fat bellies, curly hair, and an untrustworthy look.
3. Jews are responsible for the World War.

[25] Solomon Colodner, "Jewish Education under National Socialism," *Yad Washem Studies* 3 (1959): 161-180.

4. They are to blame for the armistice of 1918 and they made the Peace of Versailles.
5. They were the cause of the inflation.
6. They brought on the downfall of the Roman Empire.
7. Marx is a great criminal.
8. All Jews are communists.
9. They are the rulers of Russia.[26]

Shortly thereafter this girl's teacher became director of the school.

At first glance the School Law, along with the exclusionary laws affecting Jewish professional activity, would appear to have been an effective means of disentangling the threads of German-Jewish assimilation. The School Law supported the legislation requiring immediate exclusion of Jews from the professions by assuring that only a very limited number of Jews would be trained to enter these professions. Within a generation the vast majority of Jews would have been excluded from the life which characterized their assimilation into German society. Within two generations the exclusion would have been virtually complete. If disassimilation was the Nazi objective, its Jewish policy was at least headed in the right direction. Whether Nazi patience was equal to the leisurely pace of such a solution was, however, highly questionable.

It was also apparent to many Nazis that legislation regarding schools and professions did not strike at the heart of the Jewish problem. On April 8, the day after the announcement of the Civil Service and Lawyers Law, the *Voelkischer Beobachter* reminded the faithful that: "Our aim is the biological separation of the Jewish and German races." Only a ban on German-Jewish marriages could effect such a separation, a measure finally incorporated by the Nazis in their last significant anti-Jewish legislation—the 1935 Nuremberg Laws. The SA, too, served notice during the remainder of 1933 that it considered a few laws insufficient to deal with the Jewish problem. Boycotts and terrorization of Jews continued unabated.

[26] Dienemann, "Memoiren," p. 212.

Even the advocates of an orderly Jewish policy had little cause for satisfaction with the April Laws. They did not eliminate Jews from the civil service, law, or medicine. Of 717 non-Aryan judges and prosecuting attorneys, fewer than half (336 or 47 percent) fell under the exclusion provisions. Only 1,418 Jewish lawyers, or about 30 percent, could be removed from their professions.[27] At the same time no more than a quarter of the 4,500 Jewish doctors participating in the National Health Service could be excluded.[28] As with the boycott, the Nazis had miscalculated the nature of their Jewish problem. They had been unaware that so many Jews had served in the World War or that so many others had been active in their professions prior to the Weimar period.

Hitler, in his letter to Hindenburg, said the Civil Service and Lawyers' Law had been in preparation for only a week. In that short time it was hardly possible for the responsible authorities to do their necessary homework. The only constant factor in these early anti-Jewish actions was a lack of thorough preparation. This was as true of the legislation as it had been for the boycott, and in both cases the consequences were similar. On the first day of the boycott it had been necessary to call for a retreat. Within a week after proclamation of the Civil Service Law the regime announced that it would apply the law only to the top levels of the civil service. For the time being officials at the lower and middle ranks were exempt from its provisions. The problem of replacing even those few officials to whom the non-Aryan clause applied had not been envisioned. The thousands of highly qualified Nazi followers of whom Hitler had spoken in his letter to Hindenburg did not exist. Rigorous application of the law at all levels, as initially proposed, would have threatened the continuity of orderly administration.

The four April Laws were merely the first of some 400 pieces of anti-Jewish legislation promulgated by the Nazis between

27 *Deutsche Justiz* (1934), p. 950.
28 Bruno Blau, *Das Ausnahmerecht für die Juden in Deutschland, 1933-1945,* 2nd ed. (Düsseldorf, 1954), p. 7.

1933 and 1939. They were the first steps in a legal attack which reached its peak in late 1935. In retrospect legislation turned out to be the least important phase of National Socialism's attack upon German and European Jewry. Yet, in these early years it was the only approach officially approved by the party leadership. Hitler and his trouble shooters, Hess and Goering, expended considerable energy and ultimately the blood of the SA in suppressing or attempting to suppress a wealth of unofficial policies stemming from various quarters of the Nazi movement. For the time being he was unwilling to go beyond the reaches of the law, even though he himself defined what those reaches were.

The April Laws were followed on July 14 by a Denaturalization Law which allowed the Reich government to revoke the citizenship of people it considered undesirable.[29] The law could be applied to anyone who had settled in Germany after November 9, 1918—another way of saying anyone who had received his citizenship from the Weimar government. By order of the Interior Ministry on July 26, the law was to be applied first against the estimated 150,000 Eastern Jews in Germany.[30] An Eastern Jew (Ostjude), unless he had in some way contributed to the well-being of the German Volk, could have his citizenship revoked.

Although the law was designed to strike at the hated Ostjude, it actually served little practical purpose. Many Jews had indeed fled eastern Europe following the pogroms during the latter decades of the nineteenth century. While large numbers had used Germany only as a springboard for emigration to the United States, others had chosen to settle in the land of Kaiser Wilhelm II. Most of these were eager to attain citizenship, but the difficulties of becoming a naturalized German were almost insurmountable. Each German state government had the right to veto any application for citizenship. Only by unanimous decision was such an application approved. The result was that

29 RGB1, I, 1933, p. 480.
30 Ibid., p. 539.

most of these people, while they continued to live and even raise families in Germany, retained the citizenship of the country from which they had fled. For all practical purposes they became Germans, but unless they succeeded in acquiring citizenship, they, their children, and their grandchildren remained "foreign Jews." The situation did not improve markedly with the advent of the Weimar Republic. Naturalization procedures underwent no basic changes. Any one state government could still veto an application for citizenship and when it came to a decision on a Jewish applicant the ultraconservative government of Bavaria usually chose to exercise its veto power. Consequently thousands of Jews whose grandfathers had settled in Germany and whose fathers had been born there were still citizens of foreign states.

Following the World War the situation became even more confusing when the kaleidoscopic shift of eastern Europe's political boundaries rendered thousands more Jews stateless. During the early days of the Weimar Republic many of these people had found their way to Germany. Very few had become German citizens. The Nazis were to discover that even they could not revoke the citizenship of those who were not citizens. Outright expulsion of these foreign Jews was also out of the question. By the latter 1920's anti-Semitic regimes had captured control of many east European states. Poland, the homeland of most of Germany's Eastern Jews, was especially eager to avoid their return. Moreover, Hitler was at the outset unwilling to alienate the Pilsudski regime. The negotiations which in January 1934 would lead to a nonaggression pact with Poland were already underway. Hitler went through the motions even so. On March 23, 1934 a "Law Regarding Expulsion from the Reich"—the Denaturalization Law—was proclaimed.[31] While it laid the legal foundation for the expulsion of the Eastern Jew, no such action was carried out until mid-1938.

Because so few Eastern Jews were citizens, the Denaturalization Law was largely a meaningless gesture. The law provided,

[31] Ibid., p. 213.

however, that the citizenship of "anyone who acted contrary to the spirit of the *Volk* or state" could be revoked. For the moment such terms were more applicable to the emigrés who left Germany in the wake of Hitler's seizure of power. Between August 1933 and late 1934 such German notables as Lion Feuchtwanger, Philip Scheidemann, Kurt Tucholski, Albert Einstein, Heinrich Mann, and even Otto Strasser lost their citizenship after having fled the Third Reich.[32]

Ultimately, as with so many other early anti-Jewish measures, the Denaturalization Law backfired. Some of the Eastern Jews had been German citizens. The revocation of their citizenship undermined eventually the later policy of forcing Jewish emigration. Without citizenship papers and a passport the possibilities of emigrating to another country were greatly reduced.

Three further pieces of legislation affecting Jews came into effect in 1933. On September 29, a "Hereditary Farm Law" excluded Jews from owning farmland or engaging in agriculture.[33] The effect of this upon Jews was minimal. Very few of them were engaged in farming of any sort. The Jewish peasant did not exist. Nonetheless the terms of the law reflected a classic example of racial thinking: "The Reich government passes this law to secure the peasant foundations of our blood line through instituting the ancient customs of land inheritance." Jurist Frank's "substantive values" of blood and soil were guaranteed by the law. Paragraph thirteen established that only a German could be a farmer or *Bauer*. Persons of Jewish or colored blood were excluded. In order to inherit a peasant holding, the German *Bauer* had to be able to trace his racial purity back to the year 1800,[34] before the emancipation of west European Jewry.

Unlike the Farm Law the two remaining pieces of legislation in 1933 dealt a major blow to Germany's Jews. On September 29 German cultural life—and therefore a major portion of Jew-

32 *Deutscher Reichsanzeiger und Preussischer Staatsanzeiger*, August, 1933, through November, 1934, *passim*.

33 RGB1, I, 1933, p. 685.

34 Maxine Y. Sweezy, *The Structure of the Nazi Economy* (Cambridge, Mass., 1941), pp. 180-183.

ish cultural life—was delivered into the hands of Joseph Goebbels. Chambers of Culture were established within his Propaganda Ministry, one each to regulate the film, theater, music,
fine arts, literature, broadcasting, and the press. Each chamber
was to regulate completely the activity within its own province.
The film chamber, for example was granted authority over
everything from the producer of and actors in a movie to the
ticket collectors in the theater. To be active in any of these
areas required the licensed permission of the appropriate chamber president.[35] In one grand sweep Jews, if they were engaged
in anything related to the film, music, or the press were subject
to exclusion by Goebbels' decree. The law establishing the
Chambers of Culture contained no Aryan clause. None was necessary. Goebbels had been granted authority to refuse admission
of undesirables to any of the chambers. By avoiding the legal
problems associated with the Aryan clause, Goebbels was un-
hampered in his exclusion of Jews. A more specific law dealing
with journalists was effected on October 4.[36] Its provisions were
similar to the ones which established the chambers of culture.
Henceforth journalists and editors needed official permission
to carry on their work.

Exclusion of Jews from the professions covered by the various
chambers was eventually much more effective than it had been
through the Civil Service or Lawyers' Law. During the next
years thousands of Jewish artists, writers, actors, musicians, and
Jews in related fields were to be excluded from participating in
German cultural life. The technique of creating a bureaucratic
structure outside of the regular state apparatus allowed the
Nazis a freedom which more ordinary legislation did not.

By late 1933 the official anti-Jewish energies of the Nazi
regime seemed temporarily to have been spent. The feverish
activity surrounding the boycott and the early legislation subsided into a period of relative calm. Even the SA seemed to let

[35] See Derrick Sington and Arthur Weidenfeld, *The Goebbels Experiment: A
Study of the Nazi Propaganda Machine* (London, 1942), pp. 111-113.
[36] RGBl, I, 1933, p. 713.

up occasionally in its rowdyism. Between the stick of Hitler's call to discipline and the carrot of Roehm being invited into the Reichs Cabinet, its revolutionary enthusiasm fell to a lower ebb. In July Hitler had proclaimed the Nazi revolution to be ended.[37] By December the claim had taken on a ring of truth.

The later months of 1933 witnessed what many people—even Jews—considered to be a withdrawal from the rabid phase of anti-Jewish policy. In Jewish circles the hope that the Nazi storm was subsiding gained currency. Exclusion from the professions or even from the schools did not necessarily mean the end of the Jewish community. More likely it meant a period in which Jewish participation in German life would be circumscribed. Nazi legislation had already provided for that. But the halt to the boycotts, along with Hitler's pronouncement that the revolution was ended, at least made continued existence possible. The Jewish community began to hope for a stabilization of the *status quo*. In mid-November a leading Jewish newspaper, the *Jüdische Rundschau* reviewed the experiences of 1933 and speculated on their meaning.

> If we look at the events of the past year, we must note that many German Jews have lost their economic base for existence. Yet it appears from the pronouncements of authoritative sources that in the future our economic existence will be guaranteed, though limited, by the new legal situation. . . . In this light we can understand *Dr. Goebbels' remark that what needs to be solved concerning the Jewish question has been solved by the government.*[38]

Such hopes were buttressed in December by a joint announcement from the Economic and Interior Ministries that the Aryan clause was not applicable to the field of commerce.[39]

Nazi party radicals and many in the lower ranks feared that the stabilization for which Jews were hoping was actually being effected. Hess's orders that all spontaneous anti-Jewish

[37] *Voelkischer Beobachter,* July 17, 1933.
[38] *Jüdische Rundschau,* November 17, 1933 (italics mine).
[39] *Central Verein Zeitung,* December 7, 1933.

actions cease caused confusion and consternation among those who were pressing for more radical measures. The party leadership could hardly afford to ignore these sentiments. Goebbels addressed himself to this situation in September 1933. He chose the forum of the gigantic Nuremberg Party Rally, the gathering place for thousands of the SA and rank and file party followers. He spoke to them of domestic pressures which precluded a more radical Jewish policy and of the foreign considerations which made any sort of a Jewish policy a "heavy burden" for the Reich government. Despite these difficulties he asked for their perseverence.[40] Goebbels rarely was candid in public. His admission of internal and external pressures was a transparent effort to justify what to many of the assembled faithful seemed an unambitious Jewish policy.

Confusion in the ranks was not dispelled by Goebbels' blandishments at Nuremberg. In January 1934, a local party official from Bonn sent a letter of complaint to Julius Streicher. The official had been planning to organize a boycott of Jewish businesses locally and had just received an order from Munich demanding the boycott be cancelled. He hoped Streicher would be able to tell him why. "I have been very active in anti-Semitic affairs within our local party and have arranged among other things, many lectures on anti-Semitism. I know that you must be very busy, but I do hope you will be able to answer my question. *Please tell me in what form it is still possible, despite the existing laws and orders, to carry on anti-Semitic actions and propaganda?*"[41] His confusion was real. He was a conscientious Nazi trying to do his duty. Many others like him shared his frustrations. There was little he could do about Germany's plight, but he could assist the Fuehrer in his campaign against the Jews. There were always a few Jewish shops to be boycotted or local Jews to harass. In this he could demonstrate his loyalty to the cause and contribute to its success. It accorded him a sense of contributing to the new Germany. But without a free hand

[40] *Dokumente der deutschen Politik und Geschichte*, vol. 1, p. 183.
[41] Collection: Streicher, Folder No. 21, BDC (italics mine).

against the Jew his only meaningful contribution was severely limited.

Complaints of this sort were to no avail. During 1934 very few official measures of any public significance were being taken against the Jew. On the surface it appeared as if the Nazi regime was planning to allow Jews an economic basis for a continued, if circumscribed, existence. For what other reason would the government exclude the Aryan clause from commerce and business? Or why would it issue orders which in effect protected Jews from its own followers? There were, to be sure, continued incidents of harassment and small-scale boycotting, but they did not have the sanction of the government. The purge of radical elements within the movement, especially of the SA leadership, in June 1934 brought for the most part even these "uncoordinated" incidents to an end. To many Jews these signs seemed to point in a promising direction. An estimated 37,000 Jews had left Germany in the wake of Hitler's takeover. In 1934 the number dropped to 23,000.[42] Then, during the first months of 1935, some 10,000 of those who had fled began to return,[43] in hope of an improved situation for Jews in Germany.

Legislative action against Jews was renewed on a very subdued scale in May 1935 with the announcement of a new Military Service Law.[44] The new law reintroduced general conscription and was, therefore, a major step in Hitler's plan for German rearmament. Its effect upon Jews centered on the question of who was eligible for military service. Aryan ancestry was made an absolute prerequisite for entry into the services. Only under very unusual circumstances could a non-Aryan or a man married to a non-Aryan qualify. Even then he had to initiate an appeal to a review committee established jointly by the Ministries of Interior and War which would review the applicant's previous record, his political reliability and his general

[42] Werner Rosenstock, "Exodus 1933-1939: A Survey of Jewish Emigration from Germany," *Year Book I of the Leo Baeck Institute* (London, 1956), pp. 373-390.

[43] *Jüdische Rundschau*, May 10, 1935.

[44] RGB1, I, 1935, p. 607.

character. If he met this board's approval it was technically possible for him to be accepted for military service.

It is hardly necessary to point out that this law was not a frontal attack upon the Jew. Only those Jews convinced of the virtues of military life were directly affected. Yet German Jewry had generally prided itself on the role of Jewish soldiers in defense of the fatherland. The *Reichsbund jüdischer Front-soldaten*, a veterans group which had internalized many German military values, was bitterly humiliated. Even the Jews less committed to military life did not fail to see the implications of the military law. By deeming Jews unfit to serve in the armed forces, it also made them citizens of a lesser rank. The effect of this new status upon the morale of German Jews is impossible to assess. It must be noted, however, that an overwhelming majority of German Jews were deeply attached to Germany, an attachment which included an interest in its military defense.

The hand of the SS in Jewish affairs became publicly apparent for the first time in connection with the Military Service Law. It had been dealing with limited aspects of the Jewish question for some time, but only behind the official scene. On May 15, a few days before the Service Law was announced, the recently established voice of the SS, *Das Schwarze Korps,* published an editorial entitled "NO ROOM FOR JEWS IN THE MILITARY: We advise Jews to give up their efforts to enlist in the military service. It would be better for them to throw their enlistment papers into the waste basket, avoiding military service as Jews have always done, and let it go at that." In 1935 the bureaucratic and police network of Reichs Leader of the SS Heinrich Himmler, free from SA control, was beginning to function with some efficiency. It was also confident enough to express itself on issues related to military service and the Jews. Those who hoped for a Nazi retreat on the Jewish question were unaware that a structure entirely outside the traditional state apparatus and the restrictions of even pseudolegality was already making its influence felt.[45]

[45] The role of the SS will be treated in subsequent chapters.

Although it reintroduced the Aryan paragraph for the first time since 1933, the Military Service Law represented no progress in defining the Jew. In fact its definition of the non-Aryan was less precise than it had been in the 1933 April Laws. The question of definition could be left unresolved as long as legislation dealt only with the periphery of the Jewish problem. The entire Nazi ideological structure rested on the assumption, however, that the Jew was evil because of his blood. His most monstrous crime had been to defile the purity of the Aryan race, not the infiltration of the civil service, the various professions, or even the German economy. If this basic aspect of the Jewish problem was ever to be solved, the regulation of marriages between Jew and German was inevitable.

The logic of such a ban had not escaped racial radicals inside or outside the SA, nor the officials at the state marriage bureaus or *Standesämter*. Instances of local SA units pressuring *Standesamt* officials into refusing marriage licences to "racially mixed" couples were common. Occasionally the officials would merely warn such a couple that their marriage was inadvisable.[46] At other times a license would actually be refused. In such instances, because the marriages were not illegal, some petitioning couples brought suit in the courts. The SA naturally expected the judges faced with these cases to uphold the spirit of National Socialist ideology. Without a law upon which to base a decision, however, the courts were at a loss to give their judgments legal sanction. The judge in these cases was caught between trying to maintain the law and attempting to placate the SA.[47] Marriage officials were caught in the same uncomfortable position.

Understandably both judges and *Standesamt* officials looked to the Reichs Interior Ministry for guidance. A law, a decree, or even a directive would have given them some basis for their decisions. Nothing was forthcoming. Interior Minister Frick, in early 1934, answered queries related to mixed marriages by emphasizing the importance of Germany's image abroad: "If

46 *Dokumente Frankfurter Juden,* p. 217.
47 Lösener, "Als Rassereferat," p. 278.

our actions stay within certain legal boundaries, they will be better received at home and abroad."[48]

The question of race mixing was also of extreme interest to the obscenely minded Julius Streicher. His anti-Semitism had a peculiar sexual twist which fed upon images of illicit relationships between Aryans and Jews. The pages of his *Stürmer* were filled with reports of rich, fat Jews raping innocent Aryan maidens. It was Streicher who introduced the notion of racial treason. Sexual relations—and Streicher was mainly interested in illicit ones—came to be referred to as examples of racial treason or shame. The SA was quick to mete out punishment to racial traitors and those who brought shame upon the Aryan race. SA men took pleasure in pillorying German prostitutes who failed to be racially selective in choosing their clientele. Prostitutes suspected of having been with Jewish clients were frequently marched through the streets carrying signs advertising their racial misdeeds.[49]

The campaign to make Jewish-Aryan marriages illegal was led by Gerhard Wagner, the volatile Nazi medical chief and later Reichs Medical Leader. In November 1933, Wagner led a group of Nazi-oriented doctors to constitute themselves as the German Medical Association. This group, in a report on its research into Jewish blood characteristics, admitted failure in its efforts to identify a specifically Jewish blood type. While they could not recommend, therefore, a detailed program of racial hygiene, the doctors prescribed a preliminary ban on marriages between Aryans and Jews.[50] Failure to isolate the blood characteristics of Jewishness, however, undermined a legal solution to the Jewish problem. The neatness of legal deassimilation hinged directly upon identifying and defining the biological Jew.

Hitler and Streicher excepted, there were elements in Nazism which recognized the complexity of the problem. Not surpris-

---

[48] Ibid., p. 271.

[49] See Gerhard Schoenberner, ed., *Der Gelbe Stern, Die Judenverfolgung in Europa, 1933 bis 1945* (Hamburg, 1960), p. 21.

[50] *Deutsches Ärzteblatt*, November 11, 1933.

ingly, they were most often the lawyers charged with drafting the anti-Jewish legislation. In January 1935, the official organ of the League of German Jurists published a summary of the problems related to the racial laws. The author of the summary, Dr. Falk Ruttke, Director of the Reichs Office for People's Health (*Volksgesundheitsdienst*) called attention to the lack of clarity in racial terminology.

> While logic and consistency have traditionally been a special province of jurists and lawyers, it appears that since the *Machtergreifung* these faculties have eluded them. In looking through our racial laws it becomes apparent that we are lacking a certain conceptual clarity (*Begriffsklarheit*) in using such terms as "race," "racial hygiene," "eugenics," and others which fall into the same category. They are oftentimes used with different and contradictory meanings. . . .[51]

The final and most complete attempt to arrive at a definition of the Jew began in September 1935, with the announcement of the most spectacular anti-Jewish legislation to date at the Nuremberg Party Rally. A set of three laws, which quickly came to be known as the Nuremberg Laws, was designed to regulate a whole complex of Jewish-Aryan relationships, including intermarriage.

By the spring of 1935, there were indications that the Nazi regime felt prepared to renew its legislative attack upon German Jewry. Interior Minister Frick announced in late April that the concept of "mixed-marriage" would henceforth refer not to religious, but to racial mixing, "as when an Aryan marries a Jew."[52] On July 21, he ordered *Standesamt* officials to delay consideration of marriage license requests from racially mixed couples. The government, he said, planned shortly to issue legal regulations regarding the question of such marriages.[53] The

51 Falk Ruttke, "Erb- und Rassenpflege in Gesetzgebung und Rechtssprechung des Dritten Reiches." *Deutsches Recht*, January 25, 1933, pp. 25-27.

52 *Juristische Wochenschrift*, June 29, 1935.

53 *Dokumente Frankfurter Juden*, pp. 217-218.

guidelines which marriage officials had been requesting for two years were finally promised.

A month went by with no announcement. By then Nazi energies were absorbed in planning the annual party rally scheduled for mid-September. These massive gatherings were a high point of the Nazi calendar.[54] Hundreds of thousands of party members gathered each fall in Nuremberg for a week of parades, pageantry, and speeches. Little of lasting consequence was produced during these rallies, nor was that their aim. They were calculated to renew the spirit and enthusiasm of the movement through a meticulously planned pageantry, unmatched in the twentieth century.[55] Giant parades would follow giant parades, marching bands would be followed by more marching bands and more parades. The climactic moment would come when the Fuehrer himself would approach the Olympus-like rostrum to speak, whipping himself and his audience into an unrestrained frenzy.

As the official slogan for this year's rally Goebbels had chosen "Reichs Party Rally of Freedom." Hitler himself had decided at the last moment to add a special touch. There was to be a special session of the German Reichstag to end the rally on Sunday, September 15. For several weeks the Interior Ministry had been preparing a law prohibiting Jews from raising the Nazi colors. A solemn session of the Reichstag would make the law official.

On Friday, two days before the rally was to end, Hitler suddenly decided the Flag Law alone did not warrant so special and dramatic a meeting of the Reichstag. Something more worthy of the occasion was required. With no previous notice the Fuehrer called upon his Interior Minister Frick to draw up legislation governing the question of German-Jewish blood relationships.[56]

[54] Josef Wulf, *Die Nürenberger Gesetze* (Berlin, 1960), pp. 8-9.

[55] William L. Shirer, *Berlin Diary* (New York, 1961), p. 181.

[56] The following account of how the Nuremberg Laws came into being is told by an official of the Reichs Interior Ministry who was commissioned to prepare drafts of the laws. The official, Bernhard Lösener, has recorded his story in the

Hitler himself outlined the areas the laws were to cover. He wanted a law forbidding Jews and Aryans to marry, one forbidding them to have sexual relations outside marriage, and another regulating the employment of Aryan housemaids in Jewish homes. Together he wanted them entitled "Law for the Protection of German Blood."

If Hitler realized that he had asked for an overnight legal solution to the heart of the Jewish problem, he did not consider the complexities involved in his request. Frick, despite his earlier promise of similar legislation, was totally unprepared for such an assignment and in the holiday atmosphere of a party rally was unwilling to do the necessary work. He put his two assistants, Hans Pfundtner and Wilhelm Stuckart, both State secretaries, to work on some preliminary drafts. Without the appropriate documents and files in their Berlin offices, however, they could not go very far.

Late that same Friday evening, Stuckart telephoned Berlin to speak with Dr. Bernhard Lösener, the man responsible for "Legislation on the Jewish Question" in Section 1 of the Interior Ministry. Lösener was ordered to fly to Nuremberg early the next morning and to bring with him the files he would need to draft the legislation. When he arrived at the Nuremberg airport the next morning an automobile was waiting to take him to police headquarters where Pfundtner and Stuckart had set up a temporary command post.

Although a party member since 1931, Lösener had become disenchanted with the Nazis soon after they came to power. Instead of leaving the party, however, which would have ended his career, Lösener had decided to use his position to ameliorate the lot of Jews, a very delicate task because the slightest suspi-

previously cited "Als Rassereferat," pp. 264-313. If it were not for the existence of reliable evidence and testimony corroborating Lösener's story, it would appear highly questionable. At the Eichmann trial in Jerusalem, Heinrich Grueber, a Protestant clergyman in Berlin during the Hitler years, who risked his life to save Jews from Nazi persecutions, listed Lösener as his "contact man" in the Interior Ministry. See "Witness of Righteousness: The Work and Faith of Dean Grueber." *Wiener Library Bulletin* 16 (1962): 9.

cion of his subversive activities would have had disastrous consequences for himself and his family. Stuckart's summons now offered him the opportunity to take the cutting edge off the new legislation. The impact of the new laws, he knew, would hinge upon the inclusiveness given to the legal definition of the term "Jew." When he learned that Hitler himself planned to sign the laws, Lösener saw the chance to draft them so the least number of Jews would suffer. Nothing could be done, of course, for those whose ancestry was entirely Jewish. But the possibility existed, because of the rush, that Hitler could be maneuvered into signing a law which would actually protect people whose ancestry was only part Jewish. A major portion of assimilated German Jewry would fit into this latter category, especially the children of the many mixed marriages contracted during the Weimar period. Fortunately for Lösener's purpose, both Stuckart and Pfundtner agreed that distinctions between various degrees of Jewishness should be defined by law.

Whatever they were going to do had to be done quickly, and within the framework outlined by Hitler. The Reichstag session was scheduled for 11 o'clock the following morning.

Lösener's plan ran into unexpected obstacles shortly after work on a first draft had begun. The arrival of an emissary from Dr. Gerhard Wagner, the Reichs Medical Chief, made their task more difficult. Wagner had a direct interest in any law which protected German blood and had dispatched his representative to assure a strongly worded law. Fortunately for Lösener, Wagner's emissary was not particularly interested in legislative matters. His attention was taken up instead by a toy tank which he happened to find in the police chief's office.

With Wagner's assistant off in a corner playing with his tank, Lösener, Stuckart, and Pfundtner managed to complete a draft which included a distinction between Jew and half-Jew. The next step was to get Hitler to approve the draft. Protocol required that Frick be the one to present the committee's proposal to Hitler. Frick, however, was staying in a villa across town. Lösener decided to make the cross-town delivery himself in order to equip the Interior Minister with arguments to counter any of the Fuehrer's possible objections. But it was almost impossible to get across the city. The narrow streets were packed with wildly cheering Nazis. Twice Lösener had to dash through twelve-abreast columns of parading SS units, only to discover, when he arrived at Frick's villa, that the Minister was unwilling to hear a briefing on the draft proposals.

When Frick returned from his audience with Hitler, Lösener learned that at Gerhard Wagner's insistence, the Fuehrer had refused the draft and asked for a harsher law. The process of drafting another proposal, delivering it through Nuremberg's impossibly crowded streets—first to Frick, then to Hitler and finally back again—was repeated three times during the next fifteen hours.

Around midnight, after seeing four drafts, Hitler asked that all the proposals be typed in their final form. He would make a decision in the morning. He had an additional request which he asked Frick to relay to Lösener at police headquarters. Would Lösener please prepare a basic Reichs Citizenship Law by tomorrow morning? Without such a law, it had suddenly occurred to Hitler, regulation of the Jewish situation seemed incomplete.

It was 12:30 Sunday morning when Hitler's latest request reached the exhausted Lösener, Pfundtner, and Stuckart. Their immediate decision was to draft as meaningless a citizenship law as possible. Above all they determined not to tamper with the present citizenship status, *Staatsangehörigkeit*, of Jews. Under this status Jews were still accorded, at least in theory, the same legal protection as Aryan citizens. Within a few minutes they drafted a law creating an elevated but meaningless status to which only Aryans could aspire—"citizen of the Reich" or *Reichsangehöriger*—which entailed no special privileges. Jews remained citizens of the state and continued to enjoy the rights of regular citizens insofar as these rights had not been affected by previous legislation. Frick took this proposal to Hitler at 1:30 A.M. and returned an hour later with the news that Hitler found it acceptable. There was still no word, however, about Hitler's decision on the four Blood Law drafts.

The next morning, a few minutes before the Reichstag session was to begin, Lösener still had not heard the Fuehrer's decision. The Reichstag members were already seated in the improvised meeting hall when Lösener learned Hitler had accepted the fourth and mildest draft proposal, the one which included the provision that: "This law applies only to full-blooded Jews." Momentarily the scheme appeared to have succeeded. When Hitler read the law to the Reichstag, however, he deleted this all-important sentence. Without it the complexion of the law was changed entirely. The question of definition, or more specifically, to whom the law applied, was still unanswered.

The "Law for the Protection of German Blood and Honor,"[57] as it was finally called, made "marriages between Jews and citizens of the state with German or related blood" illegal. Such marriages contracted in spite of the law, even if performed in a foreign country, would not be recognized by the Third Reich. Extramarital relations between Jews and Germans were likewise illegal and punishable by a prison term. To make certain that the conditions for such relations were not created artificially, paragraph three made it unlawful for a Jew to employ a German housemaid who was under the age of forty-five. Violations on this count were punishable by a year in prison, a fine, or both.

The sensational circumstances in which these laws were announced has obscured their meaning in the history of Jewish persecution in Nazi Germany. Hitler's own sense of drama which led to the use of those circumstances has also contributed to the misunderstanding. After Buchenwald and Dachau it has become common to view the Nuremberg Laws as a major step in the Nazi anti-Jewish design. Not until Lösener's revelation about the *ad hoc* manner in which they came into being has a more accurate analysis of their meaning been possible.

[57] RGBl, I, 1935, p. 1146.

German Jewry's initial reaction to the Nuremberg Laws reflected the cautious hope that an area of Jewish security had been created. If in exchange for Jewish acceptance of a circumscribed existence, the Nazis brought an end to boycott actions and propaganda assaults, that hope did not appear to be an impossible one. In late September the *Reichsvertretung der Juden in Deutschland*,[58] the collective voice of Germany's Jews, issued a statement expressing its willingness to work for a *modus vivendi* with the National Socialists. The *Reichsvertretung* was willing to view the Nuremberg Laws as the beginning to such a "tolerable arrangement."[59]

Nazi reactions in the months following the Nuremberg Rally lent substance to these hopes. To a foreign correspondent Hitler hinted that the attack on Jews was finished, if Jews themselves did not create "fresh tensions."[60] Statements by Goebbels and Goering supported Hitler's contention.

In the latter part of 1935 and early 1936 the Nazi regime very deliberately soft-pedaled its anti-Jewish stance, not to encourage Jews, but to appease foreign sentiment. The 1936 Olympic Games were scheduled to be held in Berlin. A massive Olympic Stadium had been constructed and Hitler was determined to avoid any action which might lead to the games being shifted elsewhere, something which was being rumored about in international circles. The loss of the Olympics would have been a serious blow to Nazi prestige. On September 1, 1935, even before the Nuremberg Rally, the Gestapo Headquarters in Munich was ordered to avoid all untoward actions because: "Under all circumstances the 1936 Olympic Games, by will of the Fuehrer, must take place in Berlin."[61] On December 3, the Interior Min-

---

58 The *Reichsvertretung* was founded in the fall of 1933 by the Zionist Federation and Central Union of German Jews to represent the collective interests of all Jewish organizations in Germany. Rabbi Leo Baeck was chairman of the Governing Board and Otto Hirsch was Executive Director.

59 *Central Verein Zeitung*, September 26, 1935.

60 Hitler's interview is reprinted in Norman H. Baynes, ed., *The Speeches of Adolf Hitler*, vol. 1 (London, 1942), p. 735.

61 Schumacher Archiv, Folder 240 I, BDC.

istry, again upon Hitler's command, ordered that all anti-Jewish signs and posters in the vicinity of Garmisch-Partenkirchen, the scene of the Winter Games, be removed.[62] What many German Jews chose to see as a sign of good faith on Hitler's part was actually undertaken to guarantee the Olympics for Germany.

Behind this public facade a matter of utmost importance to Jews was being settled. Until it was decided to what level of "Jewishness" the Nuremberg Laws would be applied, they had little meaning. When he arrived back at his office in Berlin, Lösener saw the copy of his draft in which Hitler had penciled out the sentence, "This law applies only to full-blooded Jews." From this he could conclude only that the laws would reach further than the "full-blooded" Jew. How much further depended upon the supplementary decrees which had to follow.

The decrees would ultimately stem from the Interior Ministry itself. Lösener, as the Ministry's racial expert, was once again involved in the discussions preceding them.[63] For the next eight weeks meetings to discuss the definition of the Jews were held every day, including Sundays. Delegations of the party's racial radicals appeared almost daily to insure as inclusive a definition as possible. Their chief spokesman was usually Dr. Gerhard Wagner, whose presence in Hitler's entourage at Nuremberg may well have been responsible for striking the sentence which made these meetings necessary. The party's representatives held that the concept "Jew" should include at least those with one-quarter Jewish blood, making anyone with three German grandparents and only one Jewish grandparent legally a Jew. Wagner at first insisted upon including even one-eighth Jews.

Lösener and Stuckart carried on the struggle for a milder interpretation in the face of these demands, taking care to avoid suspicion by couching their arguments within a Nazi frame of reference. They reminded the party representatives that one-eighth Jews were also seven-eighths German. Too inclusive a

[62] Collection: Bezirksämter, Folder 35, BDC.
[63] This account of how the supplementary decrees came into being is based on Lösener, "Als Rassereferat."

definition would unnecessarily create enemies within elements which heretofore had been loyal to the regime. Moreover, it would probably raise complications abroad. After two weeks of debate the discussions reached an impasse. Only an outside authority could resolve the issue and only Hitler had that authority.

At this point, Hitler invited a wide array of party leaders, along with Stuckart and Lösener, to a conference in Munich on September 29. Reports indicated the Fuehrer was going to resolve the question of Jewish definition himself. The reports were false. The conference was finally no more than an occasion for one of those famous Hitlerian monologues. It began with Hitler delivering a detailed review of the history of German-Jewish assimilation and the problem it raised for the purity of Aryan stock. The expertness of his presentation astounded even Lösener. At the point where Lösener expected him to present his final views on Jewish definition, however, Hitler suddenly changed the subject to his plans for war. When he got back to the Jew, he concluded by saying the question of definition would have to be worked out in conference between the party and the officials in the Interior Ministry. The meeting which presumably had been called to resolve precisely that question was adjourned.

Another six weeks of negotiation followed before a solution was reached. The "First Supplementary Decree to the Reichs Citizenship Law" was published on November 14.[64] By its terms a full or three-quarter Jew was legally Jewish and therefore subject to the Nuremberg Laws. On that point Lösener and Stuckhart had lost. The point they had won was reflected in the position of the half-Jew (one with two Aryan and two Jewish grandparents) who was considered Jewish if: he was an adherent of the Jewish faith, he was married to a Jew, he was the child of a marriage with one Jewish partner, or if he was the off-spring of an illegitimate union between a Jew and Aryan.

[64] RGB1, I, 1935, p. 1333.

Someone with two Jewish grandparents, if he was not legally Jewish on the basis of these four conditions, was legally a "Jewish *Mischling*."[65] Crucial to this definition was the matter of religion. Nazi medical science had made no progress in isolating a specifically Jewish blood type. Nazi legislators had to assume, therefore, that religion somehow determined blood or otherwise that an equally mystical process forced someone with Jewish blood to accept Judaism. The absurdity of these assumptions bothered neither the doctor nor the legislator. An individual with only one Jewish grandparent was still legally Jewish if he was a member of the Jewish religious community. Anyone with less than one-quarter Jewish blood was considered to be of "German or closely related origins."

According to an estimate made by Rudolf Hess in early 1936, there were 400,000 to 500,000 full, three-quarter, or one-half Jews in Germany who fit the legal concept of "Jew" and another 300,000 one-half or one-quarter Jews who fell into the "Jewish *Mischling*" category.[66] The Nuremberg Laws protected the blood and honor of Germans by making it illegal for them to marry or consort with the newly defined Jew.[67] So there could be no doubt as to their purpose in the Nazi scheme, these marriage laws were also included in the collection of German Health Laws.

If race mixing was the basic Jewish problem—and this had been the Nazi message from the outset—the legal basis for a biological solution had been laid. Rigorous enforcement would have led eventually to the extinction of the Jewish *Mischling*. The official commentary to the Nuremberg Laws, published in 1936, stated clearly: "The aim of a legal solution to the *Misch-*

[65] *Mischling* does not bear adequate translation into English. In this context it means a person who was legally neither Jew nor Aryan, but someone whose blood was a mixture from both "races."

[66] Schumacher Archiv, Folder 240 I, BDC.

[67] For an exact listing of who could marry whom, see Dr. Rissom, "Mischehen im Lichte der neuen Gesetzgebung," *Zeitschrift der Akademie für Deutsches Recht* (January, 1936): 8-10.

ling question must be the disappearance of the *Mischling* race." [68] Within two generations the Nazis could have reasonably expected the *Mischling* to disappear and with him would have disappeared the danger of the disguised Jew, the one Nazis considered the most dangerous of all.

The Nuremberg Laws brought Nazi Jewish policy to the end of its legal phase. Thirteen supplementary decrees during the next years carried its provisions into other areas of German-Jewish contact,[69] but by that time legislation was no longer foremost in the minds of most Nazis. What happened after 1935 took place not so much because of the laws, as it did in spite of them.[70]

Because the Nuremberg Laws required proof of ancestry, their administration affected Aryans as well as Jews. Anyone applying for a position in the government or an agency of the party was required to submit proof of his non-Jewish origins. The birth certificates of parents and grandparents could well become a family's most valuable documents. A young man who aspired to membership in Himmler's racially elite SS, for example, had to offer evidence of Aryan ancestry back to 1750, before the European process of Jewish emancipation had begun.[71] Few families had such records at their disposal, or the resources necessary to hunt them down. The need for such a service led to the creation of a new profession which specialized in the search of church and state records for birth and baptismal certificates. These "genealogical researchers" or *Sippenforscher* assisted their clients in finding the necessary documents. After 1935 the *Sippenforscher* did a thriving business.

A very incomplete picture of Nazi Jewish policy would emerge

[68] Wilhelm Stuckart and Hans Globke, *Kommentare zur Rassengesetzgebung; Reichsbürgergesetz, Blutschutzgesetz, Eheschutzgesetz* (Munich, 1936), p. 17.

[69] See Marianne Sigg, *Das Rassestrafrecht in Deutschland in den Jahren 1933-1945 unter besonderer Berücksichtigung des Blutschutzgesetzes* (Aarau, Switzerland, 1951).

[70] Hans Buchheim, et al., *Anatomie des SS-Staates*, vol. 1 (Olten und Freiburg im Breisgau, 1965), pp. 19-20.

[71] "SS-Bewerber," in *Gutachten des Instituts für Zeitgeschichte* (Munich, 1958) p. 349.

from a study of discriminatory legislation alone. Laws, even of the Nazi variety, never quite fit the Nazi style, or for that matter their purposes. Had they restricted themselves to enforcement of their anti-Jewish laws the continued existence of a separate if second-class Jewish community would have been assured. Hitler became increasingly aware that laws could have precisely such an effect. He came to recognize that politically it was unwise to tie his own prestige to a law which might someday serve to restrict his own freedom to act. A particular law could always be rescinded, of course, but not without a certain loss of face. Only the higher, natural law which Hitler himself was able to divine had unquestioned legitimacy. In its lesser forms the law existed only to protect the individual against the state, and he could explain "this mental distortion only by influence of the Jews."[72]

Fully as important as the anti-Jewish legislation which culminated in the Nuremberg Laws was the light which their creation sheds upon the inner workings of Nazi officialdom. Hitler's hand appeared occasionally at crucial moments, but it was usually a vacillating and indecisive one. He did not delegate responsibility for Jewish policy, nor did he keep a close check on it. At Munich on September 29, 1935, thoughts of war pushed the Jewish problem aside. The *Fuehrerprinzip*, which should obviously have been applied, was not invoked. A few weeks earlier at the Nuremberg Rally the sight of thousands of wildly cheering National Socialists had played as great a role in his decision to call for new laws as did the apparent need for a solution to the Jewish problem. Hitler was himself prey to the emotions which Goebbels had so carefully planned to generate in his followers. He was consistent only in his continued demand on the need for a solution to the Jewish question—in private if not in public— and in his efforts to suppress nonofficial solutions if they endangered any of his other policies.

The problems associated with legislation, especially with the Nuremberg Laws, also made clear that the state bureaucracy

[72] *Trevor-Roper*, ed., *Hitler's Secret Conversations*, p. 358.

was not completely responsive to Nazi wishes. Lösener's resistance which took the form of trying to draft a milder form of legislation managed to slow down the bureaucratic process, even to delay implementation of the laws for several months. The local Nazi leader from Bonn who had complained to Streicher had another reason to be displeased. Not only were there too many laws—which had the effect of "protecting" Jews—but the occasional "good laws" were too slow in coming. The implications of this were not lost upon other more powerful Nazis who were also interested in the Jewish problem.

V. Aryanization: The Third Impasse

THE IDEOLOGICAL VALUE of the Nuremberg Laws greatly out-
weighed their practical effects. By regulating the mixing of
Aryan and Jewish races the laws presumably struck at the biological heart of the Jewish problem. That in itself was deeply satisfying to the racial purists. But there was more to be done. In its
fullest dimension the Jewish problem remained unsolved. Even
the Nuremberg Laws could effect no immediate separation of
the races. Unless the laws were the signal to attack on a much
wider front, the several generations it would take to complete
the separation were bound to stir uneasiness in radical circles.
The fact that Jews themselves could find this limited solution
tolerable merely added to the impatience.

Extremists such as Streicher and Wagner warned immediately
that the Jewish problem was not yet solved. Only continued
vigilance and steady pressures could lead to a solution. In this
they found support in the ranks of the Nazi *Mittelstand* which
was eager to launch a full-scale attack against Jewish participation in the German economy. Such an attack, it was generally
felt, would be the first stage in establishing the economic relationships promised by the National Socialist ideology. No less
than the complete elimination of the Jewish banks or department stores could satisfy this sentiment. The eagerness of many
party agencies to participate directly in this aspect of the solution had been demonstrated clearly during the first weeks of
Nazi rule. It had taken severe measures, including the spectacular purges of June 1934, to blunt the edge of anti-Jewish initiatives rising from the lower party ranks. During the months preceding the announcement of the Nuremberg Laws, however, a

new rash of anti-Jewish actions began to trouble the regime. Beginning in early 1935 the scenes which had preceded the general April boycott in 1933 again became common occurrences. Calls for the renewal of the boycott arose in many areas of the Reich. Signs such as "Jews Are Unwelcome" appeared at the outskirts of many smaller towns. In some cases the stores and shops of Jewish owners were vandalized or otherwise violated. It was against this backdrop of renewed anti-Jewish action that the Nuremberg Laws were promulgated. To the radicals the actions of the past few months were apparently ratified. The signal for more to come had been given.

Then in November, Hitler intimated to an American press correspondent that the Nazi campaign against the Jews might be at its end. The interview, published in the *Voelkischer Beobachter* on November 28, indicated that the campaign would be renewed only if the Jews stirred up further tensions. Similar statements made by Goebbels and other party leaders were duly reported in the Nazi press and such Jewish newspapers as the *Jüdische Rundschau*. The implications of these trends seemed obvious. If Hitler meant what he said, at least one area of Jewish activity—participation in the economy—was not to be rigorously circumscribed by official action. Other evidence seemed to point in the same direction. Local party officials received orders to remove their "Jews Are Unwelcome" signs. From Rudolf Hess's office came the order to avoid all efforts which might lead to unfavorable actions.[1]

Few realized, of course, that Hitler's statements and orders were less a commentary on Jewish policy than they were upon the factors circumscribing such a policy. With the Winter Games of the 1936 Olympics scheduled to begin shortly, nothing —including a new assault against the Jews—which might tarnish the image of the new Germany could be tolerated. Moreover, Hitler's Economics Minister had been conducting a month-long campaign to reduce party interference in economic affairs. Such

[1] Schumacher Archiv, Folder 240 I, BDC.

interference, he warned, endangered economic recovery and jeopardized the rearmament program. Even those who were privy to Hitler's thinking could not dismiss the possibility that Jews would ultimately be allowed some kind of separate existence based on a measure of participation in the economy. To these initiates it was certainly clear that Hitler had no intention of reorganizing the economy along lines suggested by Nazi ideology. As for Jewish policy, it was also becoming evident that Hitler had no clear idea where he wanted to go. After the Nuremberg Laws he ran out of ideas. During the next two years he was to offer nothing, other than frequent anti-Semitic outbursts, by way of suggestion to those trying to formulate a Jewish policy. He concentrated his energies instead on matters related to foreign policy and rearmament. The initiative in Jewish affairs, if there was to be one, had to come from other quarters.

Still, the most vociferous contestants for control over Jewish policy were, as might be expected, the ideological purists: the representatives of the *Mittelstand* agencies of the party, the middle level of the party apparatus—the *Gau* and district officials for example—and the rabid anti-Semites such as Julius Streicher and Gerhard Wagner. While these groups applauded the Nuremberg Laws, they were also quick to remember that the Jew was an economic parasite as well as a biological one. No one had enunciated this principle more vigorously than Hitler; yet his post-Nuremberg utterances lent themselves to the suspicion that this essential premise might be forgotten.

Mittelstand hopes for ending Jewish economic influence had suffered one severe blow with the failure of the April boycott in 1933. However reluctantly, Hitler had realized that a frontal attack was impossible. Interference with Jewish participation threatened economic recovery and therefore the security of the Nazi position. Given such a choice, Hitler was quick to sort out his priorities and opt for recovery, even at the expense of continued, though limited, Jewish economic activity. For the next years he would allow no more than peripheral attacks on the Jewish economic front. Although these attacks greatly undermined the welfare of a great number of Jews, especially those in smaller businesses, they did not drive them out of what the Nazi ideologues considered the commanding positions of the economy—the banks, department stores, and export businesses.

A policy (the radicals would have said "lack of a policy") so contrary to the party program and its years of propaganda frustrated the old-line supporters who had taken the peculiar brand of Nazi socialism seriously. Their expectations, along with those of the SA, had made the general boycott in the first weeks of Nazi rule a seeming necessity. The Roehm purges of June 1934 decimated the militant leadership of the Nazi "socialists"; they did not quell the rank-and-file sentiment for forcing Jews out of their positions in the economy.

The Nazi promise had included more than the elimination of Jewish economic influence. The party faithful had been led to expect immediate benefit from a *judenrein* German economy. Not only was the Jew to be driven from his department store; the store itself would be razed, the business going to the little German shopkeeper. The Jew and his Jewish business institutions were expected to collapse before the righteous vengeance of National Socialist power. In the wake of this collapse would be created a *Mittelstand* utopia, freed finally from interest payments to Jews, freed from Jewish banks, Jewish middlemen, Jewish lawyers, and Jewish competition. Gottfried Feder, an early Nazi who passed as the economic theoretician for this visionary Valhalla, spoke of an end to "interest-finance" which he believed to be at the root of the problem. Hitler, even if he understood what Feder meant, which is unlikely, never took these ideas seriously. They had been largely the property of the Nazi left—the Feders, the Strassers, and the Roehms. For Hitler they were propaganda tools, not ideological goals. As we have seen, however, their usefulness as tools precluded any open repudiation, and to avoid alienating a significant portion of his following, Hitler continued to pay lip service to them.

Hitler never tried to keep the economic promises which had taken a decade or more to make. If he had, Gottfried Feder should logically have become Economics Minister in the coalition of January 1933. That post went instead to a representative of big business, the conservative Alfred Hugenberg, while Feder had to reconcile himself to a minor position as Hugenberg's under-secretary. Hugenberg himself was replaced in late June 1933, when he lost his campaign to preserve the DNVP against the onslaught of Nazi *Gleichschaltung*. His successor was Dr. Kurt Schmitt, board chairman of Germany's largest insurance firm, the Munich-based Allianz. Schmitt, for reasons of health and a weak personality, failed to make adequate headway on his major assignment of retooling the German economy for military rearmament and lasted less than a year. One of his major weaknesses in Hitler's eyes was that he proved somewhat receptive to the ideas of the Nazi left.[2] Schmitt's retirement shortly after the June purges of 1934 brought Hitler face to face once more with the problem of finding a capable Economics Minister.

On July 27, 1934, Hitler interrupted his enjoyment of the annual Wagnerian Festival to summon his Reichsbank president, Hjalmar Schacht, to Bayreuth. Schacht's reputation as an economic wizard stemmed from his scheme to rescue the German mark from the inflationary chaos of 1923. Within a month after he had come to power Hitler had named Schacht to head the Reichsbank, a position second only to the Economics Minister in determining German economic policy. Now Schacht was to be offered this latter post as well, because, as Hitler explained later, he wanted a really intelligent Aryan who in the field of finance would be more than a match for any Jew.[3]

Before accepting the appointment, Schacht reports, he asked Hitler to clear up one matter. "Before I take office I should like to know how you wish me to deal with the Jewish question?" He found satisfactory Hitler's reply, "In economics the Jews

---

[2] Arthur Schweitzer, "Organizierter Kapitalismus und Parteidiktatur, 1933 bis 1936," *Schmollers Jahrbuch* 79 (1959): 37-79.

[3] Trevor-Roper, ed., *Hitler's Secret Conversations*, p. 410.

can carry on exactly as they have up to now." Schacht accepted the appointment.[4] Concerning his own role during the Nazi years, Schacht is not always the most reliable witness. In this case, however, his interest in the Jewish question was sparked by a genuine concern. Inappropriate action against the Jews could undermine seriously the work of the Economics Ministry, which he and Hitler agreed should strive to create a climate in which recovery and rearmament were possible. One of Schacht's first official acts was to dismiss Gottfried Feder. Although it was of little practical significance, Feder's dismissal symbolized the end of most hopes for the *judenrein* and fascist or corporate economy envisioned by the ideological purists.

Schacht was quick to grasp the essential difficulties of Germany's economic situation.[5] Rearmament was predicated upon economic recovery; recovery in turn was predicated upon reducing unemployment. On this level rearmament could contribute to recovery by the creation of jobs. The neatness of this arrangement was torn askew only by the fact that Germany was not economically self-sufficient, especially in those resources necessary for rearming. The lessons of the Allied blockade of 1914-1918 were abundantly clear. If Germany hoped to regain her military power, vast supplies of iron ore, copper, lead, zinc, oil, rubber, and certain foodstuffs would have to be acquired. Ideally these essentials could be produced at home, and Germany did embark upon a program of developing industries to produce these materials synthetically. Until independence from outside markets was attained, however, Germany would have to continue importing many of these basic requirements.

Germany's ability to import goods was severely restricted by numerous factors, but her most immediate handicap was the shortage of foreign exchange. The Germany which Hitler took over in 1933 was still in the depths of the Depression. Foreign

---

[4] Hjalmar H. G. Schacht, *My First Seventy-Six Years: The Autobiography of Hjalmar Schacht* (London, 1955), p. 320.

[5] Dieter Petzina, "Hauptprobleme der deutschen Wirtschaftspolitik, 1932-33," *Vierteljahrshefte für Zeitgeschichte* 15 (1967): 19-55.

exchange reserves were dangerously low, and even those available were the result of credits granted by the former Allied powers. German credit abroad was almost nonexistent. In April 1933, wishing to assure creditors abroad of his goodwill and Germany's ability to pay, Hitler authorized the transfer of RM 485 million for repayment of a loan received in 1931 from the central banks of the United States, Britain, and France.[6] This demonstration depleted German foreign exchange reserves by nearly one-half, to RM 511 million. A few weeks later a partial moratorium on such transfers was proclaimed. Reserves continued to decline, however. By the end of 1933 they had decreased to RM 200 million, which the economist Gustav Stolper has estimated to have been sufficient to meet the requirements of a two-week period.[7]

This situation was the most critical problem Schacht faced upon assuming office in the summer of 1934. It also prompted his interest in what plans Hitler had in store for the Jews. Any ill-considered interference with the economy at this stage would make a solution of any sort impossible. Investment for developing the synthetic industries had to come from inside Germany and at the expense of the consumer industries and, therefore, the consumer. The foreign exchange for imports had to be paid by German exports. Consequently, until the synthetic industries were operating effectively the import-export problem took priority.

The Nazi assault upon Jewish participation in the German economy must be understood within the framework of this complex economic situation. It had already forced an almost immediate cancellation of the general April boycott and militated against the renewal of any similar actions. For several years it made Germany unusually susceptible to a boycott of her own export wares. And most important, as far as Jews were concerned, it worked to protect a precarious area of safety, expe-

---

[6] Gustav Stolper, Karl Häuser, and Knut Borchardt, *The German Economy, 1870 to the Present* (New York, 1967), p. 149.

[7] Ibid., p. 145.

cially for those whose businesses had a share of the export market or produced goods vital to German rearmament.

The extent to which the foreign exchange deficiency was going to determine the regime's economic policy unfolded itself quickly to the radicals who had hoped for a quick exclusion of Jews from economic life. Streicher's boycott committee had not even gone through the motions of consulting Economics Minister Hugenberg in April. On May 11, 1933, however, Hugenburg had issued a "Decree for the Protection of Retail Trade,"[8] making it clear that the Aryan paragraph of the Civil Service Law and other April legislation was not applicable to commercial activities. In June Hugenberg's successor Schmitt immediately re-emphasized that boycotts must cease, and his order was supported by a similar decree from the office of Rudolf Hess in Munich. The lines of conflict were quickly drawn: the party's *Mittelstand* supporters against those in control of economic policy.

So it was that laws to regulate or limit Jewish participation in the German economy did not become common until 1938. Between 1933 and late 1937, legislation was generally employed only to assure continued Jewish participation in critical aspects of the economy, or more precisely, to protect the economy from disruptive pressures. As late as November 1937, the Economics Ministry, with support from Hess and Frick, declared that Jews were still eligible to participate in trade fairs and market places.[9] In March 1936, Justice Minister Guertner reminded the courts that the Nuremberg Laws affected only the marriages of Jews and Aryans, not the economic activity of Jews.[10]

The frustration level of the party's radicals rose in proportion to the restraining orders of the regime. Understandably the special target of their wrath was the Economics Minister. In January 1934, Jewish businesses were still advertising regularly, even in journals affiliated with NSDAP agencies. The incongruity of

8 RGBi, I, 1933, p. 262.
9 Schumacher Archiv, Folder 240 I, BDC.
10 Collection: Bezirksämter, Folder 35, BDC.

this did not escape Nazi radicals. Letters of complaint began to reach these journals, especially those with a party affiliation. The publisher of one such journal defended himself by saying:

> You must understand we are standing in a crossfire. As long-time party members we have no sympathy for such [Jewish] businesses. We would like to refuse advertisements from these firms, even if they are supported by Aryan capital. . . . The party shares our viewpoint in this matter. On the other side is the Reichs Economic Ministry which forbids sabotage of these firms in any form or manner. In some cases the Economics Ministry has even threatened punishment for anyone who indulges in such sabotage. *We are therefore caught between the Economics Ministry and the party.*[11]

Repeated attempts to get a more favorable decision from higher up, the publisher explained, had been unsuccessful. In these situations Hitler invariably avoided a public stance which would have identified him with a nonideological (or anti-ideological) position.

The tensions generated by this conflict were not consumed in the crossfires of debate. Although Streicher's committee had been divested of boycott planning activity, it continued to function at a less sensational level. It had been reduced to making investigations to determine either the Aryan or Jewish character of business firms. Any business which qualified as purely Aryan became eligible to display one of the committee's "German Enterprise" signs on its premises,[12] presumably to encourage the Aryan consumer's racial consciousness. At the same time, it was hoped, such signs would provide the Aryan businessman with an advantage over his Jewish competitor.

Efforts to steer these anti-Jewish energies into less sensitive channels were not always successful. The relatively harmless signs which Streicher wanted to post across Germany occasionally backfired. On March 21, 1934, the F. W. Woolworth Company in the United States announced its intention to cease the

---

11 Collection: Streicher, Folder 21, BDC (italics mine).
12 Ibid.

importing of German goods to sell in its American outlets.[13] The implications for Germany's foreign currency reserves were immediately clear to the party leadership and to the authorities in the Economics Ministry. Anger gripped the lower levels of the party, however, which threatened reprisals against Woolworth's numerous German branches. During the next days, irate crowds began to gather outside Woolworth stores in the larger German cities. In some cases the local police reported doubts about its ability to hold the fanatical party members in check. An unfavorable incident at this juncture was something the government could ill afford. One of the stiffest restraining orders in the twelve-year history of Nazi rule was issued to prevent any such incidents. The order emanating from party headquarters was channeled through Theodor von Renteln, who as Party Leader for the Middle Class and leader of the NS-HAGO (National Socialist Organization for Crafts, Commerce, and Trade), was a chief spokesman for *Mittelstand* economic and anti-Jewish radicalism. The order von Renteln delivered to his followers stated categorically that:

> Until the situation has been clarified, under no circumstances is anything to be done, said, or printed against Woolworth. I am making the local *Gau* officials personally responsible for the execution of this order. We are in no position to suffer another setback in foreign affairs or to take any actions contradictory to the Fuehrer's foreign policy. If any countermeasures in any *Gau* are already in progress they must be stopped immediately. . . . I ask local *Gau* officials to see to it that no private measures are undertaken either.[14]

The use of von Renteln to ward off anti-Woolworth demonstrations was effective, without, however, convincing him to soften his other appeals for radical action. At the time he was issuing his Woolworth directive he was also coordinating plans

13 *New York Times*, March 22, 1934.
14 Collection: Streicher, Folder 21, BDC.

for a boycott of Jewish businesses in selected cities of Lower Franconia, the bailiwick of Julius Streicher. Only rapid intervention by officials in the Economics Ministry prevented the boycotts from being carried out.[15] Trying to suppress *Mittelstand* sentiment on the economic aspect of the Jewish question, the Nazi leadership discovered, was fraught with difficulty. Pressure at one point merely caused an eruption elsewhere.

Small Jewish businesses, unlike the larger ones, were especially vulnerable to the unofficial actions of the lower level party agencies. Unless he was engaged in an enterprise critical to the economy, the small Jewish shopkeeper was in a precarious position. The Jewish tobacconist, publisher, or restaurateur had few resources with which to resist Nazi pressures. The Depression had softened him up, so to speak, leaving him oftentimes only one step ahead of bankruptcy. Because it was not accompanied by a significant increase in consumer purchasing power, the recovery which followed 1933 did not necessarily benefit him either.[16] Locally inspired boycotts, even when officially discouraged, weakened his position even more. Even when boycott activity waned, following periodical pronouncements from the Nazi leadership, local SA units or party agencies continued their harassment. Jewish butcher shops suddenly found themselves closed down for the slighest infraction of the Health Laws. Or if this "legal" approach failed, a Nazi group would intimidate the Jewish shopkeeper's customers, either photographing them, as the SA was wont to do, brand them as "Jew lovers," or even threaten them with physical harm.

In the smaller towns and rural areas Jews found it especially difficult to maintain their economic existence. The Jewish cattle dealer was a familiar figure in many agricultural areas, as was the grocer, clothing store owner, and so on. Many rural com-

---

15 Collection: Bezirksämter, Folder 15, BDC.
16 See "German Finances, 1933-1937" in Germanicus (pseud.), *Germany, The Last Four Years: An Independent Examination of the Results of National Socialism* (Boston, 1937), pp. 5-18.

munities began to place restrictions on the cattle dealer and eventually forbade such activity entirely for Jews.[17] Some Aryan firms, in order to gain a monopoly in their own areas, began refusing to supply Jewish firms or, whenever possible, to buy their products. In mid-1935, for example, a farmers' cooperative refused any longer to sell its grain to Jewish processors.[18] The separation·of the Jewish firm from its supplier and market quickly brought it to ruin. Many of the smaller communities added their own special touch by no longer granting municipal or county contracts to Jewish businesses. One town went so far as to threaten the expulsion of Jews from its local home for the aged.[19]

The anti-Semitic climate fostered by Nazism encouraged innumerable varieties of unofficial harassment. The small Jewish businessman, be he cattle dealer, butcher, or clothier, was particularly vulnerable. His Aryan clients could, and often did, refuse to pay their debts.[20] What could the businessman do? Threaten legal action? That would have been a dangerous course to take. A Jew suing an Aryan was enough to raise the holy wrath of local Nazis. It was much wiser simply to forget the matter.

There was little the Jewish merchant could do to ward off his persecutors. If he was not involved in foreign trade or played no immediately vital role to the economy, higher party authorities were often willing to overlook spontaneous demonstrations of anti-Semitism. In June 1935, a Jewish tobacconist in Hamburg asked for court protection from the harassment of local Nazis. He based his argument on the fact that his business was being illegally impaired. Although the court was aware of the regime's official attitude toward boycotts, it decided against the tobac-

17 Theobald Nebel, *Die Geschichte der jüdischen Gemeinde Talheim, Ein Beispiel für das Schicksal des Judentums in Württemberg* (Heilbronn, 1963), p. 40.
18 Document AR-A 372 #7/882, Leo Baeck Institute archives.
19 Allen, *The Nazi Seizure of Power*, pp. 166-167.
20 David Gruenspecht, "Memoiren," unpublished memoir in the Leo Baeck Institute archives.

conist. Its decision was based not upon the law, but "upon the program and main themes of the NSDAP."[21]

The number of Jewish firms which were liquidated in one form or other in the first two years of Nazi rule is impossible to assess, although one estimate puts it at about 75,000.[22] Such estimates, however, are no more than educated guesses. In fact, only one clear pattern emerges between 1933 and early 1938: The larger and more complex the Jewish firm, the greater were its powers of resistance. These powers alone seem to be responsible for the framework into which the anti-Jewish assault on the economic front can be fitted. By the Nazis' own estimate in April 1938, there were still some 39,532 Jewish business establishments in Germany, and many of these were in one way or another critical to rearmament or to the import-export trade.[23] As early as 1936, on the other hand, many of the smaller businesses, especially those associated with agriculture, were declared to be *judenrein*.[24]

Within this pattern, economic exclusion of Jews came first in those smaller enterprises which served primarily a domestic market. The single most important obstacle to the liquidation of Jewish firms remained the Reich's foreign exchange shortage. Some Jewish businesses able to maintain a significant volume of foreign trade managed to stay in business until shortly before the war. In Leipzig there were several large Jewish firms which specialized in publishing music and German literature for foreign markets. In 1934 they were all threatened with liquidation. Their chief adversary in this case was Propaganda Minister Goebbels who was eager to gather all elements of German culture (including publishing) under his control. To meet this threat, the publishers took their case to the Saxon Economics Minister. They reminded him that their business brought Ger-

21 Reported in *Juristische Wochenschrift*, September 28, 1935.

22 Genschel, *Die Verdrängung der Juden*, p. 125.

23 Alf Krueger, *Die Lösung der Judenfrage in der deutschen Wirtschaft, Kommentare zur Judengesetzgebung* (Berlin, 1940), p. 44.

24 Genschel, *Die Verdrängung der Juden*, p. 126.

many several million marks' worth of foreign exchange annually. Aryanization, the Nazi term for taking over a Jewish business, would probably mean the closing of this foreign market to Germany. The firm, once Aryanized, could very easily be boycotted by its clients abroad, because publishers in Vienna and Zürich would be able to supply the same materials. Austria and Switzerland, rather than Germany or the Nazis would benefit. The argument was convincing, especially when it reached Schacht in Berlin. Goebbels' ambition was thwarted; the Leipzig publishers went virtually untouched until the *Reichskristallnacht* of November 1938, and were not completely Aryanized until late 1939.[25]

Goebbels' failure to take over the Leipzig publishers must have been severely disappointing. These firms would have had a major part in the personal empire he was trying to construct. It was not, however, the only setback he suffered in 1934. From the time he became Propaganda Minister, Goebbels had also had his eye on Germany's two largest publishing houses, both of them Jewish—Mosse and Ullstein. As Germany's largest single publisher of books, newspapers, and periodicals, the Ullstein firm was an especially desirable plum. Its precarious financial situation seemed to make it ripe for plucking. Since the beginning of the decade it had been operating at a considerable deficit, a deficit which in 1933 had reached RM 2.1 million.

In January 1934, Goebbels through an intermediary, began negotiating with representatives of the Ullstein family.[26] The negotiations were already underway when Max Amann, chief of the official Nazi publishing house, the *Eher Verlag*, intervened with Hitler. Amann's point was that Ullstein should be transferred not to Goebbels, but into the hands of the party's publishing house instead. Both Goebbels and Amann had to depend finally upon Hitler for a decision. Neither one of them

25 Kurt Sabatsky, "Meine Erinnerungen an den Nationalsozialismus," unpublished memoir in the Wiener Library (London) archives.

26 See Hermann Ullstein, *The Rise and Fall of the House of Ullstein* (New York, 1943), pp. 269-272.

commanded sufficient capital to complete the transfer by themselves. Whatever amount the final agreement called for had to come from the Reich treasury and only Hitler could free the necessary funds. Amann was apparently more persuasive than his rival, although Goebbels was to learn this fact in a most surprising fashion. When Goebbels' representatives closed the deal with Ullstein on June 30, 1934, Goebbels discovered that his purchase was being transferred instead into Amann's hands.[27]

The type of deal the Nazis were able to extract from the Ullstein family is instructive. Although Ullstein holdings were valued at between RM 50 and 60 million, they received only RM 6 million in selling out to Amann's *Eher Verlag*.[28] This rate of compensation became standard for other firms which succumbed to Aryanization later on.[29]

Aryanization of the Rudolf Mosse publishing firm conformed to the precedent set in the Ullstein case. Among the most important Mosse holdings was the advertising firm *Annoncen-Expedition*, which, together with Alfred Hugenberg's firm, *Allgemeine Anzeigen*, had once dominated the German advertising field. By 1933, however, the Depression and competition from Hugenberg had brought the Mosse firm to the brink of bankruptcy. Like Ullstein, the Mosse holdings had been weakened for the Nazi assault. Although German revenue authorities had assessed the value of the Mosse properties in excess of RM 40 million, only RM 5 million were paid at the time of the 1934 sale. The Mosse holdings were placed in the hands of an Aryan concern, founded expressly to take them over.[30] Goebbels' bid for control of the business end of German publishing was off to a bad start.

In Frankfurt at the same time, the Sonnemann-Simon families, owners of the liberal and prestigious *Frankfurter Zeitung*,

[27] Hale, *Captive Press*, pp. 131-134.

[28] Ibid.

[29] *Der wirtschaftliche Vernichtungskampf gegen die Juden im Dritten Reich*, dargestellt von der ökonomischen Abteilung des jüdischen Weltkongresses (Paris, 1937), p. 57.

[30] Hale, *Captive Press*, p. 290.

saw their controlling interest being transferred to the I. G. Farben chemical trust.[31] The paper itself continued to be published on into the war, despite the fact that Hitler despised it for its tradition of liberalism and objectivity. Because of its reputation it was used as an ornament to decorate the Nazi image abroad. And, as the British ambassador observed, to have suppressed completely the renowned *Frankfurter Zeitung* "would have had a serious influence on government borrowing."[32]

There were ways other than Aryanization to keep the German press in line. In many newspaper offices the local Nazi apparatus, oftentimes against the wishes of the ruling clique, had installed commissioners who gave the management to understand what could be printed. These Nazi "commissars" also induced the management to dismiss politically or racially undesirable employees. Without central direction these kinds of initiatives invited chaos. Even within Nazism there was a rich variety of opinion seeking expression—too rich a variety to suit either Hitler's taste or his political interests. Not the least of Goebbels' tasks upon becoming Propaganda Minister was to bring order and proper direction into the business of public enlightenment and propaganda.

The apparent hit-and-miss process of Aryanization was understandably disturbing to those radical Nazis eager for Jewish spoil. If Aryanization could have taken place in the simple world constructed out of the pieces of Nazi mythology, it is likely that the Ullstein and Mosse cases would have become typical. In fact these cases became the exception. After the initial forays of 1933-1934, Aryanization of large Jewish firms was not pursued systematically again until 1938. The intervening years were disappointing and frustrating for those who did not understand the reasons for delay. Why should Jewish department stores, Jewish banks, Jewish export houses, and Jewish

31 Josef Wulf, *Presse und Funk im Dritten Reich, Eine Dokumentation* (Guetersloh, 1964), pp. 53-70.
32 Rumbold to Simon, Woodward and Butler, eds., *Documents on British Foreign Policy*, pp. 39-43.

industrial plants continue to prosper while the little Nazi was having trouble keeping his head above water?

The Nazi promise had implied that rank and file *Mittelstand* followers would be the immediate beneficiaries of Aryanization. Transfer of Ullstein to the Nazi publisher had not necessarily dissipated such hopes; neither had the transfer to I. G. Farben of the controlling shares of the Sonneman-Simon property. These holdings were too large to be given to the control of the party's rank and file. But when it came to department stores and smaller Jewish enterprises the initial ambitions were very much intact.

One of these *Mittelstand* groups, the Commission for National Socialist Economic Policy, chose to interpret the regime's official mildness toward Jews in the best possible light. While others considered the decrees concerning anti-Jewish actions as restricting, it considered them as guidelines defining the minimum of what could be done to Jews. In the aftermath to the Nuremberg Laws, this group used its journal to editorialize on the theme "Let's Not Wait for Laws": "He who sticks to the letter of the law or refuses to go beyond it, because the orders are not given to do so, confirms the fact that he is willing to do only the minimum of what the community asks of him."[33]

The vicarious satisfaction attending the Aryanization of Ullstein or Mosse was plainly insufficient to relieve this sort of frustration. In 1935, during the months preceding the Nuremberg Rally, the renewed wave of anti-Jewish actions was begun at the initiation of local Nazi groups. In various cities throughout the Reich the SA was once more warning customers to avoid Jewish shops. Streicher's committee was pushing its campaign for the adoption of "German Enterprise" signs.[34] Unofficially inspired boycotts threatened to become nationwide. Leaflets listing a town's Jewish stores were being distributed on the sly. In Lübeck during the night of August 6, the Jewish-owned

[33] "Nicht auf Gesetze warten!" *Mitteilungen der Kommission für Wirtschaftspolitik der NSDAP* 1 (August, 1936): 29-30.

[34] *Voelkischer Beobachter,* January 22, 1935.

Globus department store was virtually demolished, undoubtedly by Nazi hooligans. The local Nazi leadership excused itself by attributing the destruction to the "will of the people." Excuses could not hide the fact, however, that such destruction flew in the face of the regime's policy. In March an order from the Reich's Interior Minister had gone out to all local government and police officials enjoining against such measures and outlining the dangers they presented.[35] Globus may have been Jewish-owned, but it also employed 60 Aryans who were now jobless. What was to be done with them? "We are waiting," the local party leaders said a few days later, "for local employers to do their duty. Each one of them will have to trouble themselves about finding a job for these unemployed comrades."[36]

The Globus incident was only one of the many private measures adopted by party units throughout the Reich. Countless stores were closed down in a similar manner, their owners leaving behind a small army of suddenly jobless Aryan employees. Attempts to appease the radicals was one way of dealing with the problem. Rudolf Hess dispatched a circular letter ("not for publication") to local party units promising legislation dealing with Jews and their economic activity, a promise which may have raised hopes but took another three years to be fulfilled.[37]

Economics Minister Schacht was much more disturbed by these unsanctioned assaults. Unlike Hess, he was unwilling to play at appeasing radical Nazi sentiment. He had extracted from Hitler the assurance that the regime's Jewish policies would not interfere with the work of his ministry. Now he had every intention of holding Hitler to his word.

By mid-May, events had gone so far that Schacht began to take public issue with what appeared to be Hitler's reluctance to keep his promise. The immediate objective of Schacht's displeasure was Julius Streicher. Public designation of "German

[35] Collection: Bezirksämter, Folder I, BDC.
[36] From the *Lübecker Zeitung*, August 8, 1935. Quoted by Uhlig, *Die Warenhäuser im Dritten Reich*, p. 158.
[37] Collection: Bezirksämter, Folder 240 I, BDC.

Enterprises" not only failed to further Germany's economic interests, he declared; it actually hindered economic recovery. Party headquarters countered by proposing a conference of all interested parties. Schacht resisted all such suggestions. He considered the Economics Ministry competent to deal with economic matters by itself, and himself powerful enough to order Streicher to stop interfering in his affairs.

Schacht's power was not what he imagined it to be. On May 21, a conference was held,[38] although Schacht refused to attend. It was a subministerial conference held to discuss the role of Jews in the German economy and in no way a policy-making session. Hopefully the airing of grievances would iron out some of the differences arising from efforts to exclude Jews from the German economy. Chairman of the meeting was Wilhelm Stuckart, State Secretary in the Interior Ministry. Delegates from the Economics and Propaganda ministries were present, as were representatives from the Foreign Office, from Hess's Party Headquarters in Munich and from the National Socialist People's Welfare Office—a party agency with especially radical economic and racial views.

The immediate issue was Streicher's effort to designate a business publicly as Jewish or Aryan. The larger question centered upon jurisdiction in Jewish affairs. Chairman Stuckart declared the Interior Ministry to be generally in charge of Jewish policy, but agreed that the Streicher issue seemed to fall within the purview of the Economics Ministry. Schacht's representative pointed out the reasons for his Ministry's displeasure with Streicher. Many of the firms being branded as Jewish were actually in the hands of Aryan capital. Aryan workers and employees were being adversely affected by the harassment of Jewish businesses. Furthermore Jewish firms were often supported by foreign capital. The foreign policy implications of any interference were so obvious they hardly needed to be spelled out. Had he chosen to spell them out, Schacht's repre-

[38] Minutes of this conference are in the archives of the YIVO Institute for Jewish Research (New York), Berlin Collection: G-67.

sentative could have pointed to Germany's unfavorable trade balance for 1934 and the serious depletion of her foreign exchange reserves.[39] He did point out, however, that his chief disagreed with the purpose of this meeting and would not consider any agreements reached as binding on his own policy.

Hess's representative, on the other hand, emphasized the usefulness of the meeting. It offered him the chance to discuss what his office observed to be a very disquieting trend: the reopening of many Jewish businesses.[40] It also gave him an opportunity to stress the need for a unified Jewish policy. Given the present circumstances, he said, the German people could only feel confused about the treatment of Jews.

The representative of the National Socialist Peoples' Welfare Office agreed wholeheartedly with these latest observations. His people, too, were dissatisfied with the regime's Jewish policy. At a recent meeting of Nazi *Gauleiter* there had been complaints about Jews in the retail trade and the opening of new Jewish businesses. Were Jews to be excluded from the German economy or not? As for the Streicher-inspired "German Enterprise" dilemma, he proposed that German business firms become members of his own National Socialist Peoples' Welfare Agency. Member firms would receive a certificate which the public would soon recognize as evidence of an Aryan establishment. The proposal entailed only the applying of Streicher's measures in a little more subtle fashion. Its real importance lay elsewhere —in the transfer of the function from Streicher's hands into those of the National Socialist Peoples' Welfare Office. The issue was not the Jews or even their participation in the economy; it was the question of who would control their participation.

The meeting ended without an agreement. Schacht's delegate stood firmly on his position; the party's various representatives

39 Arthur Schweitzer, *Big Business in the Third Reich* (Bloomington, Ind., 1964), p. 428.

40 In the aftermath of the 1933 boycott many Jewish businessmen fled Germany in panic, leaving their shops and stores closed. Once the panic subsided, some of these returned and a few reopened their businesses.

on theirs. Only one thing was clear: a power conflict between Schacht and the party was developing. The course this conflict would take depended upon what further initiatives the party took and finally upon the position of the Fuehrer himself. For the time being neither side was able to impose its views upon the other and neither side disguised its dissatisfaction with the present state of affairs.

A wave of boycotts and incidents such as the one in Lübeck on August 6 kept the issue very much alive during the summer of 1935. It was the destruction of the Lübeck-based *Globus*, however which once more brought the issue to a head. Contrary to his position in May, Schacht became convinced that a high-level conference was now necessary if the issue was to be resolved. He called an interministerial conference on economic policy to be held in his office at the Reichsbank on August 20. Invited were Interior Minister Frick, Finance Minister Schwerin von Krosigk, Justice Minister Franz Guertner, Education Minister Bernhard Rust, and Adolf Wagner, who as *Gauleiter* of Bavaria, was to represent the party's interests.[41]

Schacht pulled few punches in condemning the actions of certain party authorities, the Labor Front, the NS-HAGO, and especially of Julius Streicher. Their "irresponsible Jew-baiting," he said, jeopardized the fulfillment of the economic tasks with which he had been charged: the providing of employment and building up the economy for rearmament. Streicher's activities headed the list of Schacht's complaints. In addition to his investigation of business firms, the Franconian *Gauleiter* was demanding that all German businesses dismiss the Jewish agents who represented them abroad. To illustrate the danger in this Schacht gave the example of a Jewish agent for the Allianz Insurance Company in Egypt. When party pressure had finally forced him to quit he went over to an English insurance com-

---

[41] A memorandum detailing the proceedings of this conference is published in *Documents on German Foreign Policy, 1918-1945*, series C, vol. 4 (Washington, D.C., 1962), pp. 568-570; the conference is also discussed in Hilberg, *Destruction*, pp. 21-22.

pany, taking his Allianz accounts with him. Who was the loser? The German economy. Furthermore, the party's "unlawful" activity had led a French firm to cancel a large order with the German Salamander Shoe Company. Again the German economy was the only one to suffer. The repercussions to such illegal actions could not be ignored. Jewish firms could not be liquidated at will. Many of them were essential to the German economy.

Interior Minister Frick agreed with Schacht in principle, but explained that he could order the police to intervene only if individuals were harassing Jews. In the case of anti-Semitic actions carried out by party organizations the police would have to refrain from any intervention. Responsibility in such cases had to lie with the party.

The representative of the party, Adolf Wagner, took exception to Schacht's charges. While he too disapproved of "wild actions," he was certain unlawful anti-Jewish activity would cease as soon as the regime took the "anti-Semitic public feeling into account." That feeling could be taken into account most appropriately, Wagner suggested, by prohibiting Jewish firms from receiving public contracts and ending the establishment of new Jewish businesses.

The official who drafted a report of this meeting for the record made the laconic observation that "an overall and uniform objective for Germany's policy towards the Jews did not emerge from the discussion." It was agreed only that the government should try to place its orders with German firms exclusively and that some further regulation preventing the establishment of new Jewish businesses would be desirable. Wagner readily agreed to submit suggestions from the party for such legislation. Schacht, however, had made no discernible headway on what he considered to be the major issues.

The awarding of public contracts to Jewish firms had long rankled party radicals. Schacht was candid in his explanation: Jewish firms received government contracts when it served the interests of rearmament. The question had first been raised at a cabinet meeting in July 1933, when it was decided not to discriminate against Jewish firms. At that time the main concern had been the need for reducing unemployment.[42] By mid-1935 the primary consideration had become rearmament, although knowledgeable party officials could not yet afford Schacht's candor. The complaints on this issue which reached party headquarters in Munich in the summer of 1935 were answered as if the situation had not changed. In late August every Nazi *Gauleiter* received a letter of explanation from Deputy Fuehrer Hess' office. Acting for Hess, Martin Bormann explained: "Recently numerous complaints have reached us about Jewish firms still receiving government contracts (e.g., in certain areas of rearmament). This is done, occasionally, only because of the need for reducing unemployment."[43]

In a conciliatory gesture, Bormann went on to ask each *Gauleiter* to ascertain what influence Jewish businesses still had in his district. He then asked them to make suggestions concerning further action in the light of the general economic situation. For the moment it appeared as if the party apparatus, or at least the *Gauleiter,* was being given a hand in the making of Jewish policy.

Schacht, in the meantime, continued his efforts to gain greater control over economic policy. In November he wrote to Hess at party headquarters for an authoritative definition of *Einzelaktion*,[44] a term which had been loosely applied to unlawful activity directed against Jews. *Einzelaktionen* had often been forbidden by Hess' office, but the term had never been clearly defined. Schacht suggested that it be held to mean any action not resting expressly upon orders of either the government or top leadership of the NSDAP. Although Hess agreed to Schacht's proposed definition, the latter was not empowered to enforce its terms. The basic problem remained unresolved.

In December Schacht carried his campaign against the party apparatus into a different camp. On the day before Christmas he

42 Schumacher Archiv, Folder 240 I, BDC.
43 Ibid.
44 *Dokumente Frankfurter Juden,* p. 27.

sent a "highly secret" letter to the Reich's War Minister von Blomberg stating that the importing of lead and copper requisite for rearmament was made nearly impossible for lack of "the necessary foreign currencies for these requirements."[45] Acquiring foreign exchange, Schacht told Blomberg, "has been made extremely difficult by our cultural [Jewish] policy, which is encountering opposition throughout the world."

Throughout this conflict between his economic experts and his party apparatus there is no evidence that Hitler ever intervened, although a decisive word from him could have ended the conflict at any time. As was so often the case, however, the Fuehrer avoided these kinds of conflict, probably in the hope they would burn themselves out. It would have been an uncomfortable decision for him to make. The choice lay between a continued role for Jews in his economy or endangering his rearmament program. More than that, it would have meant a public repudiation for Julius Streicher, a step Hitler would absolutely refuse to take.[46] Whether or not Hitler ever made a clear decision on the issue between Schacht and the party cannot be established. Very likely he did not. At least not at the time. The issue was not resolved until 1938, after Schacht had been replaced as Economics Minister.[47] By then circumstances had been sufficiently altered to make the issue largely irrelevant.

No major legislation directed at expelling Jews from the economy followed in the wake of the Nuremberg Laws. The legislation Hess had promised in the summer of 1935 was not forthcoming. There were ways, however, in which the Nuremberg Laws could be used against Jews to pressure them into selling out. In mid-December of that year a number of non-Aryan employees of the Jewish-owned Barasch Brothers depart-

---

45 *Nazi Conspiracy and Aggression*, vol. 7, Document 293-EC, pp. 291-293.

46 As late as 1941, after Streicher had seriously compromised himself and after receiving considerable advice to denounce him, Hitler continued to view Streicher as "irreplaceable." Trevor-Roper, ed., *Hitler's Secret Conversations*, p. 169.

47 See Amos E. Simpson, "The Struggle for the Control of the German Economy," *Journal of Modern History* 12 (March, 1959): 37-45.

ment store in Magdeburg were arrested on morals charges trumped up by the local Nazi district official or *Kreisleiter*. The accused were charged with offending the spirit if not the letter of the Nuremberg Laws. One of them allegedly kissed an Aryan girl working as an apprentice, and the other exchanged overly intimate handshakes with several Aryan salesgirls. To protest such moral laxity the Magdeburg Nazis instituted mass demonstrations, threatening to vandalize the Barasch premises. The local police simply closed the premises to avoid incidents. At this point the owners of Barasch chose to sell their store to a local Aryan competitor. Shortly thereafter the morals charges against the Jewish employees were dismissed in the local court.[48] It was a Pyrrhic victory, however, because the department store, a peculiarly Jewish institution, was reopened by its Aryan owners a week later.

Despite such dramatic exceptions, Aryanization proceeded fitfully through 1936 and most of 1937. There were, to be sure, the continual restrictions and harassments which affected especially the smaller businesses. Hundreds, perhaps thousands, of these were wiped out by local party-inspired boycotts or pressures. The Nazis who measured success by the standard of a *judenrein* economy, however, were hardly triumphant. Many large Jewish firms were still in operation, sometimes with the aid, even, of government contracts. The Jewish tannery firm of Schwabe and Heinemann in Erfurt was earning an estimated RM 70,000 to 80,000 per month during 1937 supplying leather to shoe manufacturers, some of whom were considered Jewish, who had contracts with the army.[49] And in cases where Aryanization attempts were successful, there were no plaudits celebrating the assistance of local party leaders or units. If Hitler had any dramatic solutions for the Jewish problem in the economy,

[48] *Der wirtschaftliche Vernichtungskampf*, pp. 68-69.

[49] Records of the Reichs Leader of the SS and Chief of the German Police, National Archives Microcopy T175 (409), 2932766 (hereafter cited as Himmler File).

he was obviously keeping them to himself. It was to be some time, for example, before Jews were successfully excluded from the wholesale and textile businesses where their connections in an international market were useful. As late as 1939 some Jews were still holding on in the fur and textile businesses. A striking example of the usefulness of foreign contacts was offered by two private Jewish-owned banks in Hamburg. Both of them, the Mendelssohn and Warburg houses, with their foreign contacts and close ties to Hamburg's export trade, were among the last major Jewish enterprises to be Aryanized.[50]

Aryanization of some larger Jewish firms continued through 1936 and 1937, but it usually conformed to the pattern established in the cases of Ullstein and Mosse. Through some peculiar twist of logic, the Nazis referred to these as cases of "voluntary" Aryanization. Until November 1938, the transfer of Jewish holdings into Aryan hands came about through these so-called voluntary agreements. Voluntary meant only that Jewish owners were compensated for the transfer of their properties and that the sale was negotiated and sealed by a legal contract. Compensation, of course, was never equal to the value of the property. The Ullstein and Mosse families received only ten percent of the value of their holdings. Maximum compensation rarely reached fifty percent. Nor were Jewish property owners paid in currency which could be transferred out of Germany. In one case the owners of the Orenstein and Koppel locomotive works were paid in Argentine shares supposedly worth RM 7 million, about ten or twelve percent of the firm's value.[51]

As long as Aryanization remained a voluntary process, the sheer complexity of the business world served to thwart a complete Nazi takeover. Unlike the civil service, for example, the business world was not governed by a clearly definable hierarchy with which the Nazis could deal. They were confronted instead

50 *Jews in Nazi Europe: February 1933 to November 1941*, a study prepared by the Baltimore Institute of Jewish Affairs (New York, n.d.), p. 11.
51 Ibid., p. 12.

with conglomerations of hierarchies or authorities tangled oftentimes into a seemingly inextricable web. The Nazis learned very early, if painfully, that to pull on just one thread in the web could have dangerous ramifications.

Many of the larger Jewish firms were connected with foreign interests, making the web even more complex. In such cases Aryanization became an exceedingly difficult process. The complexities of unraveling entangled international financial arrangements saved many Jewish firms from being Aryanized during the period of voluntary transfers. Some Jewish firms enhanced their bargaining position by creating dummy holding corporations abroad. Technically, then, the German firm was controlled by foreign interests and capital. Ownership became obscured in this maze of international finance. The result was an elaborate game of hide and seek, the prey hiding from the predator deep in the labyrinth of intertwined business structures. Occasionally, if temporarily, these arrangements stymied the eager Aryanizers. Clearly this was a game which called for legal, accounting, and financial expertise, commodities with which the Nazi movement had not been liberally graced.

The upswing in Aryanization which reached its peak in 1938 and early 1939 had its beginnings in the latter half of 1937. The reasons for this sudden spurt of activity are not difficult to discover. The Nazis found themselves joined by powerful and clever partners—Germany's big business interests—which were eager to assist in hunting down the Jewish prey. Since 1935 Germany had made political and economic strides which altered the circumstances related to Aryanizing the larger Jewish concerns. Political successes such as the naval agreement with Britain and reoccupation of the Rhineland had greatly enhanced German prestige and self-confidence. Gradual recovery from the depression—at least in reducing unemployment—provided for Hitler a basis of political security. Schacht's bilateral trade agreements with the countries of eastern Europe, moreover, reduced German dependence upon western Europe for the raw materials which went into rearmament, making her in the process less susceptible to pressures from her western neighbors. In the fall of 1936 Hitler drew these various strings together and appointed Hermann Goering to head a Four Year Plan designed to speed rearmament plans.

The new sense of security felt by the Nazi regime had drastic consequences for Jewish business concerns, especially those which promised to share in any economic upswing. During the first years of Nazi rule German industrialists had been wary of overexpanding their holdings, at least until they were certain of continued economic recovery.[52] In this setting of uncertainty their Jewish competitors were accorded a measure of safety. The promise of a continued upswing, seemingly assured by the regime's emphasis on rearmament, prompted a change in these cautious attitudes.[53] Huge concerns such as Mannesmann, Krupp, Flick, Wolff, Thyssen, Kirdorf, and I. G. Farben quickly became avid partners of Nazi Aryanizers.[54]

Probably the most difficult and most important Aryanization process undertaken by this new partnership was concluded during the early months of 1938. The victim was the Czechoslovakian Jewish Julius Petschek family which owned and operated a series of brown coal or lignite mining companies in central and southeastern Germany. Together with another branch of the family, the Ignaz Petschek group whose German holdings were larger, they produced an estimated thirty percent of the brown coal manufactured in Germany. The Nazi emphasis upon self-sufficiency and rearmament made the properties of both Petschek groups extremely important. Brown coal was useful as fuel and as the raw material for producing electricity, synthetic gasoline, and other chemical products. To have these firms in the hands of Jews who were also foreign citizens offended as

52 Genschel, *Die Verdrängung der Juden*, p. 221.

53 Ibid., p. 222.

54 See George W. F. Hallgarten, "Adolf Hitler and German Heavy Industry, 1931-1933," *Journal of Economic History* 12 (Summer, 1952): 222-246; Fritz Thyssen, *I Paid Hitler* (New York, 1941); and Schweitzer, *Big Business in the Third Reich*.

much against the Reich's economic interests as it did against its ideology.

The much-heralded Four Year Plan brought the Petschek problem to a head in 1937. Goering, as commissioner of rearmament plans, was immediately interested in brown coal and obviously anxious to have these resources safely in German hands. Numerous German firms, eager to profit from government contracts, were likewise eager to acquire the Petschek properties.

To Aryanize even the German holdings of foreign-based companies was no simple matter, however. Outright expropriation was out of the question. Indeed, undue coercion of any sort would have invited retaliation against German interests in foreign countries. The problem was made even more complex by the fact that both Petschek groups held their largest German properties through holding companies based in western Europe or the United States.[55] The difficulties of pressuring foreign citizens into selling property whose ownership was obscured in the maze of international finance were hard to overestimate. Only the fact that these properties were in Germany gave the Nazi a certain leverage. But it was obvious that Aryanization—if it was to come at all—would have to be through a voluntary sale.

The larger Ignaz Petschek group resisted all overtures from German business firms. The assault on the Julius Petscheks offered greater promise, perhaps because they realized the limited future of their German holdings. Through the last half of 1937 they were conducting separate negotiations with such large German industrial combines as Flick, I. G. Farben, and the Wintershall and Salzdetfurth concern. Conducting negotiations with several prospective buyers concurrently offered the Julius Petscheks a certain advantage. Conversely, it presented to the German bidders the danger of driving the price higher than necessary. By December 1937, the Wintershall concern

[55] *Trials of War Criminals before the Nuernberg Military Tribunal,* vol. 6, "The Flick Case" (Washington, D.C., 1952), p. 95.

was on the verge of agreeing to a purchase price of 11 to 12 million dollars.[56] The Julius Petscheks, it appeared, were ready to sell.

At this crucial point Friedrich Flick, director of the gigantic Flick KG combine of steel and coal companies, intervened. Earlier Flick had been reluctant to add to his industrial empire. Now, however, with the Petschek property in danger of slipping out of his hands, Flick began to pull strings. Using his friendship with Hermann Goering, he requested that the Wintershall proposal be scrapped and that he be given the sole right to negotiate with the Petscheks—Julius and Ignaz. He justified his proposal by stressing his own knowledge of the brown coal industry and pointing out to Goering the dangers of competitive bidding which had led to Wintershall's inflated offer. Flick also stressed that a voluntary deal with the Julius Petscheks might well help to soften the resistance of the more important Ignaz Petscheks. This voluntary deal, he was confident, could be concluded at a price much lower than the one currently being considered. In any event, through his negotiations "the air could be sufficiently cleared to judge whether the matter will be concluded voluntarily or not."[57]

Flick's presentation was persuasive. On February 1, 1938, Goering granted Flick the exclusive right to negotiate with the Petscheks and ordered that "all conferences initiated without my authorization are to be called off immediately and all offers to negotiate are to be cancelled."[58]

Armed with this authority, Flick immediately took over the negotiations with representatives of the Julius Petscheks. At first these talks proved fruitless. The Petschek group refused to behave according to Flick's prediction. It actually raised the price to 16 million dollars in foreign exchange, insisting this was necessary to satisfy the American holding company. Flick re-

56 Ibid.
57 Ibid., pp. 450-453.
58 Ibid., p. 464. Goering to Flick.

jected the proposal out of hand, warning the Petscheks that their resistance would eventually prove unwise.

With that the problem was taken back to Goering's headquarters where it was decided to break off the negotiations for the time being. An elaborate plan was drawn up to shock the Julius Petscheks out of their complacency. Proposals for direct action by the Reich government were discarded because Goering wished to avoid foreign diplomatic entanglements. The object was still to maintain the fiction that any eventual sale would be voluntary. In lieu of direct action it was decided to institute a massive propaganda campaign against, not the Julius Petscheks, but against the Ignaz group. Accusing the latter of tax-dodging and other financial chicanery, it was hoped, would convince the Julius group to sell out rather than risk suffering similar calumny. It was also felt that the Petscheks, being Czech, could not fail to be intimidated by the steadily mounting Nazi pressures against Austria. Could they fail to read these signs of extortion correctly? To sweeten the proposal once negotiations had been resumed, it was decided to make at least part of the offer in foreign currency.[59]

This plan, conceived by Goering and his Four Year Plan staff, was effective. When negotiations were resumed in early May they came on the heels of the propaganda campaign and, more importantly, the *Anschluss* of Austria. The Julius Petscheks had read the signs correctly. They were willing to sell. The deal was closed quickly, at a price much lower than the one demanded as recently as February. Flick bought the Petscheks' German affiliates for 6.325 million dollars payable in New York and RM 970 thousand to be paid in Berlin. He immediately turned around and sold part of these properties to his former competitors—I. G. Farben and Wintershall—at a handsome profit.[60]

The Aryanization of the Julius Petschek group was a major coup for Flick, but the bigger fish was still free. On May 25, Flick received a letter from Goering's office confirming the deal

[59] Ibid., pp. 565-566.
[60] Ibid., pp. 97-98.

with the Julius Petscheks and asking "for your proposals for the further handling of the problem Ignaz Petschek."[61] Aryanization of the Ignaz group was concluded in December 1938, although in quite different circumstances than those surrounding the purchase of the Julius Petschek holdings. The crucial difference was provided by the Munich agreements of September. Ignaz Petschek had its headquarters in the Czech Sudetenland. The Munich arrangements had provided for the transfer of Sudeten territory to Germany, thereby making Aryanization a relatively simple matter. The firm's holdings were put into Aryan trusteeship and placed under control of the Hermann Goering Works.[62] There was nothing voluntary about it. Even the facade of legality was no longer necessary.

The German *Mittelstand* never saw the rewards of Aryanization as promised by National Socialism's ideology. Instead of effecting a corporate economy of shopkeepers and small manufacturers, and thereby redistributing wealth through the *Kleinbürger* ranks, Aryanization served to concentrate wealth and industry into even fewer hands. Even the much-hated Jewish department store chains were rarely dissolved. As the Barasch case in Magdeburg demonstrated, they were merely transferred to large Aryan firms. The Petschek cases only ratified the existing trend. The little Nazi had to be satisfied that the Jew was being gradually excluded from the economy. Spoils he had once hoped to gain went into other purses.

This anti-ideological direction to Aryanization was not accidental, as the Petschek examples clearly illustrated. It was determined by factors which were only remotely related to ideology. The chief architect of Aryanization was Hermann Goering whose power was enhanced in November 1937 when upon Schacht's resignation as Economics Minister, Hitler elevated Goering to a position of control over the Reich's economic

61 Ibid., pp. 475-476.
62 *Ibid.*, p. 98. The Hermann Goering Works was established as a state-owned enterprise to make steel from low-grade ores when it became apparent that the private steel companies were unwilling to invest in such a low return venture.

affairs. When a new Economics Minister was appointed he took his direction from Goering. Goering had a cynical dislike and distrust for the lower ranks in the Nazi party. Both his social background and his inordinate taste for luxury made him more comfortable in the surroundings of the wealthy. More immediately important, the creation of a shopkeeper economy would have rendered rearmament impossible. If Germany was to rebuild her military power it would have to be in cooperation with German industry, not in opposition to it.

Goering remained deeply suspicious of the *Mittelstand* Nazi and his ambitions, fearful that he could undermine the economic achievements made in recent years. On the other hand he cultivated the friendship of German industrial magnates. His encouragements frequently inspired people such as Flick to consider the advantages of buying out a Jewish competitor.[63] Goering referred to these views on Aryanization as indicative of a "liberal attitude," in contrast to the presumably illiberal attitudes held by those who had once taken Nazi ideology at its word. To be liberal on Goering's terms was simply to ignore the dictates of ideology whenever it served the larger purpose of rearmament, or when it might serve to enrich Goering himself. His fear that other party members might profit from the expropriation of Jewish property never led him to examine his own activities. After the *Kristallnacht* pogrom of November 1938, he was concerned that some SS men might have appropriated the automobiles of their victims for private use. Petty thievery, he said, could not be condoned. Thievery on a grander scale was another matter. As chief Aryanizer of Jewish businesses and properties, especially after 1937, his own financial interests were well served. Goering's reputation as a "collector" of treasures, already established by the mid-30's, began to take on larger proportions with the extension of his powers toward the end of the decade. While his financial situation has never been sorted out, there is no doubt he used these powers to line his own purse. Technically the Hermann Goering Steel Works was a

---

[63] Genschel, *Die Verdrängung der Juden*, p. 223.

Reich-controlled enterprise. Yet a considerable portion of its assets remained in his own hands. Goering, it seemed, was successful in areas where other ambitious party officials such as Goebbels had failed.

Despite the multitude of ideological sins the terms "voluntary" and "liberal" swept aside during the first four years of Hitler's Reich, they do characterize the seemingly erratic approach to Aryanization. By no yardstick had Jewish participation in German economic life been ended. The department store, a Jewish invention, although purged of Jews, still existed; indeed, some of them were flouishing in the hands of Nazis.[64] The little shopkeeper and the cattle dealer had been eliminated; many of the big bankers and major Jewish industrialists were still in business. Four years after the *Machtergreifung*, Jewish firms were still being awarded public contracts. The hope of 1933 that Jews would quickly be eliminated from the economy remained unrealized. That thousands of Jews had been driven from earning a livelihood was undeniable. But it was unsatisfactory as well, at least as long as many other Jews still held important positions in the economy.

Driving Jews out of the economy, once considered a simple problem, had revealed itself to be bound up in nearly inconceivable complexity. It was obvious that this complexity afforded some Jews escape from the tentacles of Aryanization. The party's radical supporters were never told why Aryanization seemed to be proceeding so irregularly, making the dichotomy between promise and performance on the Jewish issue all the more exasperating. Periodically the tensions generated by this dichotomy erupted into actions against individual Jewish business places. At other times they took the milder form of protests delivered to Streicher or to one of the party journals. In late 1936 an Aryan businessman, Heinrich Schulte, noted that a Jewish salesman was still representing the Wefers & Co. textile firm with which he dealt. Until then he had believed Wefers to be completely *judenrein*. His sense of racial propriety offended,

[64] *Der wirtschaftliche Vernichtungskampf*, p. 66.

Schulte wrote the firm an indignant letter promising he would never buy another one of its products. Wefers' answer deserves quotation:

> We acknowledge your letter of November 19 and can assure you that we are an Aryan firm. Whether we employ Christian or Jewish representatives, however, is our business and not yours. We have had unfortunate experiences with some of our Christian representatives, who have not wanted to work very hard. In order to keep our business going and to keep bread on the tables of our employees we were forced, therefore, to rehire a man who took his job seriously and who was also Jewish. Your small orders do not concern us. We can easily do without them. Mit deutschem Gruss! [With German Greetings]
>
> Wefers & Co.

The enraged Schulte took the letter to the SS which in mid-December printed it along with an indignant commentary in its paper, *Das Schwarze Korps,*[65] as an example of what remained to be done regarding the Jewish question.

The fact that the base for a continued economic existence for Jews had not been entirely erased by late 1937 was obviously a failure in the eyes of the SS, Schulte, and most other radical Nazis. For Jews, however, this failure was open to another interpretation. Perhaps the Nazi regime was not striving for a completely *judenrein* economy after all. If not, the hope for an island of safety within Germany, even if it meant a return to a ghetto-like existence, remained alive. This tragic miscalculation was understandable in the circumstances, especially since the regime seemed less violent than many of its supporters. What this calculation had failed to take into account was that the regime's failure to satisfy its most radical supporters did not stem from disagreement with those radical aims.

The Jewish policy of the Nazi regime until late 1937 was determined largely by three basic economic factors; the need for creating employment, the rearmament and foreign exchange

65 *Das Schwarze Korps,* December 17, 1936.

problem, and the intricate nature of international finance. Those not privy to the decisions made in economic affairs could not appreciate their importance in the making and execution of Jewish policy.

The importance of these economic factors was increased by the fact that the Nazis themselves were not expert in any of these fields. Not until Walther Funk, a former contact man with big businessmen for the Nazis, assumed the post in February 1938, did a Nazi head the Economics Ministry, and even then Schacht continued for more than a year as president of the Reichsbank. The Minister of War, Blomberg, was in his post until January 1938. For the first four years the Nazi leadership had to rely heavily—if reluctantly—upon this non-Nazi advice in critical areas of economic and rearmament policy. Disagreement on policy goals in these circumstances was not unusual. Out of this matrix of confusion were carved the frustrations of Nazi radicals and the continued hopes of many Jews.

VI. Emigration: Signpost to the Future

THE NAZI FAILURE until shortly before the outbreak of war in 1939 to formulate a consistent Jewish policy stemmed in part from economic and political obstacles any policy had to overcome. Whether the object was systematic discrimination, elimination from the economy, or ghettoization, it was soon discovered that these efforts had unfortunate ramifications. Neither the boycott nor Aryanization could be pursued to its logical conclusion. Legislation, it was soon discovered, could serve to protect as well as circumscribe the activities of Jews.

The Nazi conception of the Jewish problem also contributed to failure of early policies. The claims of a multitude of racial scientists notwithstanding, there were no Jewish experts in the Nazi fold. The spurious scientism of a Hans F. K. Guenther or a Hans Frank was hardly a sufficient base upon which to build a racial policy. For leaders and followers alike, the understanding which the Nazis brought to the Jewish problem in 1933 was based almost entirely upon the age-worn anti-Semitic clichés spouted by Adolf Hitler.

On this very elementary level virtually every Nazi could become his own Jewish expert, and it seems that many of them did. Nearly every Nazi official felt compelled at one time or another to deliver a background report on the Jewish question. The repositories of Nazi materials are filled with these reports. Invariably they rehash the official line and they reflect not the slightest understanding of the situation of Jews in Germany or the world. Only the simple faith that a Jewish problem existed and the assumption that it was amenable to solution emerges from these reports.

The simplistic categories of this faith, insofar as they seemed to point to simple solutions, also contributed to the successive failures in Jewish policy. There was nothing complex about a boycott, anti-Jewish legislation, or even the Aryanization of Jewish property—at least not in principle. The problem arose in applying the principle to the complexities of reality. Not even Hitler (or perhaps especially Hitler, because he shared in this faith) was quite able to overcome the confusion and frustration of these early failures.

It is in this framework as well that one finds an explanation for the breakdown of the *Fuehrerprinzip* on Jewish policy. The dispute between Schacht and the party apparatus over economic policy toward the Jews provides a dramatic illustration of this breakdown. Rather than risk making an incorrect decision and accepting the consequences, Hitler chose to risk the consequences of making no decision at all. There is no reason to believe that Hitler, had he known what to do about Jewish policy, would have shied away from doing it.

The effect of Hitler's aloof stance was the exact opposite of what the *Fuehrerprinzip* would lead one to expect. Instead of authority clearly established at the top, there was no authority at all. A decision-making vacuum rather than a decision-making authority existed at the level from which decisions had to come. Hitler did not say what should be done; only occasionally in the case of boycotts or SA excesses did he say what should not be done. And since it was inconceivable that he would ever retreat from it, the Jewish question was left open to those who thought they might find a solution. It was out of this system—or lack of system—that a solution finally did emerge, but not without bitter and drawn out struggles for control over Jewish policy.

These struggles to carve out areas of influence in the making of Jewish policy encouraged the building of personal empires or power bases from which to wage the struggle. Goebbels' attempt to bring the Ullstein holdings under the control of his Propaganda Ministry provides only one example. The continued insistence of the Streicher committee that it was competent to lead boycotts and to investigate the racial character of business firms provides another. Neither of these attempts was very successful, but by 1937 it did appear as if Goering had finally managed to bring at least the problem of Aryanization under his control. To be successful in any one of these efforts was also to take a significant step upward on the Nazi hierarchical ladder.

Use of the Jewish problem for empire building took forms other than those employed by Goebbels, Goering, or Streicher. The least harmful of those forms included the establishing of research institutes devoted to investigation of Jewish matters, largely to supply justifications for anti-Semitic propaganda and policies. Before the Third Reich collapsed in 1945 at least a half-dozen major institutes had been created. The first of these, "The Institute for History of the New Germany," was established in late 1935 under the direction of the historian and Stoecker biographer, Walter Frank. A few months later a special "Research Division for the Jewish Question" was created within Frank's institute.[1] Present for the opening ceremonies of the institute had been such party dignitaries as Deputy Fuehrer Rudolf Hess and Alfred Rosenberg, the self-styled authority on ideological matters. Hess continued to take an interest in Frank's institute and for the next years it flourished. Its Jewish Research Division sponsored annual conferences at the University in Munich at which learned papers on Jewish affairs were read and discussed, oftentimes in the approving presence of chief-patron Hess or Julius Streicher.

Alfred Rosenberg, probably out of pique at the institute's self-claimed monopoly on Jewish research, did not share Hess's enthusiasm for Frank's enterprise. An open rivalry developed between Rosenberg and Frank which became increasingly bitter during the next years. Hess's patronage, however, seemed to assure Frank's position against his jealous rival. By 1940 Frank

---

[1] Weinreich, *Hitler's Professors*, p. 46.

felt confident enough to attack Rosenberg publicly in a speech at the University of Berlin. In contrast to his own work, Frank declared, Rosenberg was no more than a "publicist."[2]

Frank failed to realize that his own position rested upon the prestige of Rudolf Hess. The consequence of his shortsightedness was made clear a year later. After Hess's spectacular flight to Scotland on an unsanctioned peace mission in May 1941, Frank's star and his institute went into rapid decline. Hess's flight was also Rosenberg's signal to move. The inauguration of his own "Institute for Research into the Jewish Question" followed in a few months. Rosenberg celebrated the opening of his own institute by announcing it to be the vanguard of the "biological world revolution."[3]

The squabbles between Frank and Rosenberg afford moments of comic relief in an otherwise tragic story. Their struggles for position in the party hierarchy are revealing to the larger story of Jewish persecutions only insofar as they are caricatures of the more important conflicts and rivalries within the Nazi world. The circumstances of Frank's decline and Rosenberg's ascent reflect the highly personal and fortuitous factors at work within the Third Reich. The position which Frank—and later Rosenberg—enjoyed rested not upon the importance of their work, but upon their favor with the Fuehrer or those in his immediate circle.

Both Frank and Rosenberg demonstrated that the Jewish question, if properly exploited, offered avenues upward in the tangled Nazi hierarchy. Research into Jewish matters lent an aura of respectability and prestige to those engaged in it. Yet the information which was collected and analyzed in the various institutes was collected for its own sake. Its value was strictly nonutilitarian. The institutes were not harnessed to purposes directly useful to the regime's efforts at finding solutions to the

2 Walter Frank, *Die deutschen Geisteswissenschaften im Kriege,* Rede gehalten am 18. Mai 1940 an der Universität Berlin (Hamburg, 1940).
3 Weinreich, *Hitler's Professors,* p. 101.

Jewish problem. Policy continued to be made without the benefit of the institutes' "experts" or their advice. Hitler himself rarely took an interest in the affairs of these empires. Their irrelevance to the larger issues of the Jewish question in no way threatened to disrupt what at any given moment was the official Jewish policy. These institutes were generated by their own energies and had to maintain themselves in the same manner. Later on, during the war, Hitler admitted that he had lost sight of these many organizations which had developed within the party. "When I find myself confronted by one or another of these achievements," he confided, "I say to myself: 'By God, how that has developed.' "[4]

The anti-Semitic scholasticism to which these research institutes were addicted did nothing to further a solution to the Jewish problem. The rational, problem-solving approach which led to the Final Solution came from quite a different element within the Nazi system. But even here, the SS and its various appendages were themselves products of the empire building so characteristic of the Third Reich. The SS had been established by Adolf Hitler when he was still a peripheral figure in the topsy-turvy political world of Weimar Germany. From a small elite corps, commissioned to be the Fuehrer's bodyguard, it developed into a massive instrument of terror and death. It became the backbone of the Nazi police state, the administrator of Auschwitz and Dachau, the principal executive agency of Nazi ideology, the biggest and most powerful of the empires which the Nazi system developed.

Development of a clearly defined Jewish policy parallels very closely the development of the SS. At the time of its founding in 1922 the SS was simply a branch of the larger SA, in effect a paramilitary unit within a parent party army. By 1938 it was beginning to establish its ascendancy over the handling of Jewish policy. During the first years of Nazi rule the SS was still more concerned with the new regime's political enemies than

4 Trevor-Roper, ed., *Hitler's Secret Conversations*, p. 167.

with its racial adversaries. Only after the political enemy had been neutralized did it allow itself more than a passing interest in the Jewish question. But then the careers of Heinrich Himmler, Reichs Leader of the SS, and his deputy, Reinhard Heydrich, became crucial to the fate of German and East European Jews.

In 1929 Hitler appointed Himmler, an undistinguished young Bavarian school teacher turned poultry farmer, to head his recently reorganized bodyguard troop. Himmler had come into the Nazi movement in the early 20's through the socialist or Strasser wing of the party. His early duties seemed commensurate with his apparent abilities. Gregor Strasser had hired Himmler to be his general assistant, reportedly because he seemed sufficiently ambitious and owned a motorbike.[5] Given the state of the NSDAP at the time, the mobility represented by the motorbike was probably as important a qualification as any ambition Himmler may have possessed.

Nothing in Himmler's background seems to point to any special ambition, to say nothing of his later role as the brutal chief of the Nazi police network. Himmler's father had once been tutor to the crown prince of Bavaria. Young Heinrich's first claim to distinction was having the crown prince as godfather. Otherwise his early years seem to have been as normal as those of any German youth growing up in the period before and during World War I. He studied for a time at an agricultural college, excellent preparation for his all-too-brief career as a fertilizer salesman. For a time he taught school before turning to poultry farming, the occupation he continued even after entering the employ of Gregor Strasser. Himmler failed to develop any fierce loyalty to his new employer, despite the fact that the job allowed him to work for the party he had joined two years earlier. The bitter feud which soon developed between Strasser and Hitler apparently affected him very little. At least he seems to have had no difficulty in transfering his loyalty to

5 Roger Manvell and Heinrich Fraenkel, *Heinrich Himmler* (London, 1965), pp. 14-15.

Hitler in 1929. Nor did he seem to suffer regrets for the part he played in Gregor Strasser's murder in 1934.[6]

Himmler was only twenty-eight years old when he became chief of the SS. During those years, however, he had acquired extremely peculiar notions regarding what he considered to be mystical bonds between race, blood, and soil. He came to devote most of his spare time to these occult racial conceits. Eventually he even considered himself a reincarnation of Henry the Fowler or Henry I, the founder of the first German Reich in the tenth century. His dizziest flights of racial fancy, however, came to be reserved for schemes devoted to purifying the Nordic race. Coupled with these schemes were visions of a mystic order of Teutonic Knights which would someday be revived to rule the world. Left to himself Himmler seemed happier contemplating the misty reaches of a racist future than the more orthodox Nazi emphasis upon Jewish inferiority.

Himmler's importance, however, does not lie in his bizarre racial ideas. As a racist philosopher his future was very limited, if only because the direction of Nazi racist thought was set by the more traditional anti-Semitism of Hitler. Himmler had other qualities which eventually made him invaluable to the party and the Reich. He was to become the cold professional policeman who possessed an almost instinctual understanding of the use of power. He also understood clearly that he was subordinate to the Fuehrer's wishes, but within the limits of this subservience he gave free reign to a ruthless ambition.

In 1931, Himmler appointed Reinhard Heydrich, then only twenty-seven, to organize a secret security branch or SD (*Sicherheitsdienst*) within the SS. Heydrich had recently been forced to resign his commission in the German navy because of some alleged improprieties with a young lady. Unlike his superior, Heydrich was a man with brilliant and varied talents. While Himmler was awkward and socially modest, Heydrich was polished and flashy, an accomplished violinst, airplane pilot,

[6] For a discussion of Himmler's early career, see Gerald Reitlinger, *The SS: Alibi of a Nation, 1922-1945* (London, 1956), pp. 14-24.

skier, and fencer. He shared with Himmler only an unbridled ruthlessness and an instinct for power.

Power did not fall into the laps of Himmler or Heydrich by default. At first the SS was overshadowed by the much larger though less disciplined SA. Not until the June 1934 purges did the SS become formally independent of the SA and emerge as the Nazi's primary instrument of terror. Himmler's personal power had been increasing steadily, however, since the Nazi seizure of power in early 1933, an increase which rested on the *Gleichschaltung* of the German police system. In the federally organized Weimar Republic the German police had been controlled by the various state governments. Establishment of a police state hinged upon replacing the federal police structures with a central or unitary police system. The prime beneficiary of this centralization was Heinrich Himmler.

The Nazi *Gleichschaltung* of the police was effected hard on the heels of the March 1933 Reichstag elections. In those states where they had previously failed to gain a parliamentary majority the Nazis were now free to act. At first the prized position of police chief in the towns or cities went usually to an especially powerful or otherwise deserving SA leader, a situation which ended abruptly with the purges of 1934. More important, though, than the regular police systems were the political police of the federal states. By early 1934 Himmler had become the chief of political police in every one of the German states except Prussia.[7]

Prussia from the very outset of Nazi rule had been largely the personal bailiwick of Hermann Goering. Goering's contribution to the Nazi terror system had been the creation of the Secret State Police or Gestapo as it came to be called. The Gestapo had been created in April 1933 to serve as Goering's personal police arm in subduing Prussia.[8] The following April,

[7] See Hans Buchheim, "Die organizatorische Entwicklung der politischen Polizei in Deutschland in den Jahren 1933 und 1934," in *Gutachten des Instituts für Zeitgeschichte* (Munich, 1958): 294-307.

[8] Jacques Delarue, *The Gestapo: A History of Horror* (New York, 1965), p. 52.

when Himmler came to Berlin as Goering's police chief, the Gestapo also came under control of the SS leader.

The organizational charts which the Nazis so fondly published in their party yearbooks do not help in tracing through this maze of interlocking police structures. In fact, they serve to obscure the actual relationships, which were determined by power and not by charts. Suffice it to say that the two most important figures were Himmler and his deputy Heydrich. The structures which they commanded were the SS and its security service or the SD, both of which were police agencies of the party, and the Gestapo, the official state secret political police. Officially Heydrich headed the SD and Gestapo, but since the SD was a branch of the SS his influence within the larger SS was extensive. He was subordinate, sometimes reluctantly, only to his chief Heinrich Himmler. Because there was no clear or consistent differentiation in function between these police agencies, no organizational chart could do justice to defining their positions in the Third Reich. Together, however, they commanded the instruments of Nazi terror.

Until 1936, unity of operations in this political police network rested in the personal command of Himmler. A Central Bureau for the States' Political Police in Berlin enabled him to coordinate the work of this very complicated structure. In June 1936, a Fuehrer decree made Himmler the head of a unified German police. The decree merely made formal what already existed in fact. Himmler was now Reichs Leader of the SS and Chief of the German Police, a title which described very accurately the empire of the one-time poultry farmer from Waldtrudering.

The SS, SD, and Gestapo rarely indulged in the emotional, *ad hoc* terrorism one associates with the SA. The SA was a mass organization, its membership open to any man willing to trade his muscle and allegiance for a uniform and a meal. More than any other Nazi agency the SA provided the avenue through which the hot-blooded discontent of the late 20's and early 30's could find expression. The SS on the other hand was the elite corps of the Nazi system and as such only the perfect specimens of Aryan manhood could aspire to membership. An SS oath demanded absolute obedience and loyalty to the Fuehrer's person. In principle as well as practice it existed to carry out the whim and will of Adolf Hitler.

As important as its commitment to anti-Semitism was the SS's engagement in the general struggle for power. To have ignored the Jewish problem would have been tantamount to surrendering a basic weapon in the arsenal available for the waging of this power struggle. Moreover, in the waging of this struggle, the SS had an incomparable advantage. In contrast to the phrasemongers such as Goebbels, Frank, or Rosenberg, the SS actually controlled the means of physical coercion. The eventual victory of force over rhetoric should occasion little surprise.

Except for Himmler, the Nazi police network wasted little rhetoric on theoretical discussions of the Jewish problem. Indeed, it tended to shy away from the endless repetitions about Jewish perversity so characteristic of the Nazi movement as a whole. Instead, the SS demonstrated a certain professional rationality in its approach to the Jewish question, a rationality which distinguished the SS from the amateur excesses of the SA and most of the party apparatus.

The SS was sizing up the Jewish problem and considering possible solutions at least as early as the beginning of 1934. In the summer of that year it issued a seven-page, secret "Situation Report—Jewish Question."[9] The report, intended for Himmler, reviewed the Jewish problem, not in the propaganda clichés used by most Nazis, but in the hard cold terms of the real situation. Within the Nazi frame of reference it was a realistic appraisal of the Jewish problem and the difficulties of effecting a practical solution.

The report pointed to an aspect of the problem which very likely had not occurred to Hitler and certainly was not entertained by the party's collection of emotional Jew-haters: since the boycott of April 1933 and the subsequent anti-Jewish legisla-

9 Lagebericht—Judenfrage, May/June 1934, Himmler File, T175 (408), 2932496 —503.

tion, a significant portion of even the Nazi-oriented public felt the Jewish question to be settled. The armchair anti-Semite, who was satisfied to see the Jew made a little more modest, could view that aim as having been achieved. Just this satisfaction, the report warned, had to be avoided. A primary task of Jewish policy would have to be, therefore, "to keep alive an awareness of the Jewish problem within the *Volk*."[10]

The report went on to assess the strengths and weaknesses of the Jewish community in Germany as well as the resources which "international Jewry" could use to bring pressure upon the Nazis. These considerations, it was pointed out, would have to play a part in Nazi plans. The danger to Germany of a boycott against her goods in a foreign market was admitted. Until she became autarkic such a boycott might force the regime to reconsider its Jewish policies. At the same time the Nazi retreat from the economic attack upon Jews which had followed the April boycott was seen to be having undesirable consequences. The business volume of Jewish-owned department stores had again risen to undesired levels after having fallen drastically in the throes of the early 1933 boycott actions. A possible foreign boycott of German goods was the more immediate danger, however. This consideration alone pointed to the need for caution in any further action.

Rather than allow itself to be immobilized on the horns of this economic dilemma, a much less dangerous solution to the Jewish problem was proposed. For the first time mention was made of organizing a massive emigration of Jews from Germany. The report did not gloss over the difficulties raised by emigration. It recognized that a vast majority of German Jews would be very unlikely to consider emigrating. But there was at least one group of Jews whom the Nazis might encourage—the Zionists. Zionists at least harbored no illusions about being both Jews and Germans. Therefore, the efforts of German Zionism to create a heightened Jewish consciousness, especially since it might promote emigration to Palestine, were applauded.

10 Ibid.

Unfortunately for the Nazis, the Zionists comprised only a small minority of the German Jewish population. Two other Jewish groups, much larger than the Zionists, felt themselves to be as much German as Jewish and were oriented toward continued assimilation. The more extreme was the small but vocal League of National German Jews (*Verband nationaldeutscher Juden*), a group whose politics was conservative and exceedingly nationalistic. Between the polar extremes of Zionism and the League was by far the largest group, the assimilation-minded Central Association of German Citizens of the Jewish Faith or *Centralverein*.

To deal effectively with these groups the report stressed the need for forging some unity between the Zionists, the League, and the *Centralverein*. The object would be to erase the intolerable attitude held by most Jews that the characteristics of Jew and German were compatible. It was recognized that a unification of these three branches of Jewry would not come about by itself. Jewish unity would have to be fashioned by the regime's Jewish policy. The report proposed that such a unity might be achieved through the B'nai B'rith. This organization with its 20,000 members contained most of German Jewry's political and intellectual leaders. Eventually, it was hoped, this leadership would be able to speak for and commit most of German Jewry to emigration.

The key to these calculations was the creation of an increased Jewish self-awareness. Jewish schools, Jewish athletic associations, Jewish cultural organizations, and all other Jewish institutions devoted to promoting this self-awareness would have to receive official Nazi encouragement. Especially to be encouraged, suggested the report, was a specifically Jewish youth movement. Jews, who through these means became more aware of their Jewishness, would have instilled within them the necessary motivation for leaving Germany.

The SS report also endorsed the occupational retraining programs being sponsored by a Central Committee of Jews for Welfare and Development and by various Zionist groups. Such programs, it was felt, could not help but facilitate resettlement in Palestine. The Palestinian economy was badly in need of agricultural workers and craftsmen. Since the social development of German Jews had virtually precluded them from entering these fields, only a rigorous training program for young people could develop these skills; hence it deserved the regime's official support. One condition upon these training programs was envisioned; they would have to be carried out with a view toward emigration. Agricultural and occupational skills in Germany were not in short supply. Competition from Jews would only aggravate an already difficult problem.

Although the report emphasized the possibilities of emigration and suggested means for encouraging it, there was no suggestion that emigration could be considered a complete remedy. The day of total solutions had not yet dawned. Many of the difficulties of emigration were correctly anticipated. Settlement in Palestine for all of Germany's half-million Jews was clearly out of the question. Palestine's capacity to absorb a massive influx of refugees was limited by its physical, political, and economic circumstances. The report also pointed out that it would be unrealistic to expect Germany's neighbors—France, Great Britain, the Netherlands—to keep their doors open permanently. But, if emigration failed Germany would have to come to terms with a permanent, if unwelcome, Jewish community. The danger of the Jewish problem becoming permanent—insoluble, in other words—was recognized. In such an event the drafters of the report foresaw that "the present intermediate state, *Zwischenzustand,* will have to be given a legal definition."[11] Among the realists in 1934—the same realists who later organized the extermination—there was a willingness to accept the continued existence of a Jewish community in Germany. How circumscribed this existence might become was left undefined.

The difficulties inherent in any mass emigration did not deter these planners from making concrete suggestions. If Palestine or Germany's European neighbors proved unable or unwilling

11 Ibid.

to accept German Jews, there were still other options available. The report spoke of "positive possibilities" connected with a scheme whereby Jews themselves might be able to negotiate with France for the purchase of 30,000 square miles of territory, about the size of Austria, in the French mandate of Syria. "If this plan takes tangible form," the report concluded, "it will contribute to a basic solution of the international emigration problem."[12]

None of the concrete schemes proposed in this "Situation Report—Jewish Question" of mid-1934 provided a satisfactory solution to the Jewish problem. The projected role of B'nai B'rith in forging a Jewish unity was never realized. Eventually, in April 1937, Himmler ordered it and all its affiliates to be dissolved.[13] The proposed retraining programs did not succeed in transforming large numbers of Jews into skilled agricultural or industrial workers. Neither did the Syrian proposal ever get anywhere in facilitating emigration.

On another level, however, the report had far-reaching consequences. Its businesslike approach to the Jewish question set the tone of nearly all subsequent SS efforts to effect some kind of solution. The dreamlike world of anti-Semitic absolutes, which moved so many in the Nazi movement to uncalculated action, was never a significant part of SS racial policy. This is not to say that the SS was less absolute in its anti-Semitism. To this the unmarked mass graves of European Jewry became a macabre witness. Unlike the party apparatus, however, the SS recognized that any solution would have to be piecemeal and based on the harsh reality that Jews would not disappear simply to satisfy an ideological imperative.

In raising the "positive possibilities" of emigration as a solution to the Jewish problem, the SS report set what was to become between 1935 and the outbreak of war in September 1939 the chief objective of its Jewish policy. During these five years the SS and Gestapo were to work almost unceasingly to effect this

12 Ibid.
13 Document AR-A #1/303/193, Leo Baeck Institute archives.

massive emigration. Not until the potential of emigration had been demonstrated in Vienna after the *Anschluss* of Austria in 1938, however, was emigration officially adopted by the regime at large as the single objective of its Jewish policy, and then only after the patent failure of less grandiosely conceived schemes such as boycotts and Aryanization had failed in their larger purposes.

The Syrian project proposed in the 1934 report was never pursued seriously. Its success would have depended upon factors over which the Nazis had little control: the willingness of Jews to organize themselves for the purchase of Syrian territory and French cooperation in selling it. Furthermore, assuming both Jewish and French cooperation, the matter of paying for the purchase of 30,000 square miles in Syria or anywhere else would have run head on into Germany's foreign exchange shortage. By most standards this idea has to be ranked among the more naive proposals forwarded during these years. None of these considerations, however, deterred Himmler from carrying the proposal for some kind of Jewish state outside of Europe to Hitler.[14]

Nothing came of Himmler's discussions with the Fuehrer. Through most of 1934 Hitler seemed willing to accept a lull in the official anti-Jewish policies of the regime. But projects similar to the Syrian one continued through the next years to capture the fancy of the SS and Gestapo. According to Arthur Prinz, a member of the Jewish *Hilfsverein,* an organization devoted to helping Jews emigrate, the Gestapo and SS were "always willing to lend support to the most criminally frivolous schemes for the Jewish mass emigration."[15] In 1936 a so-called Ecuador Project was given serious consideration. The SS learned of an offbeat Jewish emigration society in Silesia which had supposedly secured permission from the government of Ecuador for large-scale Jewish immigration into its uninhabited Oriente sector. Adolf Eichmann, at that time still a minor SD official,

14 Felix Kersten, *The Kersten Memoirs* (New York, 1957), p. 162.
15 Arthur Prinz, "The Role of the Gestapo in Obstructing and Promoting Jewish Emigration," *Yad Washem Studies* 2 (1958): 209.

summoned *Hilfsverein* leaders to his office in Berlin to discuss the scheme.[16] For a time the Nazis even toyed with the idea of deporting Jews to Madagascar, an old scheme which had begun to appear in anti-Semitic literature during the 1920's. The Madagascar project, although it was never pursued systematically, enjoyed a certain currency in top-level Nazi circles, particularly during late 1938 and early 1939.[17]

The various emigration proposals which succeeded one another were symptomatic of a general Nazi approach to the Jewish problem. There was a constant illusion harbored by most Nazis—big and small—that some dramatic measure would open the way to a complete solution of the Jewish problem. For the SA and party apparatus a boycott of Jewish activities seemed to be the key. The more sophisticated SS and Gestapo recognized that boycotts created more problems than they solved. But they too were looking for a panacea. The Syrian scheme, the Ecuador project, and finally the Madagascar plan all reflected this search.

While the SS was the first to consider the possibility of massive Jewish emigration, there was at the outset very little it could do in a formal sense to expedite the process. The competent agency in such affairs was the Reichs Emigration Office, a division of the Interior Ministry. Anyone, Jewish or not, who desired to leave Germany legally had to follow the procedures prescribed by this office. And because emigration necessarily involved a host country, these procedures had to be followed. Without the cooperation of France in the Syrian scheme, for example, it was useless to consider mass emigration. Even on a more limited scale, emigration always involved a host country which required evidence of a potential immigrant's good character, health, financial stability, and so on. As long as Hitler was interested in even a minimum measure of acceptance abroad, there was little he could do to change this situation.

16 Ibid.
17 Gerald Reitlinger, *The Final Solution: The Attempt to Exterminate the Jews of Europe, 1939-1945* (New York, 1961), pp. 76-79.

While the Reichs Emigration Office was still in control, says Arthur Prinz, Jewish emigration proceeded with some concern for both the person and the substance of legality.[18] The concern was for an orderly emigration. It had to conform to the requirements of the country of destination. This meant that antisocial elements were excluded, property transfers had to be legal, and all other documents had to be in order. Such a process was inevitably tedious and time consuming and oftentimes fruitless. It seemed to offer no prospect for a *judenrein* Germany. Impatience with this process may well have inspired SS interest in Syria, Ecuador, or Madagascar as sites for a wholesale Jewish deportation. Impatience also made the SS eager to gain some measure of control over the emigration process itself.

All plans for promoting emigration, no matter how elaborate, could not escape the realities which made emigration especially difficult during the 1930's. The most immediate obstacle was the worldwide economic depression. European governments as well as those overseas, caught up in the problems of providing work for their own unemployed, were hardly willing to open their doors to an influx of immigrants. In the United States, once a haven for European emigrants, two acts of Congress in the 1920's had greatly curtailed the influx of foreigners. Following the 1929 crash, a Presidential order provided that immigrant visas be given only to people not likely to become public charges.[19] Similar obstacles were being erected in most other countries.

A second barrier was the occupational and class background of most German Jews. Some countries such as Brazil or Argentina would have welcomed an influx of farm laborers, craftsmen, or skilled industrial workers. For historical reasons Germany's Jews were mostly middle-class business or professional people. The occupational retraining sponsored by Zionist agencies and

18 Prinz, "Role of the Gestapo," p. 207.
19 Marion T. Bennett, *American Immigration Policies: A History* (Washington, D.C., 1963), p. 66.

Jewish welfare organizations was too late to meet this immediate demand. American consulates in Germany also discouraged emigration to the United States by pointing out that a German-trained doctor or lawyer would not be able to practice in his new foreign setting.[20]

In the area of occupational retraining the SS policy was consistent from the outset. Following the situation report of 1934 the SS and Gestapo kept a very close surveillance on all retraining programs. Attempts to keep abreast of these programs along with the number of people being retrained was one of Himmler's constant concerns. His awareness of their importance in promoting an eventual solution to the Jewish problem always led him to ask the decisive question: "Is retraining being undertaken to promote emigration or to provide a livelihood while staying in Germany?"[21]

The age distribution of German Jewry was yet another factor which limited prospects for wholesale emigration. Better than 35 percent of the German Jewish population was more than 50 years old. In 1933 about ten percent of this population was over 65; by 1938 this percentage had almost doubled. During these five years the over-65 category had risen from 52,000 to over 74,000.[22] Not only was emigration psychologically more difficult for these growing numbers of older people, but their prospects for taking up a new life in a foreign country, unless they were relatively wealthy, were severely circumscribed.

Even these obstacles might have been surmountable if international Jewish welfare agencies had been able to concentrate their limited resources on the problem in Germany. But the situation there was only part of a larger, general problem which presented itself throughout eastern Europe. In reaction to a growing anti-Semitism in Poland, for example, about 100,000 Jews were emigrating annually after 1933. Emigration on a

[20] Hermann Graml, "Die Auswanderung der Juden aus Deutschland zwischen 1933 und 1939," *Gutachten des Instituts für Zeitgeschicte* (Munich, 1958), p. 83.

[21] *Himmler File*, T175 (280), 2774225. Gestapo order of July 5, 1935.

[22] See *Zur Evian Konferenz*, a mimeographed report of the Reichsvertretung, Berlin, 1938.

similar scale from Germany would have made her free of Jews by 1939. Anti-Semitic policies in Latvia, Lithuania, Rumania, and Hungary also led to massive waves of Jewish emigrants. Most of these east European Jews, it seemed, were more badly in need of financial assistance from the outside than were those in Germany.[23]

In many respects, though, the most basic impediment to emigration was the deep attachment most German Jews felt for their country. Germany was their fatherland. The Jewish emancipation in Germany had coincided with the developing nationalism of the nineteenth century. Jews had shared in Germany's growth and died in her defense in World War I. Their deepest political allegiance was to Germany. To leave would be to break irrevocably the bonds of that allegiance. In their own image they were German and all of Hitler's fulminations could not shake the foundations of that self-image. Hitler's attacks were vicious, but they were also patent nonsense. Given a choice between staying in Germany or accepting the insecurities of emigration, most of them preferred to stay in Germany. Germany at least was home.

The hope that "all this Hitler business" would end the way of a bad dream undoubtedly shaped much of their thinking. In the meantime they would have to ride out the storm, as Jews had ridden out other storms in their history. Indeed, after the initial shock of 1933, there were those who thought the storm was past. Could not Goering's own favorite proverb that the soup is never eaten as hot as it is cooked be applied to this situation? Some Jewish leaders began insisting in 1934 that relief funds should be used to strengthen the Jewish position in Germany rather than for furthering emigration.[24]

The apparent lull in official anti-Jewish activity after the boycott and non-Aryan legislation of April 1933 strengthened the hopes of many Jews. Thousands of them had fled Germany

[23] Graml, "Die Auswanderung," pp. 79-85.

[24] Kurt R. Grossmann, "Zionists and Non-Zionists under Nazi Rule in the 1930's," in *Herzl Year Book* 4 (1961-1962), pp. 329-344.

in the wake of the Nazi seizure of power. Most of these had left illegally without passports, visas, or the appropriate documents necessary to begin life abroad. Without these papers the opportunities for finding employment were almost nil. They had left home without making arrangements for transferring their savings or selling their properties. By mid-1933 when the immediate panic attending the *Machtergreifung* had subsided, return to Germany seemed preferable to loneliness and insecurity abroad. Indications that the Aryan paragraph would not be applied to commercial activities made return appear more promising. Perhaps the Nazis were beginning to retreat from at least the most radical position in racial matters. During the latter part of 1933 and most of 1934 many Jews who had fled earlier gradually began to trickle back to Germany. They had no way of knowing that the lull upon which they pinned their hopes stemmed more from Nazi confusion than it did from policy.

Jewish optimism regarding the possibility of a separate and autonomous existence developed in this climate of Nazi confusion. The efforts in 1933 and 1934 to establish some kind of legal recognition for a separate Jewish community provide a revealing insight into how the Nazi system worked and the different directions in which it pulled. The first initiatives came from the Jewish side. In April 1933, an organization of anti-Zionist Jews headed by Hans Joachim Schoeps sought to protect the rights of German Jews. Schoeps' organization, the *Deutscher Vortrupp Gefolgschaft deutscher Juden,* was an outgrowth of the German Youth Movement and therefore heavily influenced by *völkisch* ideas. It considered Jews to be part of the German *Volk* in the same manner that Saxons or Bavarians might make such claim.[25] As such it believed itself to be in a better position than the Zionists to win concessions from the Nazis.[26] For one

25 George L. Mosse, "The Influence of the *Völkisch* Idea on German Jewry," *Studies of the Leo Baeck Institute* (New York, 1967), pp. 107-108.

26 Hans Joachim Schoeps, *Die letzten dreissig Jahre: Rückblicke* (Stuttgart, 1956), pp. 97-98.

thing it conceded that Jews were overrepresented in certain professions and branches of commerce. To overcome this disparity the *Vortrupp* encouraged large numbers of young Jews to enter agricultural and craft occupations. If this program produced results, much of the wind would be taken out of anti-Semitism's propaganda sails. Schoeps had something more immediate in mind as well. Together with his friends he prepared a memorandum for Hitler suggesting that German Jewry be given status as a legal entity in the corporate (*ständisch*) development of the Third Reich.

This memorandum was submitted to the Reichs Chancellory together with a request by Schoeps for a personal interview with Hitler. Schoeps received what he has described as a polite reply from Hitler's office, saying that because of a heavy schedule the Fuehrer would be unable to receive him.[27] More than likely Hitler never saw the memorandum. Schoeps tried to reach Hitler again, this time through Vice-Chancellor von Papen and Reichsbank president Schacht. The only satisfaction he received was word that his "constructive suggestion" was being discussed in the Interior Ministry.

Hopes for some kind of official recognition for Jewish autonomy were resurrected once more in late 1934. More important, this time the initiative seemed to come from the Nazi side. An article in the *Europäische Revue* by Hans Friedrich Blunk, the head of Goebbels' Chamber of Literature and presumably an authoritative source, mentioned the possibility of a concordat between the government and the Jews.[28] At the moment prospects for such an arrangement were limited, Blunk wrote, because of foreign interference in German affairs. The implications seemed fairly clear: if Jews would stop defaming Germany the government would give the concordat serious attention. What lay behind Blunk's article was never made clear. If it was

[27] Ibid.
[28] Hans Lamm, *Über die innere und äussere Entwicklung des deutschen Judentums im Dritten Reich,"* unpublished Ph.D. dissertation, University of Erlangen, 1951, p. 47.

a trial balloon, Nazi authorities failed to respond to expressions of interest from both the major Jewish newspapers, the *Jüdische Rundschau* and the *Central Verein Zeitung*.[29]

The idea of a concordat died in circumstances as obscure as those in which it was born. It was not part of the Nazi tactic to deal with Jews through such circumspect techniques as trial balloons. Nor is there any reason to believe that Hitler might have considered signing an agreement singling out Jews for special protection. For a time the Nuremberg Laws revived such hopes, but subsequent actions, especially in 1938, dashed them once and for all. Was Blunk, then, acting on his own, perhaps trying to enhance his own position by using the Jewish issue? This would have placed him in good company. Or was he acting for Goebbels who certainly was eager to build his own power base? The possibility that Blunk was seriously offering his own solution to the Jewish problem cannot be dismissed either.

The SS situation report of 1934 obviously represented an entirely different stream of thinking. Anything which might encourage Jews to stay in Germany had to be avoided. The emphasis was to be on emigration. Therefore, it was necessary to rebuild what was thought to be the diminishing anti-Jewish awareness and to facilitate, through occupational retraining, the process of emigration. If this attitude was ever to establish itself as the primary force molding Jewish policy, the hope of Jews for a separate minority status would be gone.

The establishment of SS primacy in directing racial policy is one of the main threads of continuity in the history of the Nazi persecutions of Jews. The task of establishing that primacy was not so simple as it may appear in retrospect. There were other powerful competitors for control over Jewish policy. Hitler did not give formal sanction to SS actions until it had managed several marked successes. Even the implications of these successes bothered Hitler at times and forced the SS into temporary retreat.

29 The *Jüdische Rundschau* on January 1, 1935; the *Central Verein Zeitung* on January 4, 1935.

The businesslike approach of the SS was oddly enough one of the first obstacles to its success. In calling for the encouragement of Zionist activities, it was also asking that some Jews be treated more leniently than others. Preferential treatment for Jews of any sort was bound to meet resistance at many levels in the Nazi movement. In the highly charged climate of anti-Jewish emotions such realism opened the SS to the charge that it might be soft on race issues. During the first months of Nazi rule the impulse was clearly in the direction of boycotts and pogroms. For years Hitler had lumped all Jews together in the same dirty pot. The time had come for them to stew in that pot. This attitude prevailed through the first years of Nazi rule. Most of the confusion and resentment over Jewish policy arose over the fact that anti-Jewish practice did not always conform to the clear-cut expectations of the most radical racists.

The universal nature of the early anti-Jewish actions reflected these extreme attitudes. The boycotts, the legislation, the SA in its excesses, the private initiatives from the lower party ranks all denied that some Jews were different than others. Through most of 1933, therefore, the tendency was to treat all Jews and all Jewish organizations alike. Zionists and non-Zionists, teachers, and shopkeepers, lawyers, and actors all suffered in these first convulsions of the Third Reich's anti-Semitism. Perhaps because Zionists asserted their Jewishness more openly they were a particularly desirable target. In any event the offices of the German Zionist Federation in Berlin were ransacked by the SA in April 1933.[30] During the next weeks similar incidents took place in other German cities. These incidents were sandwiched between hundreds of outrages and probably had no special meaning for the SA. Zionists were Jews; no more, no less. In July 1933, they suffered from the same general proscription placed on the activities of most Jewish organizations.[31] That

[30] Rosenbluth, *Go Forth and Serve,* pp. 247-250.

[31] See Hans Mommsen, "Dokumentation: Der nationalsozialistische Polizeistaat und die Judenverfolgung vor 1938," *Vierteljahrshefte für Zeitgeschichte* 10 (January 1962): 77-78.

some of these organizations could be used to further Nazi aims had not yet occurred to anyone.

By early 1934, however, it had occurred to the SS. The re-thinking of Jewish policy which followed in the wake of the 1933 failures raised doubts about the wisdom of banning the activity of all Jewish organizations. On March 20, 1934, shortly after Reinhard Heydrich took control of the Bavarian Political Police,[32] the original ban was lifted. Jewish organizations, as long as they did not engage in politics, were to be allowed an area of activity under the watchful eye of the political police.[33]

Heydrich's order allowed groups which contributed to the strengthening of Jewish self-awareness to resume their activities. Spelled out were several Jewish veteran organizations and especially Jewish youth associations. No special mention was made yet of Zionist organizations, but that came a few months later in the Situation Report. Even the police network of Himmler and Heydrich seemed to be backing into this new direction rather than approaching it head on. Doubts about making this new policy effective, if not about the efficacy of treating some Jews better than others, had not been entirely overcome. Policy proposals were one thing; actual policy something else. Hence the need for implementing these changes quietly and, if possible, secretly was underlined.[34]

By early 1935 the initial caution had been overcome. Henceforth the SS, and therefore the Gestapo, were clearly in the business of encouraging Zionist activities—with the proviso that these activities would foster emigration. A directive of January 28 mentioned for the first time that Jewish organizations sponsoring occupational retraining in order to prepare Jews for emigration were acting in line with the interests of the Third Reich. Furthermore, "Zionist groups which are encouraging emigration are not to be handled with the same severity as is

32 The Bavarian Political Police had been created in March 1933, and in the following month came under the command of Heinrich Himmler. It was part of the unified police network Himmler was creating.

33 Mommsen, "Dokumentation," p. 77.

34 Ibid., p. 80.

necessarily accorded to members of the so-called German Jewish assimilation-minded organizations."[35] No mention was made yet of giving these groups any more substantial encouragement.

The implementing of this policy took various forms. Himmler took an active interest in the occupational retraining programs. Throughout the spring and summer of 1935, Zionist speakers and lecturers once again began receiving permission from the police to address public gatherings.[36] The formula, repeated in countless orders granting such permission, was the same, for example: "The ban is lifted because Lubinski has shown himself to be an avowed partisan of Zionist ideas and has committed himself to tireless propagation of Jewish emigration."[37]

At the same time efforts to silence the propaganda of Jewish groups which favored staying in Germany was intensified. For the SS at least, emigration had become the solution to the Jewish question. An order of April 1935 reflected this position: "The attempts of German-Jewish organizations to persuade Jews to remain in Germany is . . . in direct contradiction to National Socialist principles and must, therefore, be prevented in any form . . . Especially the Jewish newspapers must be watched closely to see that the more subtle forms of this propaganda are not spread about."[38]

A month later the last reason for secrecy about the new policy had apparently disappeared. In an article on May 15, Heydrich made public what a year earlier had been contained in the highly secret report to SS Chief Himmler. The article, entitled "The Visible Enemy" and published in *Das Schwarze Korps*, the official SS journal, announced the position of the SS.

> After the Nazi seizure of power our racial laws did in fact curtail considerably the immediate influence of Jews. But the Jew in his tenacity has seen this merely as a temporary restriction. The

---

[35] Ibid., pp. 78-79.
[36] Schumacher Archiv, Folder 240 I, BDC.
[37] Mommsen, "Dokumentation," p. 83.
[38] Schumacher Archiv, Folder 240 I, BDC.

question as he sees it is still: How can we win back our old position and once again work to the detriment of Germany?

But we must separate Jewry into two categories according to the way in which they operate: those who work openly as Jews and those who hide behind international Jewish welfare agencies and the like.

The Jews in Germany fall into two groups: the Zionists and those who favor being assimilated. The Zionists adhere to a strict racial position and by emigrating to Palestine they are helping to build their own Jewish state. The assimilation-minded Jews deny their race and insist on their loyalty to Germany or claim to be Christians, because they have been baptized, in order to overthrow National Socialist principles.[39]

Mere encouragement did not make emigration on the massive scale desired by the SS or Gestapo any more feasible. The renewed wave of boycotts and general terrorization of Jews in early 1935, while it demonstrated that the "anti-Semitic *Volkswille*" was still alive, served only to undermine SS policy. Zionist and assimilation-minded groups suffered equally from these anti-Jewish assaults. The distinctions between the two escaped the rabidly anti-Semitic SA and party apparatus most directly responsible for the new terror. To them all Jews were alike. To favor one group over the other, even for tactical reasons, seemed to deny the basis of Nazi racial doctrine.

Then, too, as long as an emigrant had to go through the regular channels in the Interior Ministry, he remained outside the specific authority of the Nazi police network. Left to itself, the Reich Office of Emigration was bound to proceed legally and in an orderly manner. It was staffed by civil servants who were, according to Prinz, "extremely accommodating and did everything to make our work [in the *Hilfsverein*] easier."[40] Emigration organized in this fashion could never lead to the type of solution envisioned by the SS or Gestapo. It demanded respect for the laws and requirements of the country of destination.

[39] *Das Schwarze Korps*, May 15, 1935.
[40] Prinz, "Role of the Gestapo," p. 206.

Passports, visas, statements of character and financial backing had to be in order and above all conform to the realities of the situation. Any misrepresentation or falsification of documents would quickly work to prejudice the cause of emigration—for Jews or anyone else—from Germany. These terms immediately made certain people ineligible for emigration, especially the aged, the poor, or those whose character was unsatisfactory. Perhaps for this reason the SS, which was actually thinking more in terms of expulsion than emigration, was so attracted to the extravagant Syrian or Ecuadorian schemes.

From the outset one of the most stubborn obstacles to emigration was Germany's economic position. To be accepted abroad the emigrant had to take some of his capital with him. Evidence of his ability to support himself was one of the first requirements any foreign country made. Yet Germany's foreign currency problems made the transfer of capital almost impossible. Without being able to take at least a significant share of his capital with him, a potential emigrant was discouraged from emigrating at all. An individual leaving Germany in 1933 was entitled to take with him only RM 200 in foreign currency. By 1937 that figure had been reduced to RM 10.[41] Most of his property was classified as "nontransferable" by the Reich and placed into a special nontransferable account or *Sperrkonto*. In addition the special emigration tax, *Reichsfluchtsteuer,* already imposed in the Weimar period by the Bruening government, was raised by the Nazis in May 1934 to prevent, said the *Voelkischer Beobachter,* wealthy Jews from "transferring their millions—perhaps billions—abroad." Jews who fled illegally in the 1933 panic, the same paper complained, escaped their tax duties and through "Jewish financial profiteering" had already cost the Reich RM 400 million.[42] The new stipulations made emigration for the middle-class Jew almost impossible. An emigrant whose capital exceeded RM 50,000 or had an annual income exceeding

41 Mark Wischnitzer, "Jewish Emigration from Germany, 1933-1938," *Jewish Social Studies* 2 (1940): 23-45.

42 *Voelkischer Beobachter,* May 9, 1935.

RM 20,000 was forced to pay an emigration tax of 25 percent. The remaining 75 percent was deposited in the *Sperrkonto*.[43] Until some solution was found to resolve this economic dilemma, it was unrealistic to expect large-scale and voluntary Jewish emigration.

The SS policy of granting Zionist groups a freer rein raised problems of its own. To Zionists, Palestine was obviously the most desirable destination. But Palestine, since the World War, had also become a pawn in the political conflicts of the Near East. On the basis of its 1917 Balfour Declaration, Britain had committed itself to establishing Palestine as a Jewish "national home."[44] After the war Palestine had been assigned to Britain as a mandate of the League of Nations. Britain, as holder of the Palestinian mandate, was made responsible for supervising its development. During the 1920's a small but steady flow of Jewish settlers arrived, largely from eastern Europe. Since these early immigrants did not in most cases bring much capital with them, Palestine remained an underdeveloped agricultural region. Still, in the absence of any major crisis, Palestine's capacity to absorb Jewish immigrants appeared adequate.

Palestine's situation was changed drastically with the onset of worldwide depression. The Depression and the anti-Semitic measures of numerous European governments brought a significant increase in the number of Jews seeking refuge in Palestine. This increase in turn aggravated the simmering conflict between Palestinian Arabs and the Jews. In 1931, consequently, the British government announced that immigration would henceforth be limited by Palestine's economic capacity to absorb new settlers.[45] Admission to Palestine came to be selective, based on principles agreed to by the British government and the Jewish Agency, the quasi-government representing Palestine's Jews.[46] The most desirable immigrants, in recognition of Palestine's

---

[43] Prinz, "Role of the Gestapo," p. 207.

[44] Leonard Stein, *The Balfour Declaration* (New York, 1961), p. 664.

[45] Arieh Tartakower and Kurt R. Grossmann, *The Jewish Refugee* (New York, 1944), p. 57.

[46] Ibid., pp. 57-59.

need for persons of independent means, became the independently wealthy, the professional man, and the skilled craftsman or worker. Anyone likely to become a public charge was considered ineligible. There was nothing unique, of course, about these requirements. Governments throughout the world were adopting similar measures. But this new situation made Palestine uniquely unprepared to meet the emergency in Judaism brought on by Hitler's seizure of power in Germany.

German efforts to ease her own foreign currency shortage brought the first small break in Palestine's immigration restrictions. Not surprisingly, Palestine had been among the first to protest Nazism's early Jewish policies with a boycott on the importing of German goods. That such boycotts worried the Reich's economic officials became evident very quickly. Not only did they pressure the regime into ending its own Jewish boycott; they also forced it to begin looking for ways to expand the volume of Germany's foreign trade. The recognition by Palestinian authorities and the German government that they shared certain interests led in September 1933 to the so-called Haavara agreement.[47] Under Haavara's terms German Jews who were emigrating to Palestine deposited their assets in the *Sperrkonto* accounts which remained in Germany. Whenever Palestine bought German goods, it had to pay only 50 percent of the total price in its own foreign exchange. The remaining 50 percent was taken from the blocked assets of German Jews who had emigrated to Palestine. Upon his arrival in Palestine the Jewish immigrant was paid half the value of his blocked account in Germany by the Haavara trust company. Palestine's saving in foreign exchange was in effect passed on to the newly arrived immigrant. At least he recovered part of what he would otherwise have been forced to leave in Germany.

On the German side Haavara had been negotiated by the Economics Ministry and the Reich Authority for Foreign Currency Control. Schacht at the Reichsbank had been especially

[47] Ernst Marcus, "The German Foreign Office and the Palestine Question in the Period 1933-1939," *Yad Washem Studies* 2 (1958): 182.

eager to have the agreement effected. Increased export to Palestine, he emphasized, would help to ease Germany's foreign exchange shortage. Palestine's Jews on the other hand stood to benefit by the fact that emigration from Germany was being facilitated. The Haavara arrangements remained in effect until November 1938, the time of the *Kristallnacht* pogrom. During its lifetime the emigration of an estimated 45,000 German Jews to Palestine was facilitated by its terms.[48] A Haavara official also estimated that through this elaborate process around RM 94 million of German Jewish capital was transferred to Palestine.[49]

The effects of Haavara were felt in 1934 when Palestine emerged as the primary destination of Jews who left Germany. More than one-third or 8,500 of the 23,000 Jewish emigrants went to Palestine.[50] The year before only about one-fifth of the total emigrants had chosen Palestine. Most emigrants—nearly three out of four—had gone to countries in western Europe. Reasons for this European preference are not difficult to ascertain. Admission, if not the permission to work, was relatively easy to obtain. The expense of emigration was minimal. Moreover, return to Germany from points in Europe would be easiest once Nazi madness had subsided.[51] Perhaps most important of all was the fact that German Jews, themselves European, would find other European countries more to their liking. Palestine, after all, offered very few of the economic or cultural embellishments of European life.

By 1934, however, many European countries had begun to raise barriers to immigration. No more than 8,000 found entry into countries on the continent. Another five or six thousand went overseas to areas other than Palestine. The increase in the number going to Palestine reflected both the successful activity of Zionist organizations and the working of Haavara. For the

[48] Rosenstock, "Exodus 1933-1939," pp. 373-390.
[49] Werner Feilchenfeld, *Five Years of Jewish Emigration from Germany and the Haavara Transfer, 1933-1938* (Tel-Aviv, 1938), p. 6.
[50] Rosenstock, "Exodus 1933-1939," p. 380.
[51] Ibid.

next several years the annual rate of Jewish emigration to Palestine remained at about 8,000.

The disturbing factor for Nazis who were eager to see Jews leave Germany was the fact that only the annual rate to Palestine was held at a consistent level. Even the figure of 23,000 Jewish emigrants for 1934 represented a decline of 14,000 from the previous year. In fact, the 1933 total of 37,000 was never reached again. The decrease in 1934 can probably be explained by the reduction of Nazi terrorism and by the upsurge in the German economy following Hitler's announcement of German rearmament.[52]

In all, an estimated 150,000 Jews left Germany between 1933 and the end of 1938. (See Table 7.) The almost consistent an-

TABLE 7. JEWISH EMIGRATION FROM GERMANY, 1933-1938

Year	Number of Emigrants	Total Since 1933
1933	37,000	37,000
1934	23,000	60,000
1935	21,000	81,000
1936	25,000	106,000
1937	23,000	129,000
1938	20,000	149,000

nual decline was a major disappointment to Nazi proponents of emigration. It pointed also to some of the obstacles which confronted emigration in general. Emigration administered by the Reich Office of Emigration was of necessity limited to those who could meet the requirements of the law. With each succeeding year the potential number of such people declined. The young, the Zionists, the relatively well-to-do, those best equipped to take up a new life abroad were generally the first to leave. Those who remained behind tended to be, because of age, lack of wealth or skills, less able to endure the hardships of emigration. In 1938, of the 350,000 or so Jews who had stayed, over half

52 See "Verschiedene Informationen über die jüdische Situation in Berlin in den Jahren von 1933 bis 1940," Document #01/226, Yad Washem archives.

were more than forty-five years old, past the age when emigration is easily undertaken.[53] Then, too, the apparently inconsistent attitude of the regime toward Jewish persecutions served to encourage many Jews who resisted the thought of emigration. Even such weak signals as Blunk's hint of a concordat-like solution strengthened these attitudes. Hitler's announcement after the Nuremberg Laws that the Jewish question could be considered settled undoubtedly had an even more important effect. The "Jewish Section" of the SD complained that "first in the middle of 1937 did Jewish organizations begin to generally abandon their own goals and accept the idea that emigration was probably necessary."[54]

The steady decline in the rate of Jewish emigration demonstrated the need for new and more drastic approaches to the problem. The need was not merely for convincing Jews that emigration was necessary. Until the process of emigration itself was revised there was little hope for improvement. Despite their encouragement of Zionist programs, the SS and Gestapo were not equipped at the outset to deal with the many bureaucratic, political, economic, and social problems of emigration. To wield decisive influence these aspects of Jewish policy would have to come under their own administration. Neither the SS or Gestapo had been created for such a purpose.

As far as the Gestapo was concerned, its first sally into Jewish affairs had no connection with emigration. Its purpose as a political police was to ferret out the new regime's political enemies. Because he was a racial enemy, the Jew figured only incidentally in the Gestapo's immediate concerns. Just how incidentally was made clear when shortly after its birth in April 1933 the Gestapo made its first foray into the area of Jewish policy. In July, Gestapo headquarters in Berlin ordered its local units to make a list of all Jewish political organizations and lodges, or any

53 *Zur Evian Konferenz*, p. 28.
54 Himmler File, T175 (411), 2936220. From a Gestapo report on the Jewish situation in Germany. Although undated, the report was probably made in late 1938.

Jewish individuals—German or Jewish—who had ever been active politically.[55] The object was to uncover signs of Marxist activity. It was a fruitless search. The number of Marxists who used Jewish organizations as fronts for subversive activity was very small. The attempt was indicative, however, of the type of mentality which made later and more important projects possible.

The SS engaged in similar projects. To foster the biological separation of Jews and Aryans, its Race and Resettlement Office began very early to compile lists of specifically Jewish names. The assimilation of Jews into German culture had obscured the differences between many Jewish and Aryan names. The result of this effort was eventually a *Judenliste* or "Jewish List" as it came to be called, which was made available to any German official concerned with untangling the intermingled races. To help the official, each name was traced to the time and place where it had first appeared in Germany. By mid-1938 a mimeographed volume of about 175 pages listing well over 5,000 Jewish names was prepared—"for official use only."[56]

These initial efforts were hardly the stuff of which solutions to the Jewish problem were made. Neither the collecting of card files nor even the Ecuador scheme offered much promise in that direction. The SD was convinced that the preparatory work for an organized attack on Jews was hindered by a lack of coordination and a dearth of people who were specialists in Jewish affairs.[57] What was needed was more information on Jewish matters and more trained personnel to deal with that information. Overlapping jurisdictions and general incompetence imposed upon a lack of understanding had left Jewish policy open to the amateurs. The consequence had been one failure after another. If emigration was to succeed, experts were required.

In 1934, a young Austrian, Adolf Eichmann, took a lowly job at the rank of *Scharfuehrer* or sergeant in Reinhard Heydrich's

[55] *Dokumente Frankfurter Juden*, p. 338.
[56] A copy of this *Judenliste* is available at the Wiener Library in London.
[57] Himmler File, T175 (410), 2934988.

SD. Heydrich put him to work in the SD's Freemason Archive section, preparing index cards on prominent German Freemasons. The task seemed appropriate for someone with Eichmann's demonstrated abilities. He had not distinguished himself in any of his earlier jobs. A year before joining the SD he had been dismissed from the employ of an oil company.[58] But Eichmann was intelligent. He used his time well. His work on the international character of the Freemasons brought him into contact with the Jewish question. Soon he began to enjoy a certain reputation as a Jewish specialist as well. The mere fact that he attempted to acquaint himself with a few writers and other elements of Jewish culture qualified him for this role. Within Nazi circles there were very few who knew anything about the Jews, their history, their culture, or their development. To date Nazi anti-Semitism, when it did not manifest itself in street brawls and boycotts, had been largely a matter of interpretations of the text provided by Hitler. In such undistinguished surroundings it was easy for an Eichmann to stand out, especially if he also displayed some talent for organization. The latter quality, along with his "expertise," brought him to the attention of his superiors.

In late 1935, when Heinrich Himmler urged the SD to establish a Jewish museum, Eichmann was picked to head the section in charge of collecting Jewish cultural objects and literature. During the next year Eichmann familiarized himself with Jewish history and especially the Zionist movement. He even picked up a smattering of Yiddish and a few words of Hebrew. From these small beginnings fantastic legends of Eichmann's fluency in Hebrew and expertise in all aspects of Judaism were to grow. These accounts greatly exaggerated his knowledge, but they did distinguish him from his less informed colleagues.

When the SD accorded Jewish affairs their own section or *Referat*—Section II 112—in the fall of 1936, Eichmann was

---

58 For a sketch of Eichmann's pre-Nazi career see Robert Pendorf, *Mörder und Ermordete, Eichmann und die Judenpolitik des Dritten Reiches* (Hamburg, 1961), pp. 24ff.

placed second in command. In this post he demonstrated another ability which was to be essential to further promotion: the ability to keep quiet, not to test the patience of his superiors. His section chief, Leopold von Mildenstein, did not share this ability. SD chief Heydrich was keeping extremely close tabs on the work of Section II 112 and quickly became disenchanted with Mildenstein's behavior. Mildenstein fancied himself the Jewish expert and was one of the vocal exponents of solving the Jewish problem through emigration. He bombarded SD headquarters with appeals for organizing the rapid emigration of Jews. Eichmann, too, was impressed by numerous emigration plans, but he did not join in Mildenstein's appeals to headquarters. Heydrich failed to appreciate the enthusiastic meddling of his subordinate in the Jewish Section and Mildenstein was replaced. The new head of the Jewish Section was Herbert Hagen. Eichmann in the switchover was appointed the official "Specialist for Zionism."

In 1937 Eichmann took several dramatic steps upward on the bureaucratic ladder. This began when the functions of SD Section II 112 were clarified and expanded. Himmler had decided in July that it should be delegated responsibility for "general and fundamental aspects of the Jewish question" within the Nazi police system.[59] The investigation of political crimes and the measures to deal with them were purely the province of Gestapo Section II B4. The lack of coordination of which both Gestapo and SD officials had once complained, it was assumed, would be overcome by this organizational shift. "After this order," Eichmann reported, "theoretical work took second place to practical considerations. Also our concern was enlarged to cover not only Jews in Germany, but also international Jewry."[60] The practical concern to which he was referring was the organization of Jewish emigration.

During the next few months Eichmann's section worked feverishly to come up with a practical plan to make massive emi-

59 Himmler File, T175 (410), 2934988-89.
60 Ibid.

gration possible. Eichmann himself submitted numerous detailed reports on his work to his superiors. The obstacles, as he
saw them, were imposing. The majority of Jews had still not
been convinced that emigration was necessary. Furthermore,
the economic attack upon German Jews had left many of them
too poor to leave Germany. To overcome these problems it
would be essential to convince Jews that emigration was necessary and to find financial support somehow for the penniless.
Eichmann hoped that the cooperating Jewish Sections of the SD
and Gestapo would find the means to implement a successful
emigration policy. Section II 112 of the SD, he reported, after
Himmler's orders had taken effect:

> will maintain direct contact with leading Gestapo officials by in-
> viting them to participate in SD deliberations. . . . through regular
> meetings with the leaders of Jewish organizations attempts will be
> made to organize our whole Jewish policy so that especially the
> emigration of the penniless Jews will be fostered and strengthened.
> The whole object of this is the centralization of the entire work
> on the Jewish question in the hands of the SD and Gestapo.[61]

To make foreign countries more receptive to accepting the
Jews, Eichmann recommended also that the Nazi's anti-Semitic
propaganda abroad be toned down. Such propaganda, he
pointed out, served only to defeat the cause of emigration by
making Jews that much more undesirable to countries which
might accept them.

The united SD-Gestapo front which Eichmann expected
would solicit the cooperation of Jewish leaders never became
very effective. Then, too, neither SD nor Gestapo had as yet
managed to gain control over the emigration process. The Reich
Emigration Office was still in formal control of emigration,
although it was functioning under severe pressures from both
the SD and Gestapo. These pressures understandably worked to
confuse the emigration process. To Jewish leaders it appeared
that the Nazi attitude to emigration was "inconsistent, unclear,

---

[61] Himmler File, T175 (410), 2934989-90.

and torn between two opposing trends,"[62] precisely the appearance Eichmann was trying to overcome. But until emigration was entirely in the hands of the SD such confusion was likely to remain.

Most of these problems Eichmann took into account in the plan he drafted in late 1937 for the coordinated emigration of German Jewry.[63] Emigration, he stressed, would have to be carried out with ruthless energy. This energy had to be channeled and directed, however. Initiatives in Jewish policy from other Nazi agencies, and especially any initiatives related to emigration, had to come to an end. Eichmann was worried also that the upswing in the Aryanization of Jewish business—with which his SD had nothing to do—might make it impossible for Jewry to finance its own emigration. A more realistic aim for the Nazi state would be to assure that Jews were not completely pauperized. To make full-scale emigration possible, Eichmann recommended:

> The founding of a Jewish central organization to take over Jewish welfare. That way the poorer Jews would not become dependent upon the German state. (Principle: The rich Jews have to care for the poor ones.)
>
> Steps on another measure, the creation of a central organization to promote emigration, are already being taken. The purpose of this organization is to bring some uniformity to emigration. Here, too, the rich Jew is to provide the money the poor Jew needs for emigration.[64]

Eichmann hoped that the SD would have considerable influence in both the central Jewish organization and especially in the body which would organize emigration. To assure this influence (and his own), he noted that the SD had to:

1. watch very carefully the activities of once influential Jews,
2. watch the most dangerous Jews to prevent assassination attempts (on high level Nazis),

62 Prinz, "Role of the Gestapo," 208.
63 Himmler File, T175 (280), 2774476-77.
64 Ibid.

3. watch to see if dangerous Jews attempted to organize,
4. watch the activities of the central Jewish organization to
   see:
   a. are poor Jews actually receiving welfare?
   b. for what purpose are they receiving it?
   c. how are rich Jews reacting to this situation?[65]

The creation of large Jewish ghettos, Eichmann concluded, was not envisioned. Such ghettos would merely "provide cover for swindlers and all kinds of rabble." Nothing stood in the way of smaller ghettos, though; eventually "Jewish houses and villas might be packed so full of Jews that whole families would have to live in one room."[66]

Eichmann's report was still a plan for the future, although it finally earned him his commission as *Untersturmfuehrer* or second lieutenant in the SS. Until his recommendations were accepted by his superiors there was little he could do to implement them. Considering the breadth of his plan it was obvious that Hitler himself would have to approve at least the principle underlying it—the control of Jewish policy by the SD, Gestapo, and SS. At the time his proposal was submitted to Heydrich, not even the SS leadership, to say nothing of Eichmann, could feel any certainty about the direction of Jewish policy.

Throughout 1937, Eichmann's Section II 112 had been busy pursuing numerous angles to the emigration question. One of the difficulties, of course, was to find countries which would eventually accept Jewish immigrants in sizable numbers. Eichmann's approach to this problem affords an important clue into the Nazi attitude toward emigration. In January 1937, Eichmann, in a "Comprehensive Report on the Jewish Problem," warned that emigration alone might not really be a solution to the Jewish problem. As important as emigration might be, it would be self-defeating to concentrate Jews in just a few areas outside Germany. Such a concentration, Eichmann warned, would lead to "the creation in many countries of an alien lead-

[65] Ibid.
[66] Ibid.

ership (*feindliches Gremium*) which would constantly work against our interests."[67] For this reason he was worried about too many Jews settling in countries on the European continent. From here they would be well situated to continue their fight against Germany. He had only to point to Great Britain, where in 1917 a small Jewish minority had steered the government into its Balfour Declaration. South America on the other hand seemed a much safer repository for Jews. Assuming they were properly dispersed throughout the continent, South America was simply too large to succumb to "the Jewish infection."[68]

Eichmann has sometimes been thought of as being free of the ideological shackles which bound his more emotional Nazi colleagues. In most instances this is an accurate assessment, but his fears in this case seem to stem directly out of anti-Semitism's deepest and most irrational roots. What is more significant, however, is the fact that one of the earliest proponents of emigration, and later one of its chief administrators, entertained doubts about its actually solving the Jewish problem. Perhaps a *ju-denrein* Germany, the object of all emigration schemes, was not the final answer to the Jewish problem at all. Such doubts, while they did not make the Final Solution inevitable, certainly brought it a step closer.

At the time these doubts were first raised there was little reason for concern about the overconcentration of Jewish emigrants anywhere. More immediate was the problem of organizing any effective emigration scheme. True to his growing reputation as a Jewish expert, Eichmann's energies were concentrated on organizing such a scheme. The most promising avenue still seemed to be Palestine, if only because the Palestinian potential, after 1934, seemed largely untapped. Eichmann, along with most of his colleagues in the SD, Gestapo, and SS complex, were still eager to harness Zionist energies to that purpose. In February 1937, word reached Eichmann from an SD contact man in the Near East that help might be available from a very un-

[67] Himmler File, T175 (508), 9374076.
[68] Himmler File, T175 (508), 9374077.

expected source, from Palestinian Jews themselves. Zionists in Palestine were understandably anxious to encourage Jewish immigration and frequently sent emissaries abroad to assist the cause. Now one of these emissaries was eager to come to Berlin. The SD contact suggested that this one be granted permission to come to Germany. Among other things he might be able to give the SD important information about developments in Palestine which could affect emigration policy.

The trip was approved by the SD and on February 26, Feivel Polkes of the Hagana, a Jewish underground military organization, arrived in Berlin. Eichmann was selected to meet with Polkes and was instructed to learn what he could about the situation in Palestine. Polkes was not told, of course, that he was meeting with an SD official, although he knew that Eichmann was a Nazi of at least some importance. Several meetings took place at which Eichmann learned first hand of the Hagana's eagerness for Jewish immigration into Palestine. According to the SD report on these meetings Polkes offered to give the Nazis certain information in exchange for their easing the emigration of German Jews to Palestine. He suggested especially the easing of foreign currency transfer restrictions imposed by the Nazi regime. A sudden renewal of Jewish-Arab hostilities in Palestine forced Polkes to return home before the question of emigration could be discussed fully, but upon leaving, Polkes invited Eichmann to visit Palestine for further talks.[69]

Jewish-Arab tensions in Palestine frequently erupted into violence, especially during the 1930's. An increased Jewish immigration inspired by the anti-Semitic policies of numerous central and east European governments only heightened the tension. The Arab nationalism which fed upon the threat of an eventual majority of Jews made the governing of Palestine increasingly difficult for the British mandate power. In view of the apparently irreconcilable Jewish and Arab interests, the British government had sent to Palestine in late 1936 a Royal Commission to investigate the situation and to make

[69] Himmler File, T175 (411), 2936189-94.

recommendations. Its report, issued in July 1937, concluded that the present situation was unworkable and recommended that Palestine be partitioned into separate Jewish and Arab states. The British government endorsed this report and for the next year sought Arab and Jewish consent for Palestinian partition. Continual flare-ups of violence eventually convinced the British that partition was also unfeasible, but from July 1937 to late 1938 it sought to implement its commission's proposal.

The prospect of helping to populate an independent Jewish state raised second thoughts in Nazi officialdom about having Palestine serve as a prime recipient of Jewish emigrants from the Third Reich. Eichmann's section of the SD noted that with the proposal for partition the entire question of Palestine had to be reconsidered. "The proclamation of a Jewish state or a Jewish-administered Palestine would create for Germany a new enemy, one which would have a deep influence on developments in the Near East."[70] Furthermore, a Jewish state might be able to raise effectively in international councils the question of Jewish persecutions in Germany. An independent Palestine, the Race and Resettlement Office of the SS predicted, "would someday become a member of the League of Nations and would work to bring special minority protection to Jews in every country, therefore granting the exploitation activity of world Jewry legal protection."[71] Hitler, too, was haunted by the spector of an independent Jewish state. On his order, negotiations for further transfer agreements between Germany and Palestine were suspended.[72] The fear of a Jewish state continued to mount until Britain finally dropped its plans for partition. But during that time anti-Palestinian fantasies took on heroic proportions. Hitler's Foreign Minister, Joachim von Ribbentrop, circulated a memorandum in which he warned that "Germany must regard the forming of a Jewish state as dangerous, which even in minia-

[70] Himmler File, T175 (411), 2936193.
[71] Himmler File, T175 (410), 2934828.
[72] From the testimony of Dr. Benno Cohn, a Zionist leader in Germany during the 1930's, at the Eichmann Trial in Jerusalem, Session 15, April 25, 1961, p. 21.

ture would form just such an operational base as the Vatican for political Catholicism."[73] Alfred Rosenberg issued the same warning in a public speech. He cautioned the western democracies not to establish a Jewish state in Palestine. It would be wiser instead to establish Jewish reservations in various parts of the world. Ribbentrop quoted Rosenberg to support the view of how dangerous a Jewish state could be. Both Ribbentrop and Rosenberg reflected Hitler's own thinking on the matter of Palestine. Perhaps they had checked *Mein Kampf* where their Fuehrer had written: "They [the Jews] have no thought of building up a Jewish State in Palestine, so that they might perhaps inhabit it, but they only want a central organization of their international world cheating, endowed with prerogatives, withdrawn from the seizure of others; a refuge for convicted rascals and a high school for future rogues."[74]

Despite the pessimism and doubt which surrounded the Nazi plans for Palestine, the SS leadership authorized Eichmann to accept Polkes' invitation to visit the Near East. Perhaps Polkes might be able to provide certain information about world Jewry which would be useful to Nazi leaders. He had hinted during his Berlin talks with Eichmann that he knew something about the murder of a Nazi *Gauleiter* and about the attempt on the life of the Sudetan Nazi leader, Konrad Henlein. This in itself might make another contact worthwhile. In early November 1937, Eichmann together with his section chief Herbert Hagen left Berlin for Palestine. The political unrest there made it impossible to arrange a meeting with Polkes in Palestine, however, and so Eichmann and Hagen proceeded to Cairo, the operational base for the SD contact man who had arranged Eichmann's first meeting with Polkes. Polkes was now summoned to Cairo. Twice, on November 10 and again the next day, Polkes met with Eichmann and Hagen in a Cairo coffee house. These meetings were not very fruitful. Eichmann and Hagen were anxious to learn about suspected assassination plots against Nazi

---

[73] *Nazi Conspiracy and Aggression,* vol. 6, Document 3358-PS, p. 92.
[74] Hitler, *Mein Kampf,* pp. 447-448.

officials. Polkes on the other hand wanted to know what could be done to encourage German Jews to emigrate to Palestine. To advance his own cause Polkes suggested that the Nazis ease their restrictions on currency transfers. He was certain that with a $1,000 allowance for each immigrant, the British authorities would permit the entry of 50,000 Jews per year into Palestine.

In the report which Eichmann later made for Heydrich he suggested why Polkes' proposal was unacceptable. "It is not in our interest that Jewish capital be taken abroad; rather, our first concern is to effect the emigration of penniless Jews. Since the emigration of 50,000 Jews per year would greatly strengthen the Jewish position in Palestine, this [Polkes'] plan is not worth discussing. The policy of the Reich is much more to hinder the development of a Jewish state in Palestine."[75] The only reason he and Hagen even bothered to discuss Palestine's future, Eichmann went on, was not to endanger the possibility of Polkes' divulging information on assassination plots planned by international Jewry.

The fear of adding strength to a Jewish power base had a serious effect upon emigration to Palestine in 1937. The number of German Jews who emigrated to Palestine that year dropped to 3,286, less than half the 1936 figure.[76] Zionist leaders in Germany were confused at first by the shift in Nazi attitudes regarding Palestine. Not until they learned of Hitler's fear that it "might become the spiritual center for the international Jewish conspiracy"[77] did their confusion subside.

In January 1938, the SD circulated a report on the Jewish situation in Germany which reflected these new attitudes.[78] The report was not very optimistic. Only the word on Palestine was encouraging. There British policy was happily serving to limit the immigration of Jews. Otherwise the SD's assessment of the progress on Jewish policy was discouraging. Emigration to places

75 Himmler File, T175 (411), 2936104-08.
76 Rosenstock, "Exodus 1933-1939," p. 376.
77 Marcus, "The German Foreign Office," p. 191.
78 Himmler File, T175 (410), 2934012-16.

other than Palestine was being made increasingly difficult. Germany's neighboring states were imposing more and more conditions prior to accepting immigrants from the Reich. More important, South American countries were doing the same thing. The previous emigration of "Jewish capitalists" had cut off a major source of money for the Jewish organizations which promoted emigration. The upsurge in Aryanization was having a similar effect.

> The influence of the above circumstances, which reflect the worsening situation of Jews all over the world, is responsible for the resurgence of assimilation-minded Jewish circles in Germany. One could observe already in 1937 that some Jews in various parts of the Reich had decided to wait until the opportunities for emigration had improved. In the meantime they were working to improve their economic situation in Germany. Today [January, 1938] this observation appears to hold true for all of Germany.[79]

There was hardly an aspect of Jewish policy in late 1937 or early 1938 to which the Nazi observer could look with satisfaction. The Aryanization of Jewish property was far from completed. Government contracts were still being awarded to Jewish firms. The disappointment was aggravated for those who looked at the emigration statistics, unless they chose to dwell upon the negative success of reduced emigration to Palestine. Otherwise the number of Jewish emigrants from Germany had declined almost annually after the high point in 1933. During the first four years of Nazi rule only 129,000 Jews had left Germany. Those who stayed behind were for reasons of age, money, training, and restrictions abroad less likely to be able to find refuge outside Germany. Worst of all there seemed to be no clear direction to Jewish policy. No one was clearly in charge. One policy served to undermine the other. Aryanization drove Jews out of the German economy; it also made the possibility of emigration less likely. What was the ultimate purpose of Jewish policy? To drive Jews out of the economy or to drive them

[79] Ibid.

out of Germany? Those who agreed on emigration also agreed that to concentrate Jews in one place—such as Palestine—might raise a larger problem than the one it solved.

The failures in Jewish policy must have been particularly frustrating when seen in the light of Nazi successes in other areas. Rearmament was proceeding apace. The British, by concluding a naval agreement with Germany, had virtually ratified Hitler's unilateral breaking of the Versailles Treaty. German troops had reoccupied the Rhineland, and the West had contented itself with meaningless protests. The Olympic Games in Berlin's new stadium had taken place on schedule, buttressing Hitler's self-image and his image at home and abroad. A Rome-Berlin Axis had recently been lengthened to include Japan in an anti-Comintern Pact. On November 5, 1937, Hitler called a meeting of Germany's leading military and political figures. The time would soon be ripe, he explained, for a military showdown with the rest of Europe. For more than four hours Hitler unfolded his plans for the domination of Europe. He felt confident that now he could dominate events, rather than having events dominate him. Goering shortly replaced Schacht as the economic czar. Early in 1938 Hitler took personal control of the War Ministry and the army. Hitler chose as Foreign Minister one of his most pliable admirers, the spineless whiskey peddler turned diplomat, von Ribbentrop. Hitler's command of the state now seemed complete. If there seemed to be a disparity between these successes and the relatively meager results in Jewish policy, there were at least those who believed this imbalance could still be removed.

VII. 1938: A Road Is Cleared

THE WINTER MONTHS of 1937-1938 mark a decisive turning point
in the development of the Third Reich. The removal of
Schacht, Blomberg, Fritsch, and Neurath severed the remaining
threads—tenuous as they were—with the Weimar system. Fritsch,
Blomberg, and Neurath had all urged caution upon Hitler when
he revealed his plans for war in November 1937.[1] By February
1938, Hitler had countered these arguments by abolishing the
post of War Minister and assuming personally the duties of
Commander-in-Chief of the Armed Forces. Blomberg and
Fritsch fell victim to unsavory plots cooked up by Himmler and
the Gestapo. Neurath was dealt with more circumspectly. Re-
lieved of his duties as Foreign Minister, he was elevated to the
presidency of a secret cabinet council whose secrecy was assured
by the fact that it never met. Schacht, who had resisted the more
unorthodox economic schemes of Goering's rearmament commission, had already resigned in December. The last voices of
moderation in the Nazi government were silenced. Through
this last stage of the *Gleichschaltung* Hitler had finally succeeded
in filling the Reich's most vital posts with enthusiastic supporters.

Radical anti-Semites, eager for a solution to the Jewish question, had reason to applaud the departure of the moderates,
especially Schacht. His policies had been a major obstacle to
their efforts aimed at complete exclusion of Jews from the
economy. His exit signaled the ascendancy of Goering, which
in turn heralded a stronger line in Jewish affairs. Considering

[1] *Nazi Conspiracy and Aggression*, vol. 3, Document 386-PS, "The Hossbach
Protocol," pp. 295-305.

Goering's growing reputation as Nazism's chief Aryanizer, it was far less likely that the caution of his predecessor would continue to act as a restraint on Jewish policy.

Goering was unusually well placed to exercise dictatorial powers over the German economy. As Reich Marshal, Air Minister, Commissioner of the Four Year Plan and Reich Counsellor for Defense, he wore enough hats to have decisive influence on virtually all the activities of the Third Reich. For the next few years, until his vaunted air force failed to deliver on its promises, Goering was to be at the zenith of his powers. Beginning in 1938 he also became Hitler's chief troubleshooter on matters of Jewish policy. The title was never a formal one, but it was no less effective for that reason. Hitler's decisions on Jewish policy came to be announced usually through Goering. Goering, in numerous private conferences with the Fuehrer, was often successful in swaying the opinion of a vacillating Hitler. It was Goering who was to chair and guide the meeting which assessed the results and consequences of the massive November 1938 pogrom and announce the new direction for Jewish policy in early 1939.

There can be no doubt that Goering's new powers emanated directly from Hitler. But Goering was no mere mouthpiece for the Fuehrer; in fact, the two disagreed seriously over the decision to unleash Nazism's full fury against the Jews in the November pogrom. The fact that Hitler once again engaged himself directly in the matter of Jewish policy was in itself a departure from previous practice. After the failures of 1933 he had removed himself, with a few exceptions, from the everyday world of directing the anti-Jewish struggle. What sparked his renewed interest and concern in 1938 is an open question. Perhaps his successes in other areas inspired him to believe the Jewish problem could now be solved too. Perhaps the succession of failures in Jewish policy, or the threat of a "Jewish Vatican" led him to watch these matters more closely. Perhaps he was even convinced that to wait any longer would so strengthen international Jewry as to make the problem insoluble. Whatever the reason, his renewed concern led, in 1938, to an acceleration of activity on the Jewish front. Out of the cauldron of antagonisms and rivalries seething since 1933, there was forged by the end of 1938 a centrally directed and coordinated Jewish policy.

What distinguished the Nazi Jewish policies in 1938 from those of the earlier years is less their newness than it is the intensity with which they were pursued.[2] The Jews were attacked simultaneously on all fronts with a fervor unknown since the heady March and April days of 1933. Boycotts were organized, Aryanization was accelerated, legislation was promulgated, deportation was attempted, and for the first time large numbers of Jews were herded into concentration camps. In one way or another nearly every level of the Nazi movement from the Fuehrer down was caught up in this anti-Jewish fervor. Party headquarters, Goering's economic apparatus, the Foreign Ministry, the SS, the Gestapo, Streicher's boycott committee, and the SA participated in the assault. The only aspect which was entirely new was the fact that foreign Jews resident in Germany were for the first time officially singled out for special attention, itself a signal of the new confidence felt by the Nazi leadership.

The year 1938 is marked as well by a trend toward centralization of control over Jewish policy. In part this trend reflected the newly found powers of Goering, Heydrich, and Eichmann; in part it reflected the final failure of the emotional anti-Semitic wing of the Nazi movement to produce a solution to the Jewish problem through pogroms. The failure of the November pogrom finally discredited the impulsive radicals and strengthened the hand of the realists whose work in 1938 promised a more effective solution through bureaucratic means. Most important of all, Hitler finally made a choice between these two approaches to the Jewish issue. The result was to reestablish his leadership in the making of Jewish policy, and to give that policy its final direction.

[2] Shaul Esh, "Between Discrimination and Extermination (The Fateful Year of 1938)," in *From Hatred to Extermination* (Jerusalem, 1959), pp. 107-121.

No treatment of the difficulties the Nazis faced in making or executing a wide variety of Jewish policies can hide the essentially simple aims they hoped to achieve: to eliminate the Jew from the German economy and then, whether by emigration or expulsion, to drive him out of Germany. To those who did not make high level decisions or read secret situation reports, however, the aims seemed much less clear. With one hand the Reich was Aryanizing Jewish businesses; with the other it was awarding at least a few of them government contracts. In general, emigration was being encouraged, but in specific instances, such as emigration to Palestine, its prospects were being undermined. Eichmann's late 1937 complaint that Jews still did not seem convinced of the need to emigrate was an immediate product of this failure to communicate policy objectives clearly. The widespread dissatisfaction with Jewish policy manifested once again in 1938 at the lower party levels and in the SA stemmed from the same confusion. The events of late 1938, however, removed the last doubts about the aims of Jewish policy and the importance the Nazi leadership attached to them.

The removal of Schacht from his post in late 1937 and the subsuming of his main functions into Goering's Four Year Plan office signaled the first step in the accelerated campaign against Jewish participation in the economy, the end result of which was to be an economy which was virtually *judenrein*. Schacht's departure removed a major obstacle in the path of an unrestrained attack upon Jewish business activity. For the next months, until Goering too became concerned about the implications of this attack, there was to be no discussion of foreign currency problems or any of the other objections Schacht had raised. The argument about the economic aspects of Jewish policy went on, but it came to rest on a new and more simplified level. As long as Schacht had been around it was a three-way argument between Schacht himself, who raised practical if not ideological objections, the impatient party officials, and Goering, who lacking Hitler's full support remained somewhat unsure of his own powers. With Schacht gone only Goering and the party were left to dispute the manner in which Jews should be excluded from the economy.

A clash between these two sides was almost inevitable. Goering, as the new economic czar, was anxious to bring this aspect of Jewish policy under his own control, to systematize Aryanization and make it serve the interests of the state. Much of the party apparatus on the other hand was more concerned that its own *Mittelstand* interests be served. Judging from Hitler's failure to act in this dispute, one must conclude that he considered the approaches of both Goering and the party to be legitimate. Goering would do the organizational work; the party would provide the pressure. The actions of the party would push the Jews into Goering's hands. In this fashion the two would complement one another. What this failed to take into account was that the party did not share Goering's objective of concentrating former Jewish enterprises in the hands of a few Aryan industrialists. By Goering's own definition the party was not as "liberal" as he would have liked it to be. Not until the November pogrom had discredited its party organizers did Hitler conclude that a choice between Goering and the party was necessary—and then he made the only choice still open to him.

Anti-Jewish initiatives from both the party and Goering followed quickly upon Schacht's removal. Julius Streicher was the first to strike with a boycott against Jewish businesses in Nuremberg, designed to coincide with the Christmas buying season in 1937. For the first time since 1933 Streicher was given a free hand. No interference with the boycott came from the party leadership or from the economic authorities in Berlin. The Nuremburg SA and party units took full advantage of their freedom. Jewish shops were ransacked, their goods thrown onto the street and their customers and employees terrorized.[3] During the next months sporadic boycotts were organized in many German cities.

3 Uhlig, *Die Warenhäuser im Dritten Reich*, pp. 176, 205.

Goering, who in his timing was not far behind Streicher, had something more orderly in mind. Part of the problem with controlling Jewish participation in the economy had been the constant difficulty of defining precisely what constituted a Jewish business. Schacht, during his tenure as Economics Minister, had consistently resisted Nazi pressures to formulate an all-inclusive definition, and some ostensibly Jewish firms had consequently avoided Aryanization by exploiting the loopholes a loose definition provided. Without an adequate definition of a Jewish enterprise, the prospects for an orderly Aryanization seemed dim. The problems associated with the granting of public contracts to Jewish firms also had their roots in this situation. Unless one knew what a Jewish firm was, how could one avoid granting it a contract?

Goering addressed himself to this whole set of problems very early in 1938. On January 4, he admitted that before dealing with them, "it was necessary to have a legal definition of what constitutes a Jewish firm."[4] Goering himself provided the definition. If the firm was entirely owned by one or more Jews, the issue was quite clear. In other areas he ran into some of the same problems faced by the drafters of the Nuremburg Laws, but Goering sliced through these ambiguities arbitrarily. For a partnership to be considered Jewish only one of the partners had to be a Jew. Corporations presented the greatest problem. If more than one-fourth of the governing board was Jewish the entire enterprise was considered Jewish. The same definition applied if Jewish stockholders held enough votes to make corporate decisions impossible without their participation. This latter qualification, because it left the way open for almost any interpretation, was vitally important. To cover any loopholes Goering added that "an enterprise, moreover, is to be considered Jewish if it actually is under the guiding influence of Jews."[5] There was to be no nonsense, as there had been with the defini-

[4] Schumacher Archiv, Folder 240 II, BDC.
[5] Ibid.

tions established by the Nuremberg Laws, about how this order was to be interpreted. He asked that any ambiguous cases be brought to him for decision. For the next six months Goering's definition had the force of law. In June, when it was incorporated as a supplementary decree into the 1935 Reichs Citizenship Law, it also took on its substance.[6]

Cumbersome as its wording may have been, Goering's definition cleared the way for decisive action against Jewish participation in the economy. Little time was wasted in capitalizing on the opportunity. The matter of Jewish firms being awarded government contracts was given top priority. On March 1, a secret directive from the Economics Ministry—formally under the control of Walter Funk, but actually an adjunct to Goering's Four Year Plan—established new guidelines on the granting of such contracts.[7] Effective immediately it became illegal to award government contracts to firms designated as Jewish. The order was based on two premises: with some regional exceptions the unemployment problem was now solved; and German rearmament in most instances could proceed without Jewish assistance. Still, there were to be certain exceptions. Jewish firms specializing in manufacturing items vital to rearmament were, for the time being, exempted from the order, as were Jewish firms engaged in the export trade. Now that he had assumed most of Schacht's responsibilities, Goering could no longer ignore the importance of foreign exchange to the German economy. Moreover, in certain areas of Germany unemployment had still not been completely eliminated. Here it would be permissible to refuse a contract to a Jewish firm only if a nearby Aryan firm was able to fulfill it. Even then it would be necessary to proceed with "the greatest caution."[8]

To augment Goering's order concerning the definition of a Jewish enterprise, a decree of April 22 made it illegal for anyone

[6] RGB1, I, 1938, pp. 627-628.
[7] Schumacher Archiv, Folder 240 II, BDC.
[8] Ibid.

to assist in aiding the concealment of Jewish ownership.[9] Such an order gave the Nazis another lever in their Aryanization of Jewish holdings. Efforts to disguise the ownership of an enterprise—the technique employed by the Petschek negotiators at that moment—had to be discouraged.

On April 26 another decree made it compulsory for Jews to register all their property holdings, in Germany or abroad, worth more than RM 5,000.[10] Only small items for personal use did not have to be registered. The decree allowed Nazi economic authorities to arrive at an accurate assessment of the wealth still controlled by German Jewry. From here it was only a short step to the outright seizure of the Jewish property which the April decrees had finally brought out into the open.

The pace of Aryanization which had begun to pick up in late 1937 was greatly accelerated in the wake of Goering's legislative decrees. Alf Krueger, an Economics Ministry official, noted that of the 39,552 Jewish businesses still in existence on April 1, 1938, nearly 6,000 had been Aryanized by April 1939, nearly 15,000 had been liquidated altogether, and another 11,000 were either in the process of or on the verge of being Aryanized.[11] That meant that about 80 percent of the Jewish businesses which had managed to hold out until April 1938 had fallen into the Nazi clutches during the following year. The accuracy of Krueger's figures cannot be checked, but evidence from other sources indicates they are not too far wrong.[12] Throughout the Reich, Jewish businesses were liquidated or Aryanized. Falling victim to the Nazi assault were firms ranging from the renowned Bleichröder banking house to the small Jewish shopkeeper who somehow had managed to survive the earlier boycotts. Directors, managers, clerks, salesmen, and workers were dismissed immediately upon Aryanization, adding to the already alarming rate of

[9] RGBl, I, 1938, p. 404.
[10] RGBl, I, 1938, p. 414.
[11] Krueger, *Die Lösung der Judenfrage*, p. 44.
[12] Genschel, *Die Verdrängung der Juden*, p. 175, n. 159.

Jewish unemployment. A law of July 6, 1938 specifically excluded Jews from commercial enterprises.[13] An estimated 30,000 Jewish traveling salesmen alone were dismissed during the remainder of the summer.[14]

The air of drama which had surrounded the Aryanization of the Petschek firms was not always present. Jewish firms headquartered in Germany were much more vulnerable to Nazi attack. A case in point is the situation of M. M. Warburg & Co., a large Jewish banking firm in Hamburg. Founded in 1798, the firm prospered on the nineteenth-century wave of German economic expansion. One might have expected a Jewish banking firm to be first on the list of Nazi victims after 1933. M. M. Warburg & Co., hard hit by the Depression, had been weakened for the Nazi assault. Between 1930 and 1933 its number of clients had fallen by two-thirds and it did not share in the Nazi version of prosperity following Hitler's seizure of power.

Two factors had allowed it to hang on during the first years of Nazi rule, however. First, as banker to many of Hamburg's commercial interests, it was important to the generating of foreign exchange for the Reich. Secondly, it was a member of the *Reichsanleihe-Konsortium,* a group of some fifty major banks which floated loans for the Reich government. The firm's director, Max M. Warburg, credits Schacht's protective hand for maintaining the bank's position in this *Konsortium* against heavy pressures from the Nazi party.[15] Despite Schacht's assistance the firm was in steady retreat after 1933. Finally in early 1938, after Schacht's fall from favor, the Warburg firm lost its position in the *Konsortium*. Immediately the Nazis began demanding its liquidation. By the end of May a special partnership of Aryan banking, industrial, and commercial interests had formed itself to buy the firm from its Jewish owners. The price, much less than the firm's value, was determined by the Nazi

13 RGB1, I, 1938, p. 823.

14 Mark Wischnitzer, *To Dwell in Safety: The Story of Jewish Migration since 1800* (Philadelphia, 1948), p. 194.

15 Max M. Warburg, *Aus meinen Aufzeichnungen* (Privately published, 1952), p. 153.

government.[16] What may have been lacking in drama was compensated for by the quiet execution of the transfer.

In its broad outline the pattern of Aryanization established in the Warburg case was a recurring one during the remainder of 1938. Jewish firms which did attempt to hold out were subjected to pressures from all sides. The precariousness of their situation was underlined whenever they sought credit. Until 1938 German banking firms had usually been willing to grant loans to anyone able to repay them. Such was no longer the case when the Berlin-based F. A. Grünfeld Specialty House for Linens and Draperies sought a loan in June. Upon being refused credit elsewhere, F. A. Grünfeld turned to a banker in Essen, only to be told: ". . . under today's conditions it is difficult to justify any credit by regular banking standards. I hope you will understand that we cannot grant you any credit. You may justifiably ask: for what reason do we bankers exist? To that I can only answer that I do not know anymore either."[17] Without additional credit F. A Grünfeld was forced into the clutches of an Aryan buyer. A few weeks later the Reichs Economics Minister noted his pleasure at withdrawing the firm's name from the list of Jewish enterprises.

This concentrated attack upon Jewish economic life, directed as it was by Goering, still failed to satisfy large segments of the party. For one thing the massiveness of the attack seemed to signal that the days of caution and restraint were past. Obviously the conditions which allowed for a solution to the Jewish problem now existed and the party was eager to offer its assistance. Early in 1938, after being apprised that the future offered greater hope, party units began to make their bids for increased influence. In February the Racial Political Office of the NSDAP approached Heydrich's SD with an offer to help in Jewish affairs, especially in the work of overseeing the activities of Jewish organizations.[18] The gesture was politely but firmly rebuffed.

16 Ibid., p. 155.
17 From a banker to Grünfeld, in Leo Baeck Institute archives.
18 Himmler File, T175 (411), 2935554.

The party office was told to mind its own business, which, it was made specific, did not include matters within the province of the SD.

Pressures from other elements of the party, encouraged no doubt by the success of Streicher's boycott in Nuremberg, continued to mount during the early months of 1938. The retreat in Jewish policy following the 1933 boycott had created frustrated elements which demanded more extreme anti-Jewish measures. The demands of these elements had been contained only with great difficulty. They had required both the soothing and disciplinary attentions of those at higher levels who appreciated the need for a coordinated Jewish policy. While the dissatisfaction had generally been contained, it had not been eliminated. The outbreak of renewed boycotts and general harassing of Jews grew more serious as it became clear that Goering's activities introduced a new stage in Jewish policy. By March and April the SA and local action committees were once again fully engaged in "solving" the Jewish problem. Bella Fromm, a prominent Jewish German journalist, noted in her diary that by June these elements within the party had become responsible for a wholesale terrorization of the Jewish community. Along Berlin's elegant boulevard, the *Kurfürstendamm,* Jewish shops were plastered with swastikas and obscene cartoons. Elsewhere Jewish stores were broken into and looted, or their goods strewn over the sidewalk. Illustrations of Jews being beheaded and otherwise maimed were posted on poles and billboards. The effect was cumulative. Increased official activity in the form of laws, decrees, and Aryanization gave birth to increased unofficial and unsanctioned activity by the radicals. In Erfurt party officials were arranging for the "policing" of Jewish shops in order to intimidate customers.[19] Streicher, in the meantime, was planning to expand his activities by tearing down a Nuremberg synagogue and erecting an anti-Semitic museum in its place.[20]

[19] Himmler File, T175 (409), 2932699.
[20] Himmler File, T175 (410), 2934580.

This sudden upsurge in spontaneous anti-Jewish activity began to worry high-level officials. Although it cannot be documented, it is likely that Goering complained to Hitler. In June a highly secret (*Streng Geheim!*) order from the Deputy Fuehrer's office in Munich defending Goering's position was sent to all middle-ranking party officials. The order, signed by Martin Bormann and dealing with "The Elimination of Jews from the German Economy," reflected top-level concern with the turn of events.

> In the past years measures concerning the repression or elimination of Jewish participation in the German economy have been possible only within strict limits. The conditions in this area have now undergone a fundamental change. The orders of Party Comrade and Field Marshal Goering, Commissioner for the Four Year Plan, making it illegal to disguise the ownership of a Jewish enterprise and making it necessary for a Jewish business to identify itself as such, mark the beginning of final solution to this problem. I emphasize once more that all unauthorized actions against Jewish firms are to cease, because they could only jeopardize the intended total solution.[21]

Bormann issued another secret directive at the beginning of August, promising once more that a solution to the economic aspects of the Jewish question was imminent. But he also went a step beyond the economic question. Addressing a meeting of Nazi *Gauleiter,* he promised: "Goering intends to have a fundamental cleaning up (*Grundlegende Bereinigung*) of the Jewish question." He went on to assure his listeners that "this cleaning up operation will proceed in a fashion which will satisfy the demands of the party to the fullest measure."[22]

Bormann's rhetoric was designed to convince radical party elements that independent initiatives were unnecessary, that their unauthorized actions would only undermine the already prepared solution. There were other measures to which he

[21] Schumacher Archiv, Folder 240 II, BDC.
[22] Ibid.

might have pointed. Since March it was becoming increasingly clear that the Nazi regime no longer entertained seriously the thought of tolerating a separate Jewish community in Germany. A "Law Regarding the Legal Status of Jewish Communities" of March 28 deprived Jewish religious congregations of the legal protection accorded "bodies of public law."[23] Bereft of this status, Jewish congregations were no longer empowered to require financial contributions from their members. The last thread of hope Jews may have entertained about a concordat-like resolution of their crisis was removed in the process.

In the context of the other measures the March 28 law pales in significance. Certainly Goering's directives on economic matters had greater short- and long-term effect, but they had also been secret. The promulgation of a Reich Law, on the other hand, was a highly public act. It served to warn Jews that any hopes they had for a tolerable existence in Germany were in vain. The law also heralded the renewal of a legislative attack upon Jewry. It was the first piece of significant legislation since the 1935 Nuremberg Laws. There had been numerous supplementary decrees in 1936 and 1937 to already existing legislation, but none of these represented a substantial departure from earlier policies. As long as the legal basis of Jewish corporate life remained untouched there appeared to be a measure of official protection against the most radical anti-Jewish excesses. The March law created a new situation, one far less promising for the future.

That new and sharper anti-Jewish measures were in store became clear in the spring of 1938 from other sources as well. This was learned by a spy which the Zionist leadership had managed to plant in the Berlin staff headquarters of the SS. The spy was unable to discover exactly what the SS had in mind, but he did learn that Hitler was planning a war and that the time left for Jews in Germany was growing short.[24] Looming on

---

[23] RGB1, I, 1938, p. 338.

[24] The story of this episode is told by Benno Cohn. See Document #01/226, Yad Washem archives.

the horizon, if Hitler wanted a *judenrein* Germany before the war started, was the ominous prospect of forced emigration.

An indication of SS intentions had been spelled out as early as February when Himmler ordered the expulsion from the Reich of all Jews who were citizens of the Soviet Union.[25] The problem of foreign Jews had not been settled with the Denaturalization Law of 1933. The so-called Soviet Jews which Himmler was trying to expell had lived in Germany with their families for decades since the czarist pogroms of the previous century, but had not succeeded in attaining German citizenship. Until now the question of dealing with foreign Jews resident in Germany had been largely untouched. Generally Jews who were legally foreign nationals had been treated more leniently than those with German citizenship. This seemingly preferential treatment was based on nothing more solid than Hitler's desire to avoid uncomfortable diplomatic entanglements with foreign governments. Goering had once declared that foreign Jews were to be treated according to the letter of international agreements, although "all steps should be taken through either gentle or harsh pressures to maneuver [them] out of Germany."[26] Hitler himself had set the tone for the treatment of non-German Jews: They were not to be subjected to the terms of the anti-Jewish laws, but neither were they to be excluded in the wording of such legislation. When the appropriate time came he wanted no artificial barriers standing in the way of dealing with this foreign element.[27]

Himmler's order to expel the Soviet Jews indicated that "harsh pressures" had become appropriate. His order allowed them ten days to leave Germany. With the difficulties of emigration, this was patently impossible. No one could make all the necessary arrangements in that short a time. A six-week extension granted by the SS in mid-March again proved too short. Even a second six-week extension was not long enough. Finally,

[25] Collection: Bezirksämter, Folder 15, BDC.
[26] Graml, "Die Auswanderung," pp. 85, 87.
[27] Ibid.

in May, Himmler ordered the arrest of all Soviet Jews still in Germany and had them sent off to concentration camps. "As soon as the Jew is prepared to leave Germany," declared Heydrich, "the arrest is to be terminated."[28] Heydrich failed to explain how to go about preparing to emigrate from inside a concentration camp. Nonetheless, the first step in dealing with the foreign Jew had been taken, and significantly under auspices of the SS.

Following Himmler's expulsion order the attack upon Jewry was rapidly mounted on other fronts. Soviet Jews were still being rounded up when the Gestapo began arresting the ostensibly "anti-social" or criminal element of German Jewry. In its so-called June Action the Gestapo arrested some 1,500 "anti-social" Jews and transported them mostly to the Buchenwald concentration camp near Erfurt.[29] Publicly the Gestapo announced the impounding of dangerous criminals. If the Reich needed to be protected from Jews who had overparked their automobiles, the "June Action" served its purpose. Some 500 of those arrested had been convicted of crimes no more serious than traffic violations. One man arrested had not promptly paid some social security contributions for an employee; another had once made a disparaging remark about the Nazis.[30] To be sure, some of those arrested had also been convicted of more serious crimes such as tax evasion or some other type of shady financial dealing. It was unlikely that the regular authorities in the Reich Emigration Office would ever be able to rid Germany of this latter element. Armed with false documents prepared by the Gestapo, however, even this "anti-social" element could be wiped clean and prepared for "shipment" abroad.

These prisoners were the first large group of Jews to experience life inside a Nazi concentration camp. They were to be let free only if they could emigrate immediately upon leaving the

---

28 Ibid.

29 Prinz, "Role of the Gestapo."

30 Oscar Schwartz, "Mein Leben in Deutschland vor und nach dem Jahre 1933," unpublished memoir in the Leo Baeck Institute archives, p. 2.

camp, a situation which for a time made emigration even more confusing than it had been in more ordinary circumstances.

The Nazi annexation of Austria in March had added another dimension to the confusion surrounding emigration. The addition of 200,000 Austrian Jews to the Third Reich more than canceled out the emigration of those Jews who had left Germany between 1933 and early 1938. As far as the Jewish problem was concerned, the addition of Austria left the Nazis doing little more than treading water. The traditional emigration process was obviously inadequate to deal with this problem on its new scale. Both Himmler's insistence upon the expulsion of Soviet Jews and the Gestapo's arrest of anti-social elements were bold efforts to forcefeed what the Nazis themselves admitted were rapidly narrowing channels of emigration.

The boldest and most successful attempt to force Jewish emigration followed the Austrian *Anschluss*, however. Austria was made the laboratory in which new ideas concerning the Jewish problem were tested. The man assigned to head the Austrian experiment, Adolf Eichmann, had recently been promoted to *Untersturmführer* in the SS in recognition of his earlier work on the Jewish question. The confidence Himmler and Heydrich placed in their young "Jewish expert" from SD Section II 112 was well placed. It was Eichmann's big opportunity. He made the most of it.

In January Eichmann had complained to Heydrich that the lack of coordination between even those who were authorized to deal with the Jewish problem was creating difficulties for the emigration process.[31] Even more serious were the large number of unauthorized people or agencies whose interference threatened to disrupt emigration entirely. This had been Eichmann's basic complaint since mid-1937 when he began drawing up plans to organize Jewish emigration from the Reich. In this sense Austria, where the anti-Semitic policy was to be pursued for the first time, offered unique promise. Rather than being a

[31] Himmler File, T175 (410), 2935004.

late comer to the Jewish problem, as it had been in Germany, the SS was among the first on the scene.

From his headquarters in the former Viennese mansion of the Rothschilds, Eichmann applied an assembly line technique to Jewish emigration, or more accurately, deportation. The diffusion of authority which had obtained in Germany was overcome. He established in the Rothschild residence a "Central Office for Jewish Emigration" which had complete authority over emigration's every phase. What in Berlin, Hamburg, or Munich would have taken weeks of scurrying from one office to another was usually accomplished in one day by Eichmann's Central Office. The Jewish emigrant entered the office, stood in numerous lines for several hours and left at the end of the day with the stamps, papers, visas, and passports necessary for leaving Austria. If he entered wealthy, he left poor. Eichmann's principle that the rich must pay for the poor was applied ruthlessly. That part of an emigrant's wealth which did not go to pay for emigration was confiscated for the Reich's treasury.[32]

By November Eichmann's superiors could boast that "we have eliminated 50,000 Jews from Austria."[33] In six months his techniques had become responsible for the emigration of one-quarter of Austria's Jews, an astonishing success in light of the fact that emigration from the Reich proper seemed on the verge of bogging down completely. His success also demonstrated that appropriate bureaucratic and organizational measures rendered the Jewish problem amenable to solution.

But Eichmann's project also had its critics. Many of the Reich's economic officials objected to his measures because of their cost. Unlike the Haavara arrangements with Palestine, his conveyor-belt technique brought no capital into Germany. In fact, Eichmann's success in promoting emigration depended upon Jews being allowed to transfer at least some of their assets abroad. Previous emigration schemes had invariably been hin-

[32] Himmler File, T175 (411), 2935795-98, for a description of Eichmann's technique.

[33] Nazi Conspiracy and Aggression, vol. 4, Document 1816-PS, p. 450.

dered by Germany's foreign exchange shortage. This problem had in no way been solved in Vienna; Eichmann had merely chosen to ignore it. In late May a conference between a finance specialist from the Economics Ministry and the Chief of SD Section II 112 took place in Berlin to discuss this matter. The basic question was how to finance an expanded emigration without endangering foreign exchange income. Both sides agreed that emigration from Germany "was too slow and that all possibilities for simplifying the process should be studied."[34] Part of this study included a trip to Vienna to learn first hand of the economic implications to Eichmann's project. No agreement on principle was reached and the SD was undissuaded in its defense of Eichmann. The conference, which had been requested by economic officials, therefore, marked a decline in their powers to resist radical emigration schemes. Conversely it marked a major step in the SS control over Jewish policy.

Eichmann's running roughshod over generally accepted emigration procedures may have expedited emigration from Austria, but it also made immigration into possible countries of destination more difficult. First of all the emigrant processed through Eichmann's office was usually ill-prepared to take up a new life abroad. Furthermore, Britain was concerned over the problem Jewish immigration posed to her Palestinian mandate. The German immigration quota of the United States was already filled. Eichmann's "successes" shortly resulted in celebrated incidents of ships carrying Jews from port to port without being allowed to unload their unfortunate human cargo. The last resort for many of these Jews became places such as Shanghai and several of the smaller South American countries which required no immigration visas. In short, the emigration problem of Germany was being translated into a refugee problem for the rest of the world.

The Jewish refugees from Germany and the prospect of an even greater problem stemming from Nazi excesses in Austria

[34] The conference was held on May 25, 1938. For the SD report of its outcome see Himmler File, T175 (411), 2935760-63.

had prompted President Franklin D. Roosevelt in late March 1938, two weeks after the Austrian *Anschluss*, to call for an international conference to consider efforts which might alleviate the plight of Eichmann's victims. Thirty-two countries responded to the call by sending delegates to a conference convened in early July at the French resort town of Evian.

The Nazi regime allowed representatives of German and Austrian Jewry to attend the Evian Conference and present their plans for facilitating emigration.[35] Their accounts of the situation inside Germany made it obvious to most delegates that the primary objective at Evian had to be aimed at relieving the pressures inside Germany itself. The alternative would have been for each participating country to open its gates to an onslaught of refugees, something most countries were unwilling or unable to consider. Indeed, Secretary of State Cordell Hull's invitation to the various governments had specifically noted that the need for emergency emigration did not mean the respective governments would have to participate in its financing or restructure their existing legislation regarding immigration.[36] An Inter-Governmental Committee for refugees with its headquarters in London was established in the hope that some orderly emigration process could be worked out. George Rublee, an American lawyer and troubleshooter for President Roosevelt, was named its director. Agreement from the Nazi regime to enter into negotiations with the Committee was secured and Rublee was scheduled to go to Berlin in late August.

Rublee's departure for the German capital was indefinitely postponed in the face of the developing Czechoslovakian crisis of the late summer. In the meantime the Rublee committee, to

35 From Germany came a delegation of the *Reichsvertretung* and one from the *Hilfsverein;* Austrian Jewry sent representatives of the *Jüdische Kultusgemeinde Wien.* See S. Adler-Rudel, "The Evian Conference," *Year Book XIII* Leo Baeck Institute (London, 1968), pp. 235-273.

36 *Foreign Relations of the United States,* 1938, vol. 1 (Washington, D.C., 1955), pp. 740-741. The failure of the United States to consider the reassessment of its immigration quotas for Jewish refugees has been the subject of a recent book by Arthur D. Morse, *While Six Million Died: A Chronicle of American Apathy* (New York, 1967). See especially pp. 213ff.

the consternation of Jewish officials associated with emigration groups, refused to move ahead on plans designed to seek out new places for German emigrants to go. The feeling was that appropriate capital transfer agreements with the German government had to be reached first.[37] By the time Rublee came to Berlin in December an entirely new set of circumstances applied to the Jewish situation and to the ability of the major powers to deal with Germany on any level. The British and French governments, hoping to buy peace in their time, had capitulated to Hitler over the Sudetenland at Munich in September. In November a spectacular Jewish pogrom seemed to shatter the last hopes for bringing the Nazis back to reason.

When he finally did reach Berlin, Rublee found the Nazis in no mood to negotiate. They simply offered him a plan and asked for its acceptance or rejection. To cover the cost of emigration, the Nazis proposed that Jewish wage earners would be allowed to emigrate at an annual rate of 30,000 over a three- to five-year period. Their dependents were to stay behind until the wage earner had established a position abroad and could himself bear the emigration expenses of his dependents. Those who stayed behind—wives, children, the aged, and infirm—were promised reasonable treatment. At the outset the plan was to be financed by a trust fund created out of the remaining wealth of Germany's Jews.[38]

World opinion—Jewish and non-Jewish—was understandably apprehensive. Acceptance of the plan would have granted formal approval to the expropriation of what little wealth was left to German Jewry. Moreover, it would have sanctioned the creation of a hostage Jewish community, one the Nazis could have used for blackmailing Jews abroad. Rublee's objections to the Nazi offer were to no avail.[39]

The plan was never put to the test. The need at the end of

[37] S. Adler-Rudel, "Das Auswanderungsproblem im Jahre 1938, Ein Briefwechsel mit Hans Schäffer," *Bulletin des Leo Baeck Instituts* 10 (1967): 159-215.

[38] Wischnitzer, *To Dwell in Safety*, pp. 200-204.

[39] *Akten zur deutschen Auswärtigen Politik, 1918-1945*, series D, vol. 5 (Baden-Baden, 1953), p. 779 (hereafter cited as *Akten*).

1938 was for immediate emergency measures, not solutions which would take three to five years to implement. By the time this plan might have been acceptable it was tragically irrelevant. In late 1941—the earliest time at which the plan could have borne fruit—Hitler's armies controlled eastern Europe from the Baltic to the Aegean and vast expanses of western Russia. European Jewry was firmly in his clutches. The day of emigration, visas, and currency arrangements was long past.

It is doubtful whether the Nazis ever took their own proposal very seriously. The few references made to it in SS or Gestapo circles are devoid of enthusiasm.[40] Then, too, while Rublee was still in London awaiting an invitation to Berlin, Martin Bormann was already promising a solution to the Jewish problem which would satisfy the demands of the party's most radical elements. At best the plan might have served Nazi interests by promising the eventual emigration of those Jews who had no other way to leave Germany. Eichmann's example in Vienna, however, along with the November pogrom, makes it doubtful whether they were willing, even in December 1938, to wait as long as five years.

The Evian Conference had trailed off into irrelevancy long before George Rublee reached Berlin. Of much greater consequence to Jews was the continuing struggle for control over Jewish policy within Germany itself. The representatives at Evian met just as this struggle was approaching a decisive stage. Eichmann's machinery in Vienna was beginning to operate smoothly. Aryanization based upon the new legislation and decrees was gaining momentum rapidly, undercutting the last foundations for a continued existence in Germany. At the unofficial level, party functionaries, especially at the *Gau* level, were calling for sterner measures and organizing their own anti-Jewish campaigns. Many of their efforts were assisted by an SA whose anti-Jewish enthusiasm seemed suddenly revived, perhaps by the example of terrorism set by their Austrian counterparts in the wake of the *Anschluss*. The summer of 1938

[40] See SD report of February 21, 1939. Himmler File, T175 (410), 2934594.

was a period of unparalleled persecution. Boycotts, beatings, expropriation, and arrests threatened to bring down the final curtain on the German Jewish community. Still, no centralized machinery responsible for all aspects of the Jewish question had emerged. Clearly the police network of SS, Gestapo, and SD headed by Himmler and Heydrich, along with Goering who controlled the economy, outmatched any contenders for control of Jewish policy. Goering was probably at the peak of his favor with Hitler. The position of Himmler and Heydrich was greatly enhanced by Eichmann's unusual success in Vienna. Yet their interests did not coincide on a number of points. Most important, Goering could no longer avoid being concerned about the potential loss of foreign exchange. In November he challenged Heydrich's boast regarding Austrian emigration. "Have you ever thought of it," he asked Eichmann's chief, "This procedure [in Vienna] may cost us so much foreign currency that in the end we won't be able to hold out?"[41] On another level, the terror which party and SA officials excited reintroduced the confusion of early 1933. Until or unless Hitler intervened decisively, it was likely that this three-way struggle between Goering, the SS, and the radicals in the party and SA would continue with each one trying to outdo the other. Of the original contenders in this struggle, only the moderate anti-Semites, who felt the Jewish problem had already been solved, were no longer heard from.

The conflict was not resolved until November when the problems arising from the *Kristallnacht* finally convinced Hitler that the objectives of Jewish policy were unattainable without centralized control. The fact that the pogrom's engineers—the SA and radical party elements—discredited themselves in the action effectively removed them from contention and greatly strengthened the hands of Goering and the SS-Gestapo network. Once Hitler became convinced that the radical approach of the SA and party offered no solution, there was little he could do but accede to the arguments of Goering and Himmler who promised

[41] *Nazi Conspiracy and Aggression*, vol. 4, Document 1816-PS, p. 451.

to be more rational. The decision must have been a painful one for Hitler. His own sympathies tended to lie with the emotional approach of the radicals.

In one way or another the *Kristallnacht* pogrom involved all of the individuals and groups which had ever interested themselves in the question of Jewish participation in German life. This fact alone supported the easy interpretation that events on the night of November 9-10 were a carefully conceived action, coordinated in advance at the highest level and approved by all factions in the Nazi movement.[42] The evidence will not support such a conclusion. In the final analysis the *Kristallnacht* was a product of the lack of coordination which marked Nazi planning on Jewish policy and the result of a last-ditch effort by the radicals to wrest control over this policy.

The roots of the November pogrom reach back to the problem of foreign Jews residing in Germany, the problem which Himmler and Heydrich had proposed to solve by expulsion as early as February 1938. In addition to the Soviet Jews affected by the expulsion order, there was a much larger group of Polish Jews, still untouched, who posed a similar obstacle to creating a *judenrein* Germany. It was this problem with Polish Jews which led eventually to the pogrom in November. Very likely Himmler and Heydrich were deterred from issuing an order expelling Polish Jews by the size of the group, estimated to number about 70,000. Perhaps they were waiting to see whether the expulsion of Soviet Jews would provide an appropriate model for similar action against the Poles. In any event it was unlikely that the Nazis would suffer much longer the existence of so large a group of foreign Jews.

The crisis which began to develop in March was triggered, however, not by the Nazis, but by the Polish government.

---

[42] This analysis was understandably common in the outside world at the time and it has been perpetuated in such widely read works as Bullock, *Hitler*, pp. 473-474, and especially William L. Shirer, *The Rise and Fall of the Third Reich* (New York, 1960), pp. 430-431.

Whether out of anticipation of some Nazi initiative or because of its own anti-Semitic attitudes, the regime of Marshal Smigly-Ridz announced on March 31 an Expatriots Law which threatened to cancel the citizenship of Polish nationals living outside of Poland.[43] Polish citizens living outside the country were given until October 31 to have their passports reviewed and stamped by Polish consular officials. Without this special passport stamp Polish citizenship would be retracted and return to Poland denied. The effect of this order on the 70,000 Polish Jews in Germany (which now included Austria as well) was not immediately apparent. But when these people went to their consulates in Germany and were refused the vital stamp, the purpose of the Polish government became clear. Poland did not want them to return.[44]

Very few of them had any intention of returning to Poland, which recently had become nearly as unfriendly toward Jews as Germany.[45] The loss of citizenship, however, was a serious matter. Without it, prospects for emigrating from Germany were decidedly diminished at a time when it was becoming increasingly evident that emigration was the only possible escape from Nazi persecution.

The implication of the Polish action for Nazi Germany was clear as soon as Polish Jews left their consulates without the passport stamp. Germany would soon be saddled with a large community of Polish Jews rendered stateless by an action of the Polish government. Considering the difficulties faced by stateless persons who tried to emigrate, there was the immediate danger that these Jews would have no alternative to staying permanently in Germany. For a government committed to solving the Jewish problem, such a prospect was unthinkable. As the October 31 deadline drew nearer the situation took on a crisis

43 Adler-Rudel, *Ostjuden*, p. 153.

44 Waclaw Jedrzejewicz, *Diplomat in Berlin 1933-1939: Papers and Memoirs of Josef Lipski, Ambassador of Poland* (New York, 1968), p. 464.

45 See Harry M. Rabinowicz, *The Legacy of Polish Jewry: A History of Polish Jews in the Inter-War Years, 1919-1939* (New York, 1965), pp. 51-63.

atmosphere. If the Polish regime could not be persuaded to change its position, the Nazis were determined to force a solution.

In early October the Foreign Ministry inquired of Warsaw whether Poland really intended to block reentry of Jews who had failed to acquire the special stamp. Warsaw's answer that this was indeed the intention prodded the Nazis to action: "The German government cannot view such a development passively." The Foreign Office instructed its embassy in Warsaw: "The Jews of Polish nationality will, therefore, as a measure of precaution, be expelled from the Reich on the shortest possible notice."[46] On October 26, the Foreign Ministry asked the Gestapo to organize the expulsion. The following day the Gestapo began rounding up Polish Jews. The day after that, October 28, they were being transported by train and cattle truck toward the Polish frontier.

A direct confrontation between the Polish and German governments was in the making. Poland was preparing to resist the return of her citizens with force. When the transports arrived at the frontier station at Neu-Bentschen they were greeted by Polish border police who had constructed wire fences along the border and were prepared to man them with machine guns. Prevented by the border police from crossing into Poland and by the Gestapo from trying to make their way home, these thousands of people (eventually 17,000 after all the transports had arrived) found themselves in a no-man's-land between the spiritual trenches of German and Polish anti-Semitism. Some were housed temporarily in nearby barns and railway stations. Others were given no shelter at all and simply milled about in nearby fields.

It took several days for the two governments to reach even a temporary compromise. Finally Poland agreed to accept most of the refugees, and the Nazis in turn allowed the others to return to their homes in Germany to prepare for a later deportation.[47]

[46] *Akten,* p. 93.
[47] Ibid., p. 141.

The compromise was satisfactory to neither side. It merely delayed the final settlement of the issue. In the meantime, however, an unplanned and totally unexpected incident in Paris changed both the complexion and the substance of the crisis.

Early on the morning of November 7, a third secretary in the German embassy in Paris, Ernst vom Rath, was shot by a Jewish youth whose parents had been among those rounded up by the Gestapo. Rath's assailant, the seventeen-year-old Herschel Grünspan, was an ex-theology student from Frankfurt now living with relatives in Paris. When the young Grünspan learned of his parents' fate he determined to take revenge on the nearest symbol of Nazism. He bought a pistol and went directly to the German embassy, presumably to shoot Germany's ambassador to France.[48] When vom Rath rather than the ambassador appeared, Grünspan emptied his weapon into the third secretary instead, wounding him critically. The shooting of a German embassy official by a Jew led directly to the *Kristallnacht* during the early morning hours of November 10.

News of the shooting was published in the German press the afternoon of November 7 without being given special prominence. Editions of the following day relegated the story to the inside pages. The morning editions on November 9, however, headlined the story that vom Rath had died the previous afternoon and in accordance with Goebbels' directive to the German News Service announced: "The German people are entitled to identify the Jews in Germany with this crime."[49] Such infamous deeds, the Goebbels'-orchestrated press warned, would not go unpunished.

Punishment was not long in coming. By daybreak the next morning nearly 300 synagogues had been burned, hundreds of Jewish shops had been plundered and looted, some 25,000 Jews were under arrest. Property damage was estimated at several

[48] The events surrounding this affair have been painstakingly reconstructed by Helmut Heiber in, "Der Fall Grünspan," *Vierteljahrshefte für Zeitgeschichte* 5 (1957): 154-172; see also Hermann Graml, *Der 9. November 1938, "Reichskristallnacht"* (Bonn, 1958).

[49] *Voelkischer Beobachter*, November 9, 1938.

hundred million marks. The value of broken glass alone, from which the *Kristallnacht* or "night of crystal" got its name, was thought to be about 24 million marks.[50]

Except for the arrests carried out by Heydrich's Gestapo, the *Kristallnacht* was an operation conceived and executed by the radicals within the party. Vengeance for vom Rath's death was given to the "little man" in the Nazi movement, the one whose anti-Jewish energies had been so long restrained. For the first time since early 1933 the full SA was reengaged in the execution of Jewish policy. Unleashed, these energies erupted into an orgy of violence resulting in the most spectacular anti-Jewish pogrom since those of late nineteenth-century Russia. In hundreds of communities throughout Germany, large and small, the pogrom took its toll of life and property. Where there had been a breakdown in communications, the "night of crystal" was delayed for a day, but few places were spared.

That it was so widespread and created so much damage seemed to point to a new level of cooperation between elements competing for control of Jewish policy. Appearances on this point were highly deceiving.[51] There was some coordination, there was some high-level planning, but there was very little cooperation and a great deal of dissent from those elements which the *Kristallnacht* had caught almost completely off guard. A return to the spontaneous terrorism of early 1933 seriously threatened the Jewish policies of those who favored the rational approach. This threat came, moreover, at a time when the rational approaches of Goering, Himmler, Heydrich, and Eichmann seemed on the verge of achieving success in Aryanization and emigration.

The chief instigator of the *Kristallnacht* pogrom was Joseph Goebbels whose earlier attempts at influencing Jewish policy had been largely unsuccessful. Goebbels was still in the process of rescuing his reputation from the effects of his love affair with

---

[50] Lionel Kochan, *Pogrom, 10 November 1938* (London, 1957), pp. 40-50.

[51] See K.Y. Ball-Kaduri, "Die Vorplannung der Kristallnacht," *Zeitschrift für die Geschichte der Juden* 4 (1966): 211-216.

the film star Lida Baarova. The Baarova affair had brought him into considerable disfavor with Hitler who had recently confronted him with a choice between ending the liaison or stepping down as propaganda minister. The ambitious Goebbels, of course, chose to protect his position and upon Hitler's order began repairing the strained relationship with his wife and family.

The assassination of vom Rath offered Goebbels the opportunity to repair his relations with Hitler as well.[52] Fortunately for Goebbels, there was scheduled for the evening of November 9 the celebration of the fifteenth anniversary of Hitler's 1923 Beer Hall *Putsch*. Since 1933 that date had become the occasion of an annual commemorative celebration in Munich. Veterans and heroes of the Nazi movement gathered to bask in the memory of their first attempt to seize power. Hitler himself always appeared to memorialize the contributions of the "old fighters" to National Socialism. It was from the scene of this celebration, held in the festival hall of the old Munich town hall, that the signal for launching the *Kristallnacht* was sent throughout the Reich.

A special air of agitation pervaded the hall that evening. Word of vom Rath's death had just arrived from Paris. Hitler, whose speech on previous occasions had always been the highlight of these events, failed to address the assembly. Instead, reports an eyewitness, he spent most of the evening engaged in "a very serious discussion" with Goebbels, during which he was overheard to say, "The SA should be allowed to have its final fling."[53] Suddenly and without explanation Hitler got up and left the meeting. The speech making was left to Goebbels, the top-ranking Nazi official left behind. To the assembled SA chieftains, *Gauleiter*, and party comrades the propaganda minister spoke of the tragedy in Paris and its implications for the German Reich. He hinted broadly that demonstrations against Jews would not be opposed by the party. Earlier in the day he

52 Heiber, *Joseph Goebbels*, pp. 279-280.
53 Kochan, *Pogrom*, p. 51.

had already suggested in the *Voelkischer Beobachter* that the Paris crime would not go unpunished. Now, without actually saying so, he was giving the signal for what by daybreak the next morning would be dubbed the *Kristallnacht*. The reason for such circumlocution in public? It was to look as if the German populace was giving spontaneous vent to its anger over the crime of international Jewry.

Neither Himmler nor Heydrich was present at the festival hall gathering. The reason for their absence is difficult to understand, especially since they were both in Munich. Heydrich was technically ineligible to be called an "old fighter," having joined the movement only in 1931, but such a fine point had not prevented Goebbels, who had not participated in the *Putsch* either, from taking his prominent role. Himmler's credentials as an "old fighter," on the other hand, were in impeccable order. For whatever reason, neither the SS nor Gestapo chiefs had been alerted beforehand of what the evening had in store.

Himmler reacted bitterly to the news of the planned action and blamed the whole thing on Goebbels' "lust for power."[54] He was also piqued that Hitler had told him nothing about possible anti-Jewish measures when they had been together earlier in the evening. Heydrich was not let in on the plans until one o'clock the next morning, when his Gestapo was ordered to make large-scale arrests of Jewish males. The order made it clear that the SS and Gestapo were not to interfere in the action itself. Later, Heydrich emphasized that this order absolved him of any responsibility for the excesses of the pogrom, including the thirty-four Jews who had been killed. Any blame rested squarely upon undisciplined elements such as the SA.

The SA, on the other hand, seized eagerly at the opportunity for another "fling" at the Jews. Himmler and Heydrich were still in the dark about what was going on when SA units throughout the Reich were ordered into action. The case of an SA group in Kiel suffices to explain the pattern repeated through-

[54] Ibid., p. 57, n. 2.

out Germany in the late evening and early morning hours of November 9-10.

The chief of Kiel's *Nordmark* SA group, a certain Meyer-Quade, was in Munich for the reunion. At 10:00 P.M. he received a call at his hotel informing him of the plan for later that evening. He immediately phoned the *Gauleiter* of his home district to offer the services of his SA unit. About an hour later, after receiving confirmation regarding the plans, Meyer-Quade called his staff leaders in Kiel. He told them:

> A Jew has committed a crime. A German diplomat is dead. In Friedrichstadt, Kiel, Lübeck, and elsewhere useless Jewish meeting places are still standing. Even Jewish shops are still in our midst. Both of these are now superfluous. There will be no plundering. No abuses are to take place. Foreign Jews may not be touched. If you meet resistance make use of your weapons. The action must be carried out in civilian clothes and must be finished by 5:00 A.M. [tomorrow morning].[55]

Meyer-Quade's staff had difficulty in rounding up its men at first. Most of them were still celebrating the Beer Hall *Putsch* in the various taverns around Kiel. At least some of them were no longer in condition to carry out any sort of action. It took until 3:45 A.M. before the entire group had assembled and was ready to carry out its assignment. The combination of beer and darkness apparently encouraged the men in their task. By five o'clock Kiel's synagogues were aflame, Jewish stores had been vandalized, windows broken, and many Jews arrested.[56] What happened in Kiel happened in hundreds of towns and cities in Germany. Larger cities such as Berlin, Munich, Frankfurt, and Vienna were especially hard hit. In many instances instructions for the evening had been exceeded. Jewish shops were plundered. Jews were beaten and in some cases murdered. Many a

[55] From Meyer-Quade's report of December 9, 1938. Schumacher Archiv, Folder 409 SA, BDC.
[56] Ibid.

wife of an SA man woke up the next morning to find herself with a new coat or a new lamp for her sitting room.

Resentments against Goebbels, the SA, and the party apparatus made themselves felt during the next few days. Himmler and Heydrich were especially disturbed at the turn events had taken. They much preferred the cold terror of the police state to the emotional fervor of the SA. None of the objectives they had defined for Jewish policy had been forwarded by the pogrom. Among the Jews they had been ordered to arrest were many who had been instrumental in assisting the emigration process.[57] Their internment undermined the prospect of an accelerated Jewish emigration. Apparently, too, the SA was not to be satisfied with a "final fling." During the next weeks it continued to irritate the SS leadership by initiating continued anti-Jewish measures. In some areas—Hannover for example—the SS finally prepared to use force against the SA or anyone else to assure an end to all such activities.[58] A revived SA threatened the near monopoly on terror which Heydrich and Himmler had managed to put together. It took until December to bring the SA back into line. It was finally warned that all actions had to be cleared through SA Chief Victor Lutze and even then permission for any action had to be in writing and cleared through all channels of the new command structure for Jewish policy.[59]

The most immediate target of Himmler's resentment was Goebbels himself. Himmler had long been unhappy with the propaganda minister, but his latest action was too direct a challenge to ignore. The League of Nations commissioner for the Free City of Danzig, Carl Burckhardt, learned of the lengths Himmler was prepared to go when in mid-November he came to Berlin to speak against a possible Nazi-led pogrom in Danzig. Himmler's personal adjutant, Karl Wolff, told Burckhardt: "The situation in this country has become impossible. Something will have to happen. The one responsible is Goebbels who

57 Prinz, "Role of the Gestapo," pp. 213-214.
58 Himmler File, T175 (411), 2933020.
59 Schumacher Archiv, Folder 240 II, BDC.

has an intolerable influence on the Fuehrer. We had hoped . . . for sometime to bring him down [*zur Strecke zu bringen*] and this time we were sure we had him. But once again the Fuehrer has saved him. Things cannot go on like this. We'll have to deal with him." [60] Wolff's desire to reassure Burckhardt about Danzig may have led him to exaggerate somewhat the SS feud with Goebbels, but Burckhardt learned from other sources that the feud was both genuine and serious.

Goering too was upset with the situation produced by the *Kristallnacht*. In recent months he had made significant progress in Aryanization and other aspects of Jewish participation in the economy. The SA and party action of November 9-10, because of its economic implications, directly affected his concerns with the German economy. For two days following the pogrom he and Hitler engaged in lengthy talks to discuss its impact and ramifications. No minutes of these talks were taken, but they resulted in Goering gaining a much more decisive voice in control over Jewish policy. They also resulted in convincing Hitler that Goebbels' advice on Jewish matters was at best faulty, although the Fuehrer resisted whatever measures Goering may have had in mind for punishing the ambitious Goebbels.

The content of the Hitler-Goering talks was revealed on November 12, at a meeting in Goering's Air Ministry office. Most important Nazi leaders were invited and over a hundred people attended.[61] Among those present were Goebbels, Heydrich, Interior Minister Frick, the new Economics Minister Funk, a representative of the German insurance companies, and an observer from the Foreign Ministry. Goering chaired the meeting and used it as a forum to announce the conclusions of his discussions with Hitler. He began the meeting with the most important conclusion. The Fuehrer had issued an order, he said, "requesting that the Jewish question be now, once and for all,

[60] Quoted by Carl J. Burckhardt, *Meine Danziger Mission, 1937-1939* (Munich, 1960), p. 230.

[61] Bernhard Lösener, the Interior Ministry official who had been instrumental in drafting the Nuremberg Laws, attended the meeting and took notes. See Lösener, "Als Rassereferat," pp. 288-292.

coordinated or solved in one way or another."[62] It quickly became obvious that Goering was in a testy mood. He castigated the propaganda minister for failing to realize that the destruction of Jewish property hurt German insurance companies more than it did the Jews. "Demonstrations," he stressed, "don't harm the Jew, but me . . . the last authority for the German economy."[63] It was insane to loot and burn only to have insurance make good the loss.

More desirable than demonstrations would be an accelerated Aryanization of Jewish properties. But this Aryanization could not be carried out by officials in the Economics Ministry. "That way we would never finish." Goering himself promised to arrange the final expropriation process. That was necessary to prevent it from being tied up by the established bureaucracies or, even worse, being carried too far by the party's radicals. The last ties to the party's ideological position on economics were formally abandoned. Instead of being distributed to the small Ayran businessman, Jewish property was to be sold to the highest bidder.

The Aryanization of all larger establishments, said Goering, "naturally is to be my lot."[64] In these cases he would estimate the real value of the property and decide what amount the Jew should be paid. He would, of course, be paid as little as possible. The property would then be sold, according to its actual value, with the profits going to the Reich. Party members could expect no preference when Aryanized property was placed on sale. Ability to pay and ability to manage the enterprise were the considerations Goering deemed most important. Exceptions would be made for party members only if they could prove they had gone bankrupt because of corrupt Jewish business practices. Otherwise there was no intention of enriching "chauffeurs and *Gauleiter* [who already] have profited so much."[65] Redistribu-

---

[62] *Nazi Conspiracy and Aggression*, vol. 4, Document 1816-PS, p. 425.
[63] Ibid.
[64] Ibid.
[65] Ibid.

tion of property, one of the "immutable points" in the Nazi program, was going to benefit Germany's big business interests but not the party's rank and file nor even its leaders.

The amount paid to Jews for their Aryanized property, no matter how little, was to be placed immediately into blocked accounts. This, said Goering, was necessary to keep the Jew from running to the nearest jewelry store, buying diamonds, and fleeing across the border. He also suggested that payment might be made in Reich bonds or some other nontransferable assets. As it eventually turned out, it made little difference what compensation Jews received for their property. During the war all their accounts were seized by the Nazis.

The problem of insurance was the most immediately important question on the agenda. Who was to pay for the damage of the *Kristallnacht?* Most of the property had been insured. Damage estimates by the insurance representative Herr Hilgard were set at about 25 million marks. Heydrich added that when the loss of taxes on sales, property, and income were added, the total damage to the Reich might reach several hundred million marks.

Who was to pay? The insurance companies, of course, said Goering. The confidence in German insurance was at stake. Even Hilgard, who was very unhappy that day, recognized that a refusal to pay something to somebody would wreck the basis of the insurance business. The next question: who should receive the payment? The possibility of actually paying those whose property had been damaged—the Jews—was quickly eliminated. After all, the *Kristallnacht* had been punishment for the Jewish crime in Paris and for the accumulated offenses against the German people. It was suggested that Jews could be paid and some of their assets could then be confiscated to reimburse the insurance companies. Goering would have none of this. The insurance companies were liable; they would have to pay. That was the business they were in. Goering finally concluded that it was the Reich itself which had suffered the real damage. "There will be a lawful order," he told Hilgard, "forbidding you to make direct payment to Jews. You shall have to make payment . . . not to the Jews, but to the [Reich] Finance Minister. What he does with the money is his business."[66]

The insurance question settled, Goering returned once more to the matter of Jews participating in the economy. Economics Minister Funk, little more than Goering's mouthpiece, announced a piece of legislation which would greatly facilitate Aryanization. Effective January 1, 1939, Jews would be prohibited from operating retail or wholesale establishments as well as independent artisan shops. The law also enjoined them from having employees or offering goods on the market. In these circumstances the Jewish businessman was left no alternative to selling to the Aryanizers. Jewish employees who so far had managed to hold onto their positions were also hit by the new law. An Aryan employer was empowered to cancel any contract with his Jewish employees on the first of the year. Another of the law's provisions required the retiring of Jewish corporation board members by the same date. As the order was finally implemented, certain Jewish wholesale and large manufacturing enterprises were temporarily exempted.[67] There was to be no doubt, however, what implications the order had for Jews. Their last foothold on the German economy was being torn from beneath them.

Heydrich, except for answering a few questions, had remained silent through much of the meeting, but Funk's announcement prompted him to raise another problem, "In spite of the elimination of the Jew from the German economy, the main problem, namely to kick the Jew out of Germany, remains," he warned. He mentioned the difficulties emigration continued to face in Germany, but then pointed to the success of Eichmann's operation in Vienna, for which he as Gestapo and SD chief could take some credit. Eichmann's extortion of money from wealthy Jews to assist their less affluent brothers had achieved remarkable results. At least 45,000 Austrian Jews had been

66 Ibid.
67 Himmler File, T175 (280), 2774192.

forced to emigrate during the last months largely because Eichmann had succeeded in centralizing the administrative apparatus. From Germany on the other hand, where no central apparatus existed, the number of Jewish emigrants during the same time had been significantly less.

Goering was at first reluctant to accept Eichmann's success at face value. The loss of foreign currency, even if it was Jewish money helping to rid the Reich of Jews, bothered him, but he did eventually consent to Heydrich's suggestion that Eichmann's example be imitated in the Reich proper. Given the present circumstances, however, Heydrich did not expect the spectacular successes in Vienna to be all that transferable. His estimate that 8,000 to 10,000 Jews could be gotten out of Germany every year envisioned an eight- to ten-year continuation of concentrated effort. In the meantime there was the question of what to do with those Jews who remained behind. The latest economic restrictions imposed on top of a rapid increase in Aryanization offered very little prospect for German Jewry to support itself. The destruction during the recent pogrom had only exacerbated the problem of growing destitution. In Frankfurt, moreover, local party units had closed down and seized the assets of the largest Jewish welfare agency.[68]

Goering proposed the establishing of Jewish ghettos in the larger cities, self-contained communities which would exist at a bare subsistence level, but to this Heydrich raised strenuous objections. The problem of ghettos had been studied earlier by Adolf Eichmann who concluded they would be uncontrollable. Echoing the conclusions of his very able subordinate, Heydrich pointed out that ghettos would become the permanent hideouts of criminal elements and the breeding ground for epidemics. The Jewish population would be much easier to control if it were forced to wear some kind of identifying insignia. Goering immediately thought of a special Jewish uniform, but Heydrich insisted the insignia would suffice.

The discussion of emigration ended with Goering's mention

[68] *Dokumente Frankfurter Juden*, p. 297.

that he had discussed the whole problem with Hitler a few days before. The Fuehrer had said that if foreign countries were so concerned about the Jew, they would simply have to take him.

By now the meeting, which had begun at 11:00 A.M., was well into its third hour. No one seemed anxious to discuss any of the remaining aspects of the Jewish question in detail. Goebbels, the man most responsible for the actions which had made this meeting necessary, made a few suggestions about restricting Jews from movie theaters, railway coaches, and schools, but his proposals were quickly shouted down. If he was hoping to re-assert some influence on Jewish policy, it was obvious that Goering and Heydrich had no intention of brooking any inter-ference from the despised little propaganda minister. The fact that some of his proposals were shortly implemented added noth-ing to Goebbels' standing on the Jewish question.[69]

A last-minute announcement by Goering that German Jews would be forced to pay a one-billion-mark fine as punishment for the vom Rath assassination elicited almost no response. After three hours no one seemed surprised, or even especially inter-ested. In its audacity the fine exceeded even the terms of the agreed-upon insurance settlement. Goering then concluded the meeting with the comment that "If, in the near future, the German Reich should come into conflict with foreign powers, it goes without saying that we in Germany should first of all let it come to a showdown with the Jews." No one asked what this meant and Goering did not elaborate. The meeting was ad-journed.

That same afternoon there appeared in the official *Reichs-gesetzblatt* the decree regarding the one-billion-mark fine.[70] It was entitled the "Order Regarding the Atonement for Jews of German Citizenship." The fine was to be exacted for: "The hostile behavior of Judaism against the German people and

69 A decree of November 15, 1938, by the Reichs Education Minister expelled the few remaining Jewish students from German schools. Schumacher Archiv, Folder 240 II, BDC.

70 RGBl, I, 1938, p. 1579.

Reich, which does not shrink even from cowardly assassination. . . ."

It was quite apparent from the lengthy meeting of November 12 that a *Kristallnacht* was no solution to the Jewish problem. Goering was unhappy because of the economic difficulties the action had caused. Heydrich certainly had something more rational in mind when he spoke of a solution to the Jewish question. Not that they objected to violence; it was uncontrolled violence to which they were opposed. Both Goering and Heydrich had made themselves unmistakably clear on that point.

A "night of crystal" is what the radicals in the Nazi movement had been waiting for since the day Hitler seized power. It is probably what they had anticipated the general boycott of April 1933 would turn out to be. It is what they had been rehearsing for every time they threw a stone through the shop window of a Jewish proprietor or scrawled a swastika on the door of a synagogue. Time and time again their violent ambitions had been thwarted by some circumstance which demanded a degree of restraint. When the great orgy was finally permitted they made the most of their opportunity. For the first time the SA, the Nazi *Gauleiter,* and other radical anti-Semites had no reason to complain about the supposed mildness of Jewish policy.

The "final fling" about which Hitler had spoken on the evening of November 9 turned out to be a brief one, however. The primary purpose of the meeting in the Air Ministry was to prevent any repetition of the *Kristallnacht.* Exactly what Goering and Hitler talked about in their conversations which preceded the meeting is not known, but it is clear that Hitler agreed to ending radical participation in solving the Jewish problem. A few evenings before he had been talked into something quite different by Goebbels.

The *Kristallnacht* was not repeated and for that reason it marked the end of an era in Nazi Jewish policy. It had made clear the difficulties which lack of coordination raised. The making of Jewish policy, even its execution, could no longer be left to amateurs. If there were to be successes on the scale envisioned by Hitler the cold steady hand of the professional was the first requirement. Only from this hand could come a coordinated policy, one with a single direction and a clearly defined objective.

During the last six weeks of 1938 Goering clearly and officially came to be in charge of Jewish policy. The phrase "The Fuehrer upon my suggestion has reached the following decisions" preceded his policy announcements to leading party and government authorities. On December 14, he sent a letter to all Reich officials announcing that he had taken charge of Jewish affairs: "To secure the necessary unity in the handling of the Jewish question, upon which rests the handling of economic matters, I am asking that all decrees and other important orders touching upon Jewish matters be cleared through my office and have my approval. Remind all of the officials under your authority that absolutely no independent initiatives on the Jewish question are to be undertaken."[71] For the first time the lines of authority on the Jewish problem were clearly established.

Goering used his newly assigned authority to remove the last important props supporting a Jewish community in Germany. All Jewish political organizations, including the Zionist Federation and the *Centralverein,* were disbanded.[72] All Jewish newspapers except the *Jüdische Nachrichtenblatt* were forbidden to publish. The use of dining and sleeping cars on trains was forbidden to Jews, and Jews who received pension payments found these payments reduced.[73] Jews who had their property Aryanized found the little that was being paid them confiscated and figured toward the fine levied against Jews for the vom Rath murder.[74]

The subsidiary aim of Goering and the SS leadership of bringing about the fall of Propaganda Minister Goebbels was not realized. But Goering and Heydrich did hound the SA and

[71] Schumacher Archiv, Folder 240 II, BDC.
[72] Rosenbluth, *Go Forth and Serve,* p. 271.
[73] *Dokumente Frankfurter Juden,* pp. 233-234.
[74] Nebel, *Geschichte der jüdischen Gemeinde,* p. 43.

party officials who had participated so eagerly in what they considered to be the Goebbels-inspired pogrom. In late November Goering appointed a commission to investigate the many reports of irregularities on the part of SA and party people during the evening of the *Kristallnacht*.[75] A good deal of Jewish property, including an occasional automobile, had found its way into the hands of local officials. In Franconia the activities of *Gauleiter* Julius Streicher seemed to warrant special attention. Much of the property which had been confiscated or was later unofficially Aryanized never found its way to the state, but remained somewhere in the *Gau*. On January 14, 1939, Goering reminded the SA once again that eliminating Jews from the economy was exclusively his business and any profits belonged to the state. "Persons or party units which take any unauthorized advantage of the transfer of Jewish goods or property may expect a settling of accounts from the side of the Reich."[76] In February the Gestapo was still complaining that countless things such as typewriters, radios, and jewelry had not been turned in.[77]

The measures taken against Jews in the economy all pointed to renewed emphasis upon emigration. Eichmann's results in Vienna had convinced Hitler, and Goering too, that his measures were applicable to the old Reich as well. Rublee, who in the weeks after the *Kristallnacht* had been in contact with lower German officials, was once again ignored. The problem was to be solved without outside interference. On January 24, 1939, Goering commissioned Heydrich to organize the emigration of Jews who were still in Germany, using the model Eichmann had established in Vienna. A Central Office for Jewish Emigration on the Vienna model was to be created in the larger cities of Germany and was to be responsible for all aspects of emigration. In addition Goering instructed Heydrich to:

1. prepare all measures for a stepped up process of emigration, including coordination of the activities of all Jewish

[75] *Nazi Conspiracy and Aggression*, vol. 2, Document 1757-PS, pp. 700-703.
[76] Schumacher Archiv, Folder 240 II, BDC.
[77] Himmler File, T175 (280), 2774187.

organizations which might be of assistance; make all the arrangements regarding the necessary transfer of money, and together with the Reich establish which countries are the most willing to accept emigrants.

2. steer matters so that especially poor Jews emigrate.

3. concern himself with individual cases so that emigration in all phases might be facilitated.[78]

The Jew—every Jew—was supposed to emigrate, and Heydrich was placed in charge of the machinery.

At the Air Ministry meeting in November, Goering had summed up his attitude toward the first five years of Jewish policy: "To our shame, we made only pretty plans, which we executed very slowly."[79] That situation was now changed. Heydrich's assignment was to implement what had always stood as the Nazi ideal—a *judenrein* Germany. It remained to be seen whether he would succeed. If he did not, the machinery and the command structure for even more drastic measures existed. The "experts" were finally in charge of Jewish policy.

---

[78] Ibid.

[79] *Nazi Conspiracy and Aggression*, vol. 4, Document 1816-PS, p. 425.

ON JULY 31, 1941, a dispatch from Hermann Goering reached Reinhard Heydrich at the latter's Security Police headquarters in Berlin. It was a day of delirious excitement in the Reich capital. Five weeks earlier Hitler's armies had invaded the Soviet Union. At that very moment German troops were racing across the broad expanse of western Russia in pursuit of a disorganized and retreating Red Army. Smolensk was already in Hitler's grasp; Moscow and Leningrad, it seemed certain, would fall shortly. Never before had Hitler been so fully in command of events on the European continent. Within a few months at the most the grip of bolshevism upon Russia would be wrenched loose and Nazi Germany could go about the business of establishing its European New Order.

Goering's dispatch to Heydrich had to do with that business. It was brief and to the point. The time had come, he informed Heydrich, "to make all the preparations in organizational, practical, and material matters necessary for a total solution [*Gesamtlösung*] of the Jewish question in territories under German influence." Moreover, said Goering, "I am asking you to prepare and submit to me in the near future, a master plan for carrying out the final solution [*Endlösung*] of the Jewish problem."[1]

In the earlier order of January 14, 1939, Heydrich had been commissioned to arrange for the emigration or evacuation of Jews from German territory. The chain of command created in 1939 remained the same; only the orders had changed. For the first time the Nazi leadership had begun to think in practical terms of a total and final solution. Like so many of its earlier

[1] Reinhard Heydrich Personal Akten, H22/A, BDC.

policies, emigration too had failed to solve the Jewish problem in Germany. As early as June 1939, Heydrich's SD had reported that emigration was faltering, "first of all because of the failure to organize effectively the Central Offices for Emigration and a similar failure on the part of the Jewish *Reichsvereinigung;* secondly because of the growing tendency for other countries to lock their doors against immigration."[2] The report might also have made mention of the fact that with each of Hitler's foreign policy successes and conquests more Jews were being added to Germany's territory. The annexation of Austria, then the Sudetenland, and finally the takeover of Czechoslovakia had added at least 300,000 Jews who had to be dealt with. The Nazi conquest of Poland alone had added another 3,000,000, and eventually Nazi acquisitions brought the total number of Jews within the German grip to about 10,000,000.

An emigration policy which had not been able to keep pace with Hitler's peacetime acquisitions fell apart almost completely with the outbreak of war. Yet with each wartime acquisition the Jewish problem took on larger and larger dimensions. It was the Jewish problem on this new level to which Goering addressed himself in July 1941. The imminent collapse of Russia would bring another 4,000,000 Jews (there were no exact figures on the number of Jews in Russia) under Nazi control. If there was to be a solution to the Jewish problem, it would require a drastically new approach.

The spector of 10,000,000 Jews did nothing to weaken the Nazi commitment to finding a solution to the Jewish problem. Having arrived in 1941 at the pinnacle of its power and self-assurance, the Third Reich leadership could finally afford to think in terms of a solution which would be total and final. Questions of world opinion were now, of course, irrelevant, as were the earlier concerns with foreign exchange, immigration quotas, and Jewish Vaticans. A Germany at war with the world's major powers and fully confident of victory was for the first time

2 Report on the Jewish situation in Germany by SD Section II 112, dated June 15, 1939. Himmler File, T175 (411), 2936198.

in a position to define unlimited aims for its Jewish policy. "Fortunately," commented Goebbels on this new situation, "a whole series of possibilities presents itself for us in wartime that would be denied us in peacetime."[3]

From the summer of 1941, the problems of effecting a solution were to be, as Goering suggested to Heydrich, organizational and administrative. Questions related to transport and gas and the harnessing of technical and administrative talents had become paramount. Once these problems had been solved, the limits to any solution of the Jewish problem had to be imposed by the Nazis themselves. The limits became the unthinkable. To this Auschwitz, Treblinka, Dachau, and their sister camps are the grisly reminders.

We have traced in the preceding chapters the paths which led eventually to the gates of these extermination camps, paths which were by no means direct or, for that matter, charted far in advance. During the early years of the Third Reich no one in the Nazi movement, from the Fuehrer down, had defined what the substance of a solution to the Jewish problem might be. The biological premises of Aryan superiority and Jewish inferiority might logically have led to the conclusion that there was no real problem at all, but the Nazi Aryan was hardly satisfied to bask comfortably in the knowledge of his own superiority. Given the fashion in which the Nazis purported to understand the Jewish problem, one might have expected the biological separation of the races. Yet such a separation came into being relatively late, and even then rather haphazardly in the form of the Nuremberg Laws which were really the product of a Hitlerian afterthought. Only in the broadest sense are the anti-Semitic premises of National Socialism useful in explaining the course which a wide variety of Jewish policies eventually took.

The fact that there was no widespread agreement on what might comprise a solution to the Jewish problem rested ultimately on lack of agreement about the nature of the Jewish

[3] Louis P. Lochner, ed., *The Goebbels Diaries, 1942-1943* (Garden City, N.Y., 1948), p. 148.

257

problem itself. To many of those who supported Hitler before 1933 the Jewish problem was an economic one. The exclusion of Jewish competition would undoubtedly have been satisfactory to the vast majority of his lower-middle-class followers. But then Hitler did very little to satisfy the demands of the lower middle classes, the ones to whom he had made the most grandiose promises. To other groups, such as his own SA, the Jews offered a target for venting their addiction to violence. Even here, however, Hitler had to step in when SA violence interfered with the more nonideological aims such as strengthening the traditional economy in order to rearm Germany. By late 1934 it was becoming increasingly clear that a solution to the Jewish problem was not going to come about merely to satisfy the interests of pressures from inside or outside the Nazi movement. When a proposal to institute the formal separation of Jews and Aryans by preventing future interracial marriages crossed Hitler's desk in 1933, it received little if any attention despite the fact that such marriages lay at the heart of what Hitler proclaimed to be the Jewish problem. If there was a logic in the Nazi search for a solution it is not to be found in the premises or even the promises of Nazi propaganda.

The figure of Adolf Hitler during these years of search is a shadowy one. His hand appears only rarely in the actual making of Jewish policy between 1933 and 1938. One can only conclude from this that he occupied his time with more important concerns. In part the vagaries and inconsistencies of Jewish policy during the first five years of Nazi rule stem from his failure to offer guidance. A clear and consistent policy was virtually impossible without the Fuehrer himself making basic decisions or delegating to a subordinate the authority to make such decisions for him. The fact that he avoided both of these options until late 1938 encouraged the independent and often rival policies pursued by factions within the Nazi movement. It also made inevitable the trial and error approach to the Jewish problem which marked the period to November 1938. There were definite advantages for Hitler in such an aloof stance, of course. He could learn from the trials and disassociate himself from the errors.

At no point did Hitler consider retreating on the Jewish issue, an option which his aloofness to the fray left open. There were numerous points at which a quiet retreat would have been possible. In fact there were times when it was feared by the radical racists that Hitler was doing just that. The Nuremberg Laws were followed by Hitler's announcement that the persecution of Jews was to be ended after the discriminatory measures had taken effect. While they were less explicit, the temporary retreats after the boycott of 1933 and the statement that an Aryan clause was not applicable to commerce had seemed to point in a similar direction. These turned out to be no more than tactical retreats, however, or tacit admissions of failure. Naturally these failures were always publicized as significant successes. That has been a politician's prerogative since politics began and Hitler was not the one to violate such a time-honored tradition. What made Hitler different was that he did not accept failure. Reluctant as he was to offer specific guidelines on Jewish policy, he was not looking for a convenient way to abandon the struggle against the Jews.

Each one of the failures during these first years of Nazi rule— whether of boycott, legislation, Aryanization, or emigration— was the signal for renewed effort. The failure of a specific policy or action might discredit a particular group; it did not discourage others from trying their own hand at finding a solution. Failure in these circumstances was relative, of course. The thousands of Jews who suffered from the legislation, who lost their businesses, or professional practices, or were forced to emigrate leaving behind their friends, families, and fortunes would have been hard to convince that Nazi efforts at persecution had failed. That the Nazis considered these efforts to have failed, however, indicates that failure was considered to be anything less than absolute success. If one Jew was boycotted, all Jews had to be boycotted. If one Jewish business was to be Aryanized, all had to be Aryanized. The same held true for any other policy, be it emigration or finally murder.

The absolute objectives envisioned for these Jewish policies prior to the war virtually insured their failure. No Jewish policy could be pursued in the fantasy world created by Nazi propaganda. After January 30, 1933, this policy, like any other, had to be pursued in a world structured by unemployment, foreign currency shortages, a need for imports, German military weakness, pressures from outside Germany, and the very real fact of bitter intraparty rivalries. The search for a solution to the Jewish problem had been set into motion by the anti-Semitic energies which constituted the heart of Nazism; it was driven forward by the frustrations of each successive failure. A more extreme approach appeared to be the only alternative to the less-than-total solutions which had proved unsatisfactory or unworkable.

The manner in which these various Jewish policies were pursued is highly revealing of the nature of the Nazi movement itself. Both Nazi propaganda and the totalitarian model later used to explain the functioning of the Nazi system tried to make of it a monolithic structure. It was nothing of the sort. The gruesome efficiency of the wartime death camps came only after the voices of numerous contestants for control over Jewish policy had been silenced. It took violence and bloodshed to satisfy the SA. The lower party apparatus could be ignored, while those of the stripe of Rosenberg and Streicher could be shunted aside by allowing them to engage in essentially irrelevant propaganda or research. The party slogan, "Complete authority from above; absolute obedience from below," which supposedly gave substance to Hitler's *Fuehrerprinzip* was, as we have seen, rarely applied to Jewish policy until after the *Kristallnacht*.

The *Fuehrerprinzip* model, at least as it was understood by Hitler, does little to explain the workings of the Nazi system.

It has recently been suggested that feudalism serves as a more useful model for understanding Nazi authority relationships.[4] The suggestion that Hitler held and wielded power less as an absolute dictator than as a feudal lord helps to explain his peculiar neutrality to the bitter rivalries seething between party factions beneath him. Not until he had seen the direction these struggles were taking and assessed the advantage he might gain from them did he intervene. The factional struggle for control over Jewish policy was not resolved until late 1938, after the SS had clearly emerged with the most effective proposals for a solution. Then, and only then, did Hitler commission it to prepare a coordinated policy toward the Jews.

That Hitler was able to contain the rivalries and maintain his position at the top of this tangled and shifting hierarchy is testimony to his political acuity and charismatic power.[5] It was the Jew who helped hold Hitler's system together—on the practical as well as the ideological level. The Jew allowed Hitler to ignore the long list of economic and social promises he had made to the SA, the lower party apparatus, and the lower middle classes. By steering the attention of these groups away from their more genuine grievances and toward the Jew, Hitler succeeded in blunting the edge of their revolutionary wrath, leaving him freer to pursue his own nonideological goals of power in cooperation with groups whose influence he had once promised to weaken or even destroy. An ideological retreat on the Jewish issue in these circumstances was impossible. Even the tactical retreats served to remind segments of his following of a long list of unfulfilled promises. The continued search for a solution to the Jewish problem allowed Hitler to maintain ideological contact with elements of his movement for whom National Socialism had done very little. This situation, which Hitler had

---

[4] Robert Koehl, "Feudal Aspects of National Socialism," *American Political Science Review* 54 (December 1960); 921-933.

[5] See Joseph Nyomarky, *Charisma and Factionalism in the Nazi Party* (Minneapolis, 1967), pp. 9-15.

created for himself, made the Jewish problem and the promise of its solution a functional necessity. When such a necessity was supported also by the convictions of a Hitler and a Himmler there could be no retreat. The search had to continue, whatever the obstacles. Out of these circumstances emerged the logic of the boycott, and finally of the extermination camp.

BIBLIOGRAPHIES AND GUIDES TO DOCUMENTS

American Historical Association, Committee for the Study of War Documents. *Guides to German War Records Microfilmed at Alexandria, Va.,* no. 39, *Records of the Reichs Leader of the SS and Chief of the German Police,* part 3. Washington, D.C.: National Archives, 1963.

Ball-Kaduri, K.Y. "Testimonies and Recollections about Activities Organized by German Jewry during the Years 1933-1945: Catalogue of Manuscripts in the Yad Washem Archives." *Yad Washem Studies* 4 (1960): 317-333.

Robinson, Jacob, and Philip Friedman, eds. *Guide to Jewish History under Nazi Impact.* New York: YIVO Institute for Jewish Research, 1960.

Wiener Library. *Persecution and Resistance under the Nazis.* Wiener Library Catalogue Series, no. 1 and 2, London: Vallentine, Mitchell, 1960.

UNPUBLISHED DOCUMENTS

BERLIN DOCUMENT CENTER: Berlin, Germany. (Since this study has been completed, these records at the Berlin Document Center have been transferred to the Federal Archives of the West German Federal Republic at Koblenz.)

The following document collections have been vital to this study:
Collection: Bezirksämter, Folder 15, Behandlung der Judenfrage
Collection: Bezirksämter, Folder 35, Massnahmen gegen Juden
Collection: Streicher, Folder 21, Zentralkomitee für Boykottbewegung
Feststellung der Emigranten, Folder 21
Schumacher Archiv: Folder 240 I, Judenfrage
Schumacher Archiv: Folder 240 II, Judenfrage
Hauptarchiv der NSDAP: Folder 504, Nazis und Judenfrage

EICHMANN TRIAL TRANSCRIPT:

Transcript of the trial in the case of the Attorney-General of the Government of Israel v. Adolf, the son of Karl Adolf Eichmann, in the District Court of Jerusalem. Criminal Case No. 40/61. (An unedited and unrevised transcript of the simultaneous translation.) Washington, D.C.: Microcard Editions, 1962.

LEO BAECK INSTITUTE: New York

Selected documents from the archives have been useful in this study as well as the following:

Dienemann, Mally. "Memoiren"
Gruenspecht, David. "Memoiren"
Heilberg, Adolf. "Pro-Memoria 1933"
Schwartz, Oscar. "Mein Leben in Deutschland vor und nach dem Jahre 1933"

MICROFILMED RECORDS OF THE REICHS LEADER OF THE SS AND CHIEF OF THE GERMAN POLICE: National Archives, Washington, D.C.

The following microfilm reels have been especially useful:

T175 (280)	T175 (411)
T175 (403)	T175 (491)
T175 (408)	T175 (496)
T175 (409)	T175 (508)
T175 (410)	

WIENER LIBRARY: London

Judenliste. Mimeographed list of Jewish names compiled by the SS during the 1930's.
Sabatsky, Kurt. "Meine Erinnerungen an den Nationalsozialismus." Typewritten manuscript.
Zur Evian Konferenz. Mimeographed report of the Reichsvertretung. Berlin: 1938.

YAD WASHEM ARCHIVES: Jerusalem

Selected documents

YIVO INSTITUTE FOR JEWISH RESEARCH: New York

"Berlin Collection"

PUBLISHED DOCUMENTS AND MEMOIRS

Akten zur deutschen Auswärtigen Politik, 1918-1945, series D, vol. 5. Baden-Baden: Imprimerie Nationale, 1953.

Baynes, Norman H., ed. *The Speeches of Adolf Hitler,* vol. 1. London: Oxford University Press, 1942.

Blau, Bruno. *Das Ausnahmerecht für die Juden in Deutschland, 1933-1945.* 2nd ed. Düsseldorf, Verlag Allgemeine Wochenzeitung der Juden in Deutschland 1954.

Deutscher Reichsanzeiger und Preussicher Staatsanzeiger, August, 1933, through November, 1934.

Die Glaubensjuden im Deutschen Reich. vol. 451, no. 5 of *Statistik des deutschen Reiches* (Volks-Berufs—und Betriebszählung vom 16. Juli 1933. Die Bevölkerung des deutschen Reiches nach den Ergebnissen der Volkszählung 1933). Berlin: Verlag für Sozialpolitik, Wirtschaft und Statistik, 1936.

Diels, Rudolf. *Lucifer Ante Portas: es spricht der erste Chef der Gestapo.* Stuttgart: Deutsche Verlagsanstalt, 1950.

Documents on German Foreign Policy, 1918-1945. series C, vol. 4. Washington, D.C.: U.S. Government Printing Office, 1962.

Dokumente der deutschen Politik und Geschichte. 4 vols. *Nationalsozialistischer Diktatur, 1933-1938.* vol. 1. Berlin: Dokumenten-Verlag Herbert Wendler, n.d.

Dokumente zur Geschichte der Frankfurter Juden, 1933-1945. Herausgegeben von der Komission zur Erforschung der Geschichte der Frankfurter Juden. Frankfurt a.M.: Verlag Waldemar Kramer, 1963.

Foreign Relations of the United States, 1938. vol. 1. Washington, D.C.: United States Government Printing Office, 1955.

Goebbels, Joseph. *Revolution der Deutschen.* Oldenburg: Gerhard Stalling Verlag, 1933.

―――. *Vom Kaiserhof zur Reichskanzlei, Eine historische Darstellung in Tagebuchblättern.* Munich: Franz Eher, 1934.

Hitler, Adolf. *Mein Kampf.* New York: Reynal and Hitchcock, 1939.

Hofer, Walther, ed. *Der Nationalsozialismus: Dokumente, 1933-1945.* Frankfurt a.M.: Fischer, 1957.

Kersten, Felix. *The Kersten Memoirs.* New York: Macmillan, 1957.

Lochner, Louis P., ed. *The Goebbels Diaries, 1942-1943.* Garden City, N.Y.: Doubleday, 1948.

Michaelis, Herbert, and Ernst Schraepler, eds. *Das Dritte Reich, Die Zertrümmerung des Parteienstaates und die Grundlegung der*

Diktatur: Dokumentensammlung. Berlin: Dokumenten-Verlag Herbert Wendler, n.d.

Nazi Conspiracy and Aggression. 8 vols. Washington, D.C.: United States Government Printing Office, 1946.

Reichsgesetzblatt. Part I, 1933-1938. Berlin: Reichsverlagsamt, 1933-1938.

Ritter, Gerhard, ed. *Hitlers Tischgespräche im Führerhauptquartier, 1941-1942.* Bonn: Athenaeum Verlag, 1951.

Rosenbluth, Martin. *Go Forth and Serve: Early Years and Public Life.* New York: Herzl Press, 1961.

Schacht, Hjalmar H.G. *My First Seventy-Six Years: The Autobiography of Hjalmar Schacht.* London: Wingate, 1955.

Thyssen, Fritz. *I Paid Hitler.* New York: Farrar and Rinehart, 1941.

Trials of War Criminals before the Nuerenberg Military Tribunal. vol. 6 (The Flick Case). Washington, D.C.: United States Government Printing Office, 1952.

Warburg, Max M. *Aus meinen Aufzeichnungen.* Privately published: 1952.

Weiss, George. "Einige Dokumente zur Rechtstellung der Juden und zur Entziehung ihres Vermögens." *Schriftenreihe zum Berliner Rückerstattungsrecht,* 7. n.p. or d.

Weizmann, Chaim. *Trial and Error: The Autobiography of Chaim Weizmann.* New York: Harper, 1949.

Woodward, E.L., and Rohan Butler, eds. *Documents on British Foreign Policy, 1919-1939.* series 2, vol. 5, 1933. London: Her Majesty's Stationery Office, 1956.

BOOKS

Adler-Rudel, S. *Ostjuden in Deutschland, 1880-1940.* Schriftenreihe Wissenschaftlicher Abhandlungen des Leo Baeck Instituts. Tübingen: J.C.B. Mohr (Paul Siebeck), 1959.

Allen, William Sheridan. *The Nazi Seizure of Power: The Experience of a Single German Town, 1933-1935.* Chicago: Quadrangle, 1965.

Bennett, Marion T. *American Immigration Policies: A History.* Washington, D.C.: Public Affairs Press, 1963.

Bölsche, Wilhelm. *Haeckel, His Life and Work.* trans. Joseph McCabe. London: T. Fischer Unwin, 1906.

Bracher, Karl Dietrich. *Die Auflösung der Weimarer Republik.* 3rd ed. Villingen/Schwarzwald: Ring-Verlag, 1960.

————, Wolfgang Sauer, and Gerhard Schulz. *Die nationalsozial-istische Machtergreifung. Studien zur Errichtung des totalitären Herrschaftssystem in Deutschland 1933/34.* Cologne: Westdeutscher Verlag, 1960.

Bramstedt, E. K. *Dictatorship and Political Police: The Technique of Control by Fear.* New York: Oxford University Press, 1945.

Buchheim, Hans, et al. *Anatomie des SS-Staates.* vol. 1. Olten und Freiburg im Breisgau: Walter-Verlag, 1965.

Bullock, Alan. *Hitler: A Study in Tyranny.* rev. ed. New York: Harper, 1964.

Burckhardt, Carl J. *Meine Danziger Mission, 1937-1939.* Munich: Verlag Georg D.W. Callwey, 1960.

Daim, Wilfried. *Der Mann der Hitler die Ideen gab.* Munich: Isar Verlag, 1958.

Delarue, Jacques. *The Gestapo: A History of Horror.* New York: Dell, 1965.

Demeter, Karl. *The German Officer-Corps in Society and State, 1650-1945.* trans. Angus Malcolm. New York: Praeger, 1965.

Der Wirtschaftliche Vernichtungskampf gegen die Juden im Dritten Reich. Paris: Dargestellt von der ökonomischen Abteilung des jüdischen Weltkongresses, 1937.

Dorpalen, Andreas. *Heinrich von Treitschke.* New Haven: Yale University Press, 1957.

Dubnow, Simon. *Die neueste Geschichte des jüdischen Volkes, 1789-1914.* Berlin: Jüdischer Verlag, 1920.

Ergang, Robert R. *Herder and the Foundations of German Nationalism.* New York: Octagon Books, 1966.

Fackenheim, Emil L. *Hermann Cohen: After Fifty Years.* Leo Baeck Memorial Lecture 12. New York: Leo Baeck Institute, 1969.

Feilchenfeld, Werner. *Five Years of Jewish Emigration from Germany and the Haavara Transfer, 1933-1938.* Tel-Aviv: Trust and Transfer Office "Haavara" Ltd., 1938.

Fischer, Ruth. *Stalin and German Communism: A Study in the Origins of the State Party.* Cambridge, Mass.: Harvard University Press, 1948.

Frank, Walter. *Die deutschen Geisteswissenschaften im Kriege.* Rede gehalten am 18. Mai 1940 an der Universität Berlin. Hamburg: Hanseatische Verlagsanstalt, 1940.

Fromm, Bela. *Blood and Banquets: A Berlin Social Diary.* New York: Harper and Brothers, 1942.

Geiger, Theodor. *Die soziale Schichtung des deutschen Volkes.* Stuttgart: Ferdinand Enke Verlag, 1932.

Genschel, Helmut. *Die Verdrängung der Juden aus der Wirtschaft im Dritten Reich.* Göttingen: Musterschmidt, 1966.

George, Margaret. *The Warped Vision: British Foreign Policy, 1933-1939.* Pittsburgh: University of Pittsburgh Press, 1965.

Germanicus (pseud.). *Germany, The Last Four Years: An Independent Examination of the Results of National Socialism.* Boston: Houghton Mifflin, 1937.

Graml, Hermann. *Der 9. November 1938, "Reichskristallnacht."* Bonn: Schriftenreihe der Bundeszentrale für Heimatdienst, 1958.

Hale, Oron J. *The Captive Press in the Third Reich.* Princeton, N.J.: Princeton University Press, 1964.

Hamerow, Theodor S. *Restoration, Revolution, Reaction: Economics and Politics in Germany, 1815-1871.* Princeton, N.J.: Princeton University Press, 1958.

Heberle, Rudolf. *From Democracy to Nazism: A Regional Case Study of Political Parties in Germany.* Baton Rouge, La.: Louisiana State University Press 1945.

Herr, Georg. *Die Geschichte des deutschen Burschenschaft.* vol. 2. Heidelberg: Carl Winters, 1920.

Heiber, Helmut. *Joseph Goebbels.* Berlin: Colloquium Verlag, 1962.

Hilberg, Raul. *The Destruction of the European Jews.* Chicago: Quadrangle, 1961.

Janowsky, Oscar I., and Melvin M. Fagen. *International Aspects of German Racial Policies.* New York: Oxford University Press, 1937.

Jedrzejewicz, Waclaw. *Diplomat in Berlin 1933-1939: Papers and Memoirs of Josef Lipski, Ambassador of Poland.* New York: Columbia University Press, 1968.

Jewish Black Committee. *The Black Book: The Nazi Crime Against the Jewish People.* New York: Stratford Press, 1946.

Jews in Nazi Europe: February 1933 to November 1941. New York: Baltimore Institute of Jewish Affairs of the American Jewish Congress, n.d.

Kochan, Lionel. *Pogrom, 10 November 1938.* London: Andre Deutsch, 1957.

Kogon, Eugen. *Der SS-Staat, Das System der deutschen Konzentrationslager.* Frankfurt a.M.: Europäische Verlagsanstalt, 1946.

Kohn, Hans. *Pan-Slavism.* New York: Vintage, 1966.

Kruck, Alfred. *Geschichte des Alldeutschen Verbandes, 1890-1939.* Wiesbaden: Franz Steiner Verlag, 1954.

Krueger, Alf. *Die Lösung der Judenfrage in der deutschen Wirtschaft, Kommentare zur Judengesetzgebung.* Berlin: Limpert, 1940.

Lakeman, Enid, and James D. Lambert. *Voting in Democracies: A Study of Majority and Proportional Election Systems.* London: Faber, 1955.

Lamm, Hans. *Über die innere und äussere Entwicklung des deutschen Judentums im Dritten Reich.* Unpublished Ph.D. dissertation, University of Erlangen, 1951.

Lichtheim, Richard. *Die Geschichte des deutschen Zionismus.* Jerusalem: Verlag Rubin Mass, 1954.

Lipset, Martin Seymour. *The First New Nation.* New York: Basic Books, 1963.

Lorenzen, Sievert. *Die Juden und die Justiz.* 2nd ed. Berlin: R.V. Decker Verlag, 1943.

Manvell, Roger, and Heinrich Fraenkel. *Heinrich Himmler.* London: Heinemann, 1965.

Massing, Paul W. *Rehearsal for Destruction: A Study of Political Anti-Semitism in Imperial Germany.* New York: Harper, 1949.

Meinecke, Friedrich. *Weltbürgertum und Nationalstaat, Werke.* vol. 5. Munich: R. Oldenbourg Verlag, 1962.

Menzel, Curt. *Minderheitenrecht und Judenfrage.* (Zwei Vorträge gehalten am 17. Februar und 28. April 1933 im Bund Nationalsozialistischer Deutscher Juristen zu Hamburg) Beuern/Hessen: Edelgarten Verlag, n.d.

Morse, Arthur D. *While Six Million Died, A Chronicle of American Apathy.* New York: Random House, 1967.

Mosse, George L. *The Crisis of German Ideology.* New York: Grosset and Dunlap, 1965.

Nebel, Theobald. *Die Geschichte der jüdischen Gemeinde Talheim, Ein Beispiel für das Schicksal des Judentums in Württemberg.* Heilbronn: Gemeinde Talheim, 1963.

Nyomarky, Joseph. *Charisma and Factionalism in the Nazi Party.* Minneapolis: University of Minnesota Press, 1967.

Pendorf, Robert. *Mörder und Ermordete, Eichmann und die Judenpolitik des Dritten Reiches.* Hamburg: Rütten und Loening Verlag, 1961.

Pinson, Koppel S., ed. *Essays on Antisemitism.* New York: Conference on Jewish Relations, 1946.

————. *Modern Germany.* 2nd ed. New York: Macmillan, 1966.

Pulzer, P. G. J. *The Rise of Political Anti-Semitism in Germany and Austria.* New York: John Wiley and Sons, 1964.

Pye, Lucian. *Politics, Personality, and Nation Building: Burma's Search for Identity.* New Haven: Yale University Press, 1962.

Rabinowicz, Harry M. *The Legacy of Polish Jewry: A History of Polish Jews in the Inter-War Years 1919-1939*. New York: Thomas Yoseloff, 1965.

Rauschning, Hermann. *The Voice of Destruction*. New York: G. P. Putnam's Sons, 1940.

Reitlinger, Gerald. *The Final Solution: The Attempt to Exterminate the Jews of Europe, 1939-1945*. New York: A. S. Barnes, 1961.

_____. *The SS: Alibi of a Nation, 1922-1945*. London: Simon and Schuster, 1956.

Rosenberg, Arthur. *Der Mythos des 20. Jahrhunderts*. Munich: Eher Verlag, 1931.

Ruppin, Arthur. *The Jews in the Modern World*. London: Macmillan, 1934.

_____. *Soziologie der Juden*. vol. 2. Berlin: Jüdischer Verlag, 1930.

Sacher, Howard Morley. *The Course of Modern Jewish History*. New York: Dell, 1963.

Schoenberner, Gerhard. ed., *Der Gelbe Stern, Die Judenverfolgung in Europa, 1933 bis 1945*. Hamburg: Rütten und Loening Verlag, 1960.

Schoeps, Hans Joachim. *Die letzten dreissig Jahre: Rückblicke*. Stuttgart: Ernst Klett Verlag, 1956.

Schwartz, Mildred. *Public Opinion and Canadian Identity*. Berkeley: University of California Press, 1967.

Schweitzer, Arthur. *Big Business in the Third Reich*. Bloomington: University of Indiana Press, 1964.

Shirer, William L. *Berlin Diary*. New York: Popular Library, 1961.

_____. *The Rise and Fall of the Third Reich*. New York: Simon and Schuster, 1960.

Sigg, Marianne. *Das Rassestrafrecht in Deutschland in den Jahren 1933-1945 unter besonderer Berücksichtigung des Blutschutzgesetzes*. Aarau, Switzerland: Verlag H.R. Sauerlaender, 1951.

Sington, Derrick and Arthur Weidenfeld. *The Goebbels Experiment: A Study of the Nazi Propaganda Machine*. London: John Murray, 1942.

Sombart, Werner. *The Jews and Modern Capitalism*. London: T. Fischer Unwin, 1913.

Stein, Leonard. *The Balfour Declaration*. New York: Simon and Schuster, 1961.

Stern, Fritz. *The Politics of Cultural Despair: A Study in the Rise of the Germanic Ideology*. New York: Doubleday, 1965.

Stolper, Gustav, Karl Häuser, and Knut Borchardt, *The German Economy, 1870 to the Present*. New York: Harcourt, Brace and World, 1967.

Stuckart, Wilhelm, and Hans Globke. *Kommentare zur Rassengesetzgebung Reichsbürgergesetz, Blutschutzgesetz, Eheschutzgesetz.* vol. 1. Munich: Beck'sche Verlagsbuchhandlung, 1936.

Sweezy, Maxine Y. *The Structure of the Nazi Economy.* Cambridge, Mass.: Harvard University Press, 1941.

Tartakower, Arieh, and Kurt R. Grossmann. *The Jewish Refugee.* New York: Institute of Jewish Affairs, 1944.

Tenenbaum, Joseph. *Race and Reich: The Story of an Epoch.* New York: Twayne, 1956.

Tobias, Fritz. *The Reichstag Fire.* New York: G. P. Putnam's Sons, 1963.

Toury, Jacob. *Die politischen Orientierungen der Juden in Deutschland, von Jena bis Weimar.* Tübingen: J.C.B. Mohr (Paul Siebeck), 1966.

Trevor-Roper, H. R., ed. *Hitler's Secret Conversations, 1941-1944.* New York: New American Library, 1961.

Turner, Henry Ashby. *Stresemann and the Politics of the Weimar Republic.* Princeton, N.J.: Princeton University Press, 1963.

Uhlig, Heinrich. *Die Warenhäuser im Dritten Reich.* Cologne: Westdeutscher Verlag, 1956.

Ullstein, Hermann. *The Rise and the Fall of the House of Ullstein.* New York: Simon and Schuster, 1943.

Valentin, Hugo. *Antisemitism: Historically and Critically Examined.* New York: Viking Press, 1936.

Weinreich, Max. *Hitler's Professors: The Part of Scholarship in Germany's Crimes against the Jewish People.* New York: Yiddish Scientific Institute, YIVO, 1946.

Wheeler-Bennet, J. W. *The Nemesis of Power: The German Army in Politics, 1918-1945.* 2nd ed. London: Macmillan, 1964.

Wischnitzer, Mark. *To Dwell in Safety: The Story of Jewish Migration since 1800.* Philadelphia: Jewish Publication Society of America, 1948.

Wulf, Josef. *Die Nürenberger Gesetze.* Berlin: Arani Verlag, 1960.

————. *Presse und Funk im Dritten Reich, Eine Dokumentation.* Guetersloh: Sigbert Mohn Verlag, 1964.

Zielenziger, Kurt. *Juden in der deutschen Wirtschaft.* Berlin: Der Heine-Bund, 1930.

ARTICLES

Adler-Rudel, S. "Das Auswanderungsproblem im Jahre 1938, Ein Briefwechsel mit Hans Schäffer." *Bulletin des Leo Baeck Instituts* 10 (1967): 159-215.

_____. "The Evian Conference." *Year Book XIII of the Leo Baeck Institute* (1968): 235-273.

Ball-Kaduri, K. Y. "Die Vorplannung der Kristallnacht." *Zeitschrift für die Geschichte der Juden* 4 (1966): 211-216.

Bennathan, Esra. "Die demographische und wirtschaftliche Struktur der Juden." Werner E. Mosse, ed: *Entscheidungsjahr 1932, Zur Judenfrage in der Endphase der Weimarer Republik.* 2nd ed. Tübingen: J.C.B. Mohr (Paul Siebeck), 1966. pp. 87-131.

Buchheim, Hans. "Die organizatorische Entwicklung der politischen Polizei in Deutschland in den Jahren 1933 und 1934." *Gutachten des Instituts für Zeitgeschichte* Munich: Selbstverlag, 1958: 294-307.

Colodner, Solomon. "Jewish Education under National Socialism." *Yad Washem Studies* 3 (1959): 161-180.

Esh, Shaul. "Between Discrimination and Extermination: The Fateful Year of 1938." In *From Hatred to Extermination.* Jerusalem: Yad Washem, 1959.

Graml, Hermann. "Die Auswanderung der Juden aus Deutschland zwischen 1933 und 1939." *Gutachten des Instituts für Zeitgeschichte* Munich: Selbstverlag, 1958: 79-85.

Grossman, Kurt R. "Zionists and Non-Zionists under Nazi Rule in the 1930's." In *Herzl Year Book* 4 (1961-1962): 329-344.

Hagelstange, Rudolf. "Metamorphosen des Antisemitismus." *Deutsche Rundschau* 80 (1954): 1255-1260.

Hallgarten, George W. F. "Adolf Hitler and German Heavy Industry, 1931-1933." *Journal of Economic History* 12 (Summer, 1952): 222-246.

Heiber, Helmut. "Der Fall Grünspan." *Vierteljahrshefte für Zeitgeschichte* 5 (1957): 154-172.

Kahn, Ernst. "Die Judenpresse." *Leo Baeck Institute Bulletin* 1 (1958): 13-18.

Kaltenbrunner, Gerd-Klaus. "Houston Stewart Chamberlains germanischer Mythos." *Politische Studien* 175 (1967): 568-583.

Koehl, Robert. "Feudal Aspects of National Socialism." *American Political Science Review* 54 (December, 1960): 921-933.

Lasswell, Harold D. "The Psychology of Hitlerism." *Political Quarterly* 4 (1933): 373-384.

Lipgens, Walter. "Bismarck, die öffentliche Meinung und die Annexion von Ellass-Lothringen, 1870." *Historische Zeitschrift* 199 (1964): 31-112.

Lösener, Bernhard. "Als Rassereferat im Reichsministerium des Innern." *Vierteljahrshefte für Zeitgeschichte* 9 (July, 1961): 264-313.

Marcus, Ernst. "The German Foreign Office and the Palestine Question in the Period 1933-1939." *Yad Washem Studies* 2 (1958): 179-204.

Mommsen, Hans. "Dokumentation: Der nationalsozialistische Polizeistaat und die Judenverfolgung vor 1938." *Vierteljahrshefte für Zeitgeschichte* 10 (January, 1962): 68-87.

Mosse, George L. "The Influence of the *Völkisch* Idea on German Jewry." *Studies of the Leo Baeck Institute* (1967): 83-114.

Needler, Martin. "Hitler's Anti-Semitism: A Political Appraisal." *Public Opinion Quarterly* 24 (Winter, 1960): 665-669.

"Nicht auf Gesetze warten!" *Mitteilungen der Komission für Wirtschaftspolitik der NSDAP* 1 (August, 1936): 29-30.

Oncken, Hermann. "Deutsche geistige Einflüsse in der europäischen Nationalitätenbewegung des 19. Jahrhunderts." *Deutsche Vierteljahrsschrift für Literatur—Wissenschaft—und Geistesgeschichte* 7 (1929): 607-627.

Peterson, E. N. "The Bureaucracy and the Nazi Party." *Review of Politics* 28 (April, 1966): 172-192.

Petzina, Dieter. "Hauptprobleme der deutschen Wirtschaftspolitik, 1932-33." *Vierteljahrshefte für Zeitgeschichte* 15 (1967): 19-55.

Pfitzner, Josef. "Heinrich Luden und František Palacký, Ein Kapital deutsch-slawischer Kulturbeziehungen." *Historische Zeitschrift* 141 (1930): 54-96.

Pflanze, Otto. "Nationalism in Europe, 1848-1871." *Review of Politics* 28 (April, 1966): 129-143.

Prinz, Arthur. "The Role of the Gestapo in Obstructing and Promoting Jewish Emigration." *Yad Washem Studies* 2 (1958): 205-218.

Rissom, Dr. "Mischehen im Lichte der neuen Gesetzgebung." *Zeitschrift der Akademie für Deutsches Recht* 1 (January, 1936): 8-10.

Roloff, Ernst-August. "Wer wählte Hitler?" *Politische Studien* 15 (1964): 293-300.

Rosenstock, Werner. "Exodus 1933-1939: A Survey of Jewish Emigration from Germany." *Year Book I of Leo Baeck Institute* (1956): 373-390.

Rothfels, Hans. "Grundsätzliches zum Problem der Nationalität." *Historische Zeitschrift* 174 (1952): 339-358.

Ruttke, Falk. "Erb- und Rassenpflege in Gesetzgebung und Rechtssprechung des Dritten Reiches." *Deutsches Recht* (January 25, 1935): 25-27.

Schorske, Carl E. "Politics in a New Key: An Austrian Triptych." *Journal of Modern History* 39 (December, 1967): 343-386.

Schweitzer, Arthur. "Organizierter Kapitalismus und Parteidiktatur, 1933 bis 1936." *Schmollers Jahrbuch* 79 (1959): 37-79.

Simon, Walter B. "Motivation of a Totalitarian Mass Vote." *British Journal of Sociology* 10 (1959): 338-345.

Simpson, Amos E. "The Struggle for the Control of the German Economy." *Journal of Modern History* 12 (1959): 37-45.

"SS-Bewerber." *Gutachten des Instituts für Zeitgeschichte*. Munich (1958).

Wischnitzer, Mark. "Jewish Emigration from Germany, 1933-1938." *Jewish Social Studies* 2 (1940): 23-44.

"Witness of Righteousness: The Work and Faith of Dean Grueber." *Wiener Library Bulletin* 16 (1962).

Zmarzlik, Hans-Günther. "Der Antisemitismus im Zweiten Reich." *Geschichte im Wissenschaft und Unterricht* 14 (1963): 273-286.

————. "Der Sozialdarwinismus in Deutschland als geschichtliches Problem." *Vierteljahrshefte für Zeitgeschichte* 11 (July, 1963): 246-273.

NEWSPAPERS AND PERIODICALS (NOT LISTED ABOVE)

Allgemeine Wochenzeitung der Juden in Deutschland
Central Verein Zeitung
Das Schwarze Korps
Deutsche Allgemeine Zeitung
Deutsche Justiz
Deutsches Ärzteblatt
Frankfurter Zeitung
Jüdische Rundschau
Juristische Wochenschrift
New York Times
Voelkischer Beobachter

Bibliographical Essay

WHEN *The Twisted Road to Auschwitz* was published in 1970 the debate among historians about the nature of Nazi decision making and the manner in which Nazi policies in general—the Jewish policy in particular—had been made during the Third Reich was not yet fully joined. The thesis of *The Twisted Road,* implied in the title, contributed to the joining of the debate. The controversy that ensued came to be labeled as one between intentionalists and functionalists. Functionalists argued, as did *The Twisted Road,* that the Nazi persecutions of the Jews during the 1930s underwent an incremental radicalization that was as much a product of dynamics within the functioning of the Nazi system—its stresses and tensions—as it was the result of conscious planning and design on the part of the Nazi leadership. Intentionalists, on the other hand, interpreted the radicalization as the product chiefly of the unfolding designs and intentions of Adolf Hitler. The interpretive implications of these two basic positions are brilliantly analyzed by Tim Mason in his essay "Intention and Explanation: A Current Controversy about the Interpretation of National Socialism" in *The "Führer State," Myth and Reality: Studies on the Structure and Politics of the Third Reich* (Stuttgart: 1981), ed. Gerhard Hirschfeld and Lothar Kettenacker.

The scholarly literature on the Nazis and their facinorous persecutions that culminated in their construction of six factories of death, the largest being Auschwitz, has grown immensely since the publication of *The Twisted Road,* a reflection of the extraordinary growth of scholarly and public interest in the events that collectively are most often labeled the Holocaust.

The following is intended merely as a guide pointing toward some of the more important literature published on this subject since 1970. The guide focuses upon literature about the period between 1933 and the outbreak of the war in 1939. No such listing can be exhaustive; some critically important work will inevitably be overlooked. For that reason the reader should begin by consulting two important guides to the scholarly literature available on the Holocaust and National Socialism, Michael Marrus's *The Holocaust in History* (Hanover, N.H.:

1987) and Ian Kershaw's *The Nazi Dictatorship: Problems and Perspectives of Interpretation,* 2d ed. (London: 1989), especially the latter's chapter five "Hitler and the Holocaust." Useful also is Saul Friedländer's "From Anti-Semitism to Extermination: A Historiographical Study of Nazi Policies toward the Jews and an Essay in Interpretation" in *Yad Vashem Studies* 16 (1984). Also to be consulted is Otto Dov Kulka's "Major Trends and Tendencies in German Historiography on National Socialism and the 'Jewish Question,' 1924–1984" in the *Leo Baeck Institute Yearbook* 30 (1985). Saul Friedländer's introduction to Gerald Fleming's *Hitler and the Final Solution* (Berkeley: 1984) is important both for its discussion of the literature and for its cogent comments on the functionalist-intentionalist debate.

Gerald Fleming's *Hitler and the Final Solution* is perhaps the most avowedly intentionalist and effectively constructed intentionalist interpretation of Nazi Jewish policy to appear since the controversy began, claiming that Hitler's murderous intentions were clear since the early 1920s and that they led in an absolutely straight line to the exterminations at Auschwitz. Fleming's case is argued more carefully than is the more popular statement of the intentionalist position by Lucy S. Dawidowicz in her widely read *The War against the Jews, 1933–1945,* 2d ed. (New York: 1986). Eberhard Jäckel's essay "Hitler Orders the Holocaust," a chapter in his *Hitler in History* (1984), presents a strong case for the importance of understanding Hitler's intentions regarding the Jews. See also his essay "The Elimination of the Jews" in his *Hitler's World View: A Blueprint for Power* (Cambridge, Mass., 1981). Among intentionalists the debate centers on when it was that Hitler decided to exterminate the Jewish people. Fleming and Jäckel argue that it was in the early 1920s. Sarah Gordon in her important work *Hitler, Germans, and the "Jewish Question"* (Princeton, N.J.: 1984), traces that decision to 1936.

An intentionalist interpretation of Nazi efforts to drive the Jews out of the German economy is effectively argued by Avraham Barkai in *From Boycott to Annihilation: The Economic Struggle of German Jews, 1933–1943,* trans. William Templer (Hanover, N.H.: 1989). The intentionalist position is also being vigorously defended by the Israeli scholar David Bankier. See his "Hitler and the Policy-making Process on the Jewish Question" in *Holocaust and Genocide Studies* 3 (1988).

Although its interpretation is not expressly intentionalist, and certainly not functionalist, no listing of books on Nazi persecution and murder can overlook Raul Hilberg's monumental three-volume *The Destruction of the European Jews,* 2d ed. (New York: 1985). Hilberg emphasizes the role of bureaucratic momentum in propelling the Nazis toward Auschwitz. A rigorously Marxist point of view regarding the

Nazi persecution of Jews is to be found in Kurt Pätzold's *Faschismus, Rassenwahn, Judenvervolgung: Eine Studie zur politischen Strategie des faschistischen deutschen Imperialismus, 1933–1935* (East Berlin: 1975). For more on the Marxist position see Konrad Kwiet, "Historians of the German Democratic Republic on Antisemitism and Persecution" in the *Leo Baeck Institute Yearbook* 21 (1976).

The interpretations of the functionalists, wide-ranging as they are, are all deeply indebted to Martin Broszat's *The Hitler State: The Foundation and Development of the Internal Structure of the Third Reich* (London: 1981; German original in 1969), which very early called attention to the internal strains within the structure of the Nazi regime. In 1977 Broszat applied that understanding to a devastating critique of David Irving's revisionism in "Hitler und die Genesis der 'Endlösung': Aus Anlass der Thesen von David Irving" in the *Vierteljahrshefte für Zeitgeschichte* 25 (1977). The first full-blown history in German of the Nazi Jewish persecutions that was clearly functionalist in its argument was Uwe-Dietrich Adam's *Judenpolitik im Dritten Reich* (Königstein: 1972), which, like *The Twisted Road*, was published before the functionalist label had been invented. A few years later the functionalist position was pushed an important step forward by Christopher Browning in *The Final Solution and the Foreign Office: A Study of Referat D III of Abteilung Deutschland, 1940–1943* (New York: 1978). The functionalist position has been stated most boldly by Hans Mommsen in his essay "The Realization of the Unthinkable: The 'Final Solution' of the Jewish Question in the Third Reich" (originally in German in 1983) in *The Policies of Genocide: Jews and Soviet Prisoners of War in Nazi Germany*, ed. Gerhard Hirschfeld (Boston: 1986).

An effort to clarify, if not to resolve, the issues surrounding Nazi decision making was made at an international conference held in Stuttgart, West Germany, in 1984. The proceedings of that conference are available in *Der Mord an den Juden im Zweiten Weltkrieg*, ed. Eberhard Jäckel and Jürgen Rohwer (Stuttgart: 1985). The controversy between functionalists and intentionalists is not likely to be resolved in favor of either side, and certainly not in the terms that either side has produced. Much more likely is that the questions themselves will be transformed by new research and new insights into the nature of the Nazi system. A case in point is the recent work by Ian Kershaw whose *The "Hitler Myth": Image and Reality in the Third Reich* (Oxford: 1987) shows that Hitler, by virtue of the charismatic aura surrounding him, could be the central figure in the Nazi system without at the same time being the programmatic designer of every policy or the maker of every decision.